AF540142

CLINICAL LINGUISTICS
AN OVERVIEW

CLINICAL LINGUISTICS
AN OVERVIEW

By

Brajesh Priyadarshi
Lecturer in Linguistics
Deptt. of Speech-Language Pathology
All India Institute of Speech & Hearing (AIIH)
Mysore (India)

&

Dr. Shyamala K. Chengappa
Professor & Head (Language Pathology)
Deptt. of Speech-Language Pathology
All India Institute of Speech & Hearing
Mysore (India)

DISCOVERY PUBLISHING HOUSE PVT. LTD.
NEW DELHI-110 002

Published by:
Tilak Wasan

DISCOVERY PUBLISHING HOUSE PVT. LTD.
4383/4B, Ansari Road, Darya Ganj
New Delhi-110 002 (India)
Phone : +91-11-23279245, 43596064-65
Fax : +91-11-23253475
E-mail : parul.wasan@gmail.com
discoverypublishinghouse@gmail.com
web : www.discoverypublishinggroup.com

***First Edition:* 2013**

ISBN: 978-93-5056-241-3

Clinical Linguistics: *An Overview*

Printed at:
Dynamic Printers
Delhi

Foreword

Clinial Lingustics : An Overview authored by Mr. Brajesh Priyadarshi and Dr. Shyamala Chengappa is a timely contribution to the field of Clinical Linguistics in India and South Asia. There is an impressive growth of acilities in India in recent decades to help train speech and language specialists, to diagnose a variety of speech and language disorders and to devise suitable therapy programmes. A talented pool of teachers, researchers and therapists was developed through the hard work of pioneering teachers like Professors N. Ratna, Nataraj, Nagaraja, Pratibha Karanth, Shyamala Chengappa and others. Yet, Indian and South Asian practitioners have to depent on manuals prepared of non-Indian contexts. **Clinial** ***Linguistics : An Overview*** presents materials that are directly relevant to Indian and South Asian contexts.

Clinical Linguistics : An Overview by Brajesh Priyadarshi and Shyamala Chengappa is a comprehensive work that present in five chapters the essentials of what constitutes clinical linguistics. Chapter I presents aspects of language, communication and linguistics (Concept and their Clinical Relevance). Chapter 2 deals with phonetics and phonology : (Concept, Acquisiton/Development, Disorder and their Clinical Relevance). Chapter 3 discusses morphology and syntax (grammar) (Concept, Acquisition/Development and Disorder and their Clinical Relevance). Chapter 4 present aspects of semantics (Concepts/Acquisition/Development,

Disorder and its Clinical Relevances). Chapter 5 introduces pragmatics (Concept, Acquisition/Development, Disorder and its Clinical Relevance).

This book is a great introduction to the field of Clinical Linguistics. Teachers, trainers, therapists, students and researchers in all speech and language institutions and clinics will find this book very useful.

M.S. Thirumalai, Ph.D.

Retired Professor-cum-Deputy Director
Central Institute of Indian Languages
Mysore-570 006
Karnataka, India
Managing Editor, Language in India
www.languageinindia.com

Preface

This book is the outcome of the lectures that were undertaken for students of All India Institute of Speech and Hearing during their course work in Linguistics and Clinical Linguistics during their B.Sc. (Speech and Hearing), PG Diploma in Clinical Linguistics (PGDCL) and M.Sc. (Speech-Language Pathology) classes. This publication is expected to cater to the needs of students of Linguistics, Clinical Linguistics, Speech and Hearing, Special Education and allied disciplines. The book is designed in such a way that each section tries to present the basic linguistic concepts related to the title at the first instance; then, proceeds to discuss the acquisition process involved and lastly, the disorders related to it. It also tries to bring out the clinical relevance of these linguistic concepts for the clinical practitioners. The experience has been greatly beneficial all along and we have been helped immensely by several people.

We are greatly indebted to The Director, All India Institute of Speech and Hearing, Manasa Gangotri, Mysore for the encouragement and cooperation extended during the preparation of this book.

We owe a lot to our students who have helped us to refine our ideas while teaching their classes.

Brajesh Priyadarshi
Shyamala Chengappa

Contents

of Consonants—Place of Articulation—Manner of Articulation—Voicing—Vowel—Classification of Vowels—Tongue Height—ackness of the Tongue—Roundedness (lip orification)—Classifications Based on other Qualities—Syllable—Syllable Structure—Syllabification—Syllabic Consonants and Non-Syllabic Vowels—Diphthong—Types of Diphthongs—Supra-Segmentals—Phonology—Types of Phonology—Segmental/Linear Phonology—Natural Phonology and Its Clinical Implications—Generative Phonology and Its Clinical Implications—Nonsegmental/Nonlinear Phonologies/Multilineared/Multitiered Phonology—Autosegmental Phonology and Its Clinical Implication—Metrical Phonology and Its Clinical Implication—Feature Geometry and Its Clinical Implication—Optimality Theory and Its Clinical Implication—Minimal Pairs—Transcription of Segments—Narrow and Broad Transcription—Extended IPA—Distinctive Feature—Clinical Application of Distinctive Feature Theory—Distinctive Feature Approaches Used in Therapy—Distinctive Features in Developmental Phonology—Phonotactics—English Phonotactics—Principles and Practices of Phonemic Analysis—Principle of Contrastive Distribution—Principles of Complimentary Distribution—Principle of Phonetic Similarity—Principle of Free Variation—Principle of Pattern Congruity—Principle of Economy—Application of Phonemic Analysis in Speech-Language Pathology—Phonological Processes—Assimilation—Dissimilation—Metathesis—Lenition—Haplology—Vowel Harmony—Phonological Acquisition/Development—Stages of Acquisition—Prelinguistic Stages—Babbling and Its Relationship to Later Language Development—Prosodic Feature Development—Transition from Babbling to Meaningful Speech—Linguistic Stage—Segmental Form Development—Prosodic Feature Development—Preschool Child—Segmental form

CHAPTER

1

Language, Communication and Linguistics

Concept and their Clinical Relevance

Language

Language is a dynamic set of sensory symbols of communication and the elements used to manipulate them. It can also refer to the use of such systems as a general phenomenon. Strictly speaking, language is considered to be an exclusively human mode of communication. Although other animals make use of quite sophisticated communicative systems, sometimes casually referred to as animal language, none of these are known to make use of all of the properties that linguists use to define language.

In Western Philosophy, language has long been closely associated with reason, which is also a uniquely human way of using symbols. In Ancient Greek philosophical terminology, the same word logos, was used as a term for both language or speech and reason. More commonly though, the English word "language", derived ultimately from lingua, Latin for tongue, typically refers only to expressions of reason which can be understood by other people, most obviously by speaking.

Speech

Speech refers to the processes associated with the production and perception of sounds used in spoken language.

Communication

Communication is the process whereby information is imparted by a sender to a receiver via a medium. Communication requires that all parties have an area of communicative commonality. There are auditory means, such as speaking, singing and sometimes tone of voice, and nonverbal, physical means, such as body language, sign language, paralanguage, touch, eye contact, by using writing. Communication is defined as a process by which we assign and convey meaning in an attempt to create shared understanding. This process requires a vast repertoire of skills in intrapersonal and interpersonal processing, listening, observing, speaking, questioning, analyzing, and evaluating.

Communication is a process of sending a message through different media, whether it be verbal or nonverbal, so long as a being transmits a thought provoking idea, gesture or action. Communication is a learned skill. Most babies are born with the physical ability to make sounds, but must learn to speak and communicate effectively. Speaking, listening, and our ability to understand verbal and nonverbal meanings are skills we develop in various ways. We learn basic communication skills by observing other people and modelling our behaviours based on what we see. We also are taught some communication skills directly through education, and by practicing those skills and having them evaluated.

Communication as an academic discipline relates to all the ways we communicate, so it embraces a large body of study and knowledge. The communication discipline includes both verbal and nonverbal messages. A body of scholarship all about communication is presented and explained in textbooks, electronic publications, and academic journals. In the journals, researchers report the results of studies that are the basis for an ever-expanding understanding of how we all communicate. Communication happens at many levels (even for one single action), in many different ways, and for most beings, as well as certain machines. Several, if not all, fields of study dedicate a portion of attention to communication, so when speaking about communication it is very important to be sure about what aspects of communication one is speaking about. Definitions of communication range widely, some recognizing that animals can communicate with each other as well as human beings, and some are narrower, only including human beings within the parameters of human symbolic interaction.

Nonetheless, communication is usually described along a few major dimensions: Content (what type of things are communicated), source, emisor, sender or encoder (by whom), form (in which form), channel (through which medium), destination, receiver, target or decoder (to whom), and the purpose or pragmatic aspect. Between parties, communication includes acts that confer knowledge and experiences, give advice and commands, and ask questions. These acts may take many forms, in one of the various manners of communication. The form depends on the abilities of the group communicating. Together, communication content and form make messages that are sent towards a destination. The target can be oneself, another person or being, another entity (such as a corporation or group of beings).

Human languages are usually referred to as natural languages, and the science of studying them, falls under the purview of linguistics. A common progression for natural languages is that they are considered to be first spoken, then written, and then; an understanding and explanation of their grammar is attempted.

Languages live, die, move from place to place, and change with time. Any language that ceases to change or develop is categorized as a dead language. Conversely, any language that is in a continuous state of change is known as a living language or modern language

Animal Communication

Animal communication is any behaviour on the part of one animal that has an effect on the current or future behaviour of another animal. The study of animal communication, sometimes called zoosemiotics (distinguishable from anthrop semiotics, the study of human communication) has played an important part in the development of ethology, sociobiology, and the study of animal cognition.

The term *animal language* is often used for non-human languages. Linguists do not consider these to be "language", but describe them as animal communication, because the interaction between animals in such communication is fundamentally different in its underlying principles from human language. Nevertheless, some scholars have tried to disprove this mainstream premise through experiments on training chimpanzees to talk. Karl von Frisch received the Nobel Prize in 1973 for his proof of the language and dialects of the bees. Current research indicates that signalling codes are the most fundamental precondition for coordination within and between cells, tissues, organs and organisms of all organismic kingdoms. All of these signalling codes follow combinatorial (syntactic), context-sensitive (pragmatic) and content-specific (semantic) rules. In contrast to linguists, biolinguistics and biosemiotics consider these codes to be real languages.

In several publicized instances, non-human animals have been taught to understand certain features of human language. Chimpanzees, Guerrillas and Orang-utans have been taught hand signs based on American Sign Language (ASL). The African Grey Parrot, which possesses the ability to mimic human speech with a high degree of accuracy, is suspected of having sufficient intelligence to comprehend some of the speech it mimics. Most species of parrot, despite expert mimicry, are believed to have no linguistic comprehension at all.

While proponents of animal communication systems have debated levels of semantics, these systems have not been found to have anything approaching human language syntax. Let us see, how these two differ:

Difference between Human Language and Animal Communication System

Human Language	Animal Communication System
(1) Unlimited and infinite	(1) Limited and finite
(2) Open system (for changes)	(2) Closed system
(3) Extendable, modifiable	(3) Unextendable, unmodifiable.
(4) Flexible and full of variety	(4) Inflexible and without variety.
(5) Non-instinctive	(5) Instinctive (learnt).
(6) Acquired	(6) Inherited.
(7) Conditioned by Geography	(7) Not conditioned by Geography.
(8) Full of novelty and creativity	(8) Bereft of novelty and creativity.
(9) Has grammaticality	(9) Has no grammaticality.
(10) Cognitive as well as behavioural.	(10) Only behavioural.
(11) Descriptive and narrative.	(11) Non-descriptive and non-narrative.

Properties of Language

A set of commonly accepted signs (indices, icons or symbols) is only one feature of language; all languages must define (i) the structural relationships between these signs in a system of grammar, (ii) the context wherein the signs are used (pragmatics) and (iii) dependent on their context the content specifity, i.e. its meaning(semantics). Rules of grammar are one of the characteristics sometimes said to distinguish language from other forms of communication. They allow a finite set of signs to be manipulated to create a potentially infinite number of grammatical utterances.

Another property of language is that its symbols are arbitrary. Any concept or grammatical rule can be mapped onto a symbol. In other words, most languages make use of sound, but the combinations of sounds used do not have any necessary and inherent meaning – they are merely an agreed-upon convention to represent a certain thing by users of that language. For instance, there is nothing about the Spanish word nada itself that forces Spanish speakers to convey the idea of "nothing". Another set of sounds (for example, the English word nothing) could equally be used to represent the same concept, but all Spanish speakers have acquired or learned to correlate this meaning for this particular sound pattern. For Slovenian, Croatian, Serbian or Bosnian speakers on the other hand, nada means something else; it means "hope".

This arbitrariness even applies to words with an onomatopoeic dimension (i.e. words that to some extent simulate the sound of the token referred to). For example, several animal names (e.g. cuckoo), are derived from sounds the bird/animal makes, but these forms did not have to be chosen for these meanings. Non-onomatopoetic words can stand just as easily for the same meaning. For instance, the katydid is called a "bush cricket" in British English, a term that bears no relation to the sound the animal makes. In time, onomatopoeic words can also change in form, losing their mimetic status. Onomatopoeic words may have an inherent relation to their referent, but this meaning is not inherent, thus they do not violate arbitrariness.

Functions of Language

1. ***Instrumental:*** In this function, language is used by the child/adults to express material needs.

2. ***Regulatory:*** One controls the behaviour of others through language.

3. ***Interactional:*** This is 'me and you' function, used specifically to interact socially with some other person. Eg: It is nice to see you, How are you? Etc.

4. ***Personal:*** One uses language to express feelings about, reactions to, and interests in things in the environment.

5. ***Heuristic:*** The heuristic or learning function is used by

a person to explore and find out new things. It includes demands for names or things: 'What is that?' and later develops into a wide variety of questioning, such as, When, Why, Where, etc.

6. Imaginative: Pretend play, story, and make believe, and moving into the world of fantasy are the imaginative function of language.

7. Informative: Language is used to pass on information from one place to other, one person to other.

Characteristics of Language (According to Charles Hockett)

(1) Interchangeability: All members of the species can both send and receive messages.

(2) Feedback: Users of the system monitor what they are transmitting (and can correct it).

(3) Specialization: The communication system serves no other function but to communicate. Human language represents reality-both external (real world) and internal (states, beliefs)-symbolically in the mind.

(4) Semanticity: The system conveys meaning through a set of fixed relationships among tokens, referents and meanings.

(5) Arbitrariness: There is no natural or inherent connection between a token and its referent.

(6) Discreetness: The communication system consists of isolatable, repeatable units. Human language shows distinctive features, phonemes, syllables, morphemes, words, and still larger combinations. Bee dancing may be thought as consisting of two (or three) discrete types, but these dances are not recombinable. There is some evidence for subunits in birdsong. They are also present in primate call systems.

(7) Displacement: Users of the system are able to refer to events remote in space and time.

(8) Productivity: New messages on any topic can be produced at any time.

(9) Duality of Patterning: Meaningless units (phonemes) are combined to form arbitrary signs. These signs in turn can be recombined to form new, meaningful larger units. In human language, phonemes can be combined in various ways to create different symbolic tokens: spot, tops, opts, pots. These tokens in turn can be combined in meaningful ways: spot the tops of the pots.

(10) Tradition: At least certain aspects of the system must be transmitted from an experienced user to learner.

(11) Prevarication: The system enables the users to talk nonsense or to lie.

(12) Learnability: A user of the system can learn other variants.

(13) Reflexiveness: The ability to use the communication system to discuss the system itself.

The Scientific Study of Language

Linguistics

Linguistics is the scientific study of language. Scientific study means the systematic and objective investigation of a clearly defined subject (K.Grundy, 1989).

According to D. N. S Bhatt, it is the study of language. It deals with topics such as the nature of language, its internal organization, the nature of its acquisition by children, as well as by adults, the influence of language upon society and that of society upon the language, the way in which the languages undergo change and so on. Of these the study of internal organization of language i.e., its grammar, is considered to be the most important goal in linguistics.

The word 'linguistics' has been derived from Latin words- 'lingua' meaning tongue and 'istics' meaning knowledge or science. Therefore linguistics is the scientific study of human language. It is concerned with the structures, principles and patterns of a language, its development and relation to other languages.

It is that science which studies the origin, organization, nature and development of language descriptively, historically, comparatively and explicitly and formulates the general rules related to language.

Linguistics is the scientific study of language, encompassing a number of sub-fields. At the core of theoretical linguistics are the study of language structure (grammar) and the study of meaning (semantics). The first of these encompasses morphology (the formation and composition of words), syntax (the rules that determine how words combine into phrases and sentences) and phonology (the study of sound systems and abstract sound units). Phonetics is a related branch of linguistics concerned with the actual properties of speech sounds (phones), non-speech sounds, and how they are produced and perceived.

Theoretical linguistics is mostly concerned with developing models of linguistic knowledge. The fields that are generally considered as the core of theoretical linguistics are syntax, phonology, morphology, and semantics. Applied linguistics attempts to put linguistic theories into practice through areas like translation, stylistics, literary criticism and theory, discourse analysis, speech therapy, speech pathology and foreign language teaching.

The linguistic study of language confines itself to a study of the verbal utterances of human beings. Its aims are to describe the structure of these utterances and to do so by setting up a theory of linguistic structure- grammar. This means that it does not concern itself with the motives of the speaker, what he is trying to achieve through using language. The linguist is not concerned with the situational context in which his data were produced, the relations between speakers and hearers, their social characteristics, what is happening while they talk the results of their speech, the accompanying paralinguistic behaviour and so on. The linguist's data are of two sorts:

(*a*) Sequences of sounds, or an acoustic waveform.

(*b*) Certain sorts of judgments on these sequences. Eg. Their acceptability, their similarity and difference.

The Subfields of Linguistics

(1) ***Phonetic or phonological information*:** For every word, we have learned a pronunciation. Part of knowing the word 'tree' is knowing certain sounds or a certain sequence of sound. Phonetics and phonology deals with the study of the structure and systematic patterning of sounds in human language.

(2) ***Morphology*:** Every word has an internal structure. Eg. The word 'tree' cannot be broken down into any meaningful parts. But the word 'trees' is made up of two parts- the word 'tree' and an additional element, '-s' (plural marker). Morphology studies the internal structure of words and the relationships among words.

(3) ***Syntax*:** For every word we learn, we learn how it fits into the overall structure of sentences in which it can be used. Eg. The word 'reads' can be used in a sentence like 'Mark reads the book' and the word 'readable' (related to the word 'read') can be used in a sentence like 'the book is readable'. We may not know that 'read' is called a verb and 'readable' is called an adjective; but we intuitively know how to use those words in different kinds of sentences. Syntax is the study of internal structure of sentences. It lays how words combine to form grammatical sentences.

(4) ***Semantics*:** Every word has a meaning or several meanings. Semantics is the study of the nature of meaning of individual words and the meaning of individual words and the meaning of words grouped into phrases and sentences.

(5) ***Stylistics*:** It is the study of style used in languages.

(6) ***Pragmatics:*** We learn how to use every word in the context of discourse and conversation. Pragmatics is the study of the use of words (and phrases and sentences) in the actual context of discourse.

(7) ***Grammar:*** It allows sounds and meanings to be paired by the construction of sentences.

Contribution of Linguistics in Developing New Fields

Researchers and practitioners have been using or applying linguistic techniques in new developments which might be useful for special fields like teaching, communication, psychology, etc. The use of linguistic ideas in new fields has led to the development of fields as follows:

Bio linguistics: It includes not only the anatomical and physiological foundations of speaking and hearing, but also the place of the speech event in human ecology, the development of an individual and human evolution. Bio linguistics is a fairly recent field.

Ethno linguistics: The ethnology of language is ethnolinguistics. It studies man's linguistic customs (eg. those relating to naming children, joking, greeting, swearing, etc.) relates them to language as studied intrinsically and to non-linguistic customs and finally places language in relation to the larger problems of the science of culture group, tradition and innovation, cultural relativism and ethnocentrism and cultural evolution.

Developmental Linguistics: A developmental linguist will try to describe the child's development in terms of a sequence of grammars. They suppose that children too have an access to a mentally represented grammar. They move towards this through a sequence of 'incomplete' or 'immature' grammars. Children between the age one-and-a-half and two-and-a-half have a spurt in their grammatical development. This uniform and rapidity in the pattern of children's linguistic developments are central facts which a theory of language acquisition must seek to explain.

Many theories have been put forth to explain child language acquisition. Chomsky's hypothesis that the course of language acquisition is determined by an innate language faculty is known popularly as the innateness hypothesis. This entails, that the language faculty must incorporate a set of Universal Grammar principles. This language faculty is species specific and the ability to develop a grammar of a language is unique to human beings.

Psycholinguistics: Psycholinguistics is the study of the mental mechanisms that make it possible for people to use language. A psycholinguist addresses the question of how the mentally represented grammar (linguistic competence) is employed in the production and comprehension of speech (linguistic performance).

The goals of psycholinguists are to understand the language acquisition, how the acquired language is used to speak and understand one another, and how it is represented and processed by the brain. An important area of psycholinguists is the acquisition of first language. Children do this without effort and without being taught, just as any other developmental skills. Psycholinguists think that the rapid effortless and natural acquisition of language by children is the result of the fact that language is a product of the human brain. As the brain develops, it naturally organizes the language the child is exposed to in ways that are common to all humans.

Neurolinguistics: It is a branch of linguistics that deals with the representation of linguistic knowledge in the brain. The study of patients with various types of brain damage has revealed that different parts of the brain are associated with different functions. It is possible to localize different functions in the brain.

Broca's aphasia, a language disorder resulting from brain damage has its site of lesion in left hemisphere, implying a defect in symbolic formulation and expression. In Wernicke's aphasia, however, comprehension is affected more than expressive speech due to lesion in posterior temporal and tempero-parietal regions. As the site varies in the left hemisphere, the areas of language affected vary. It has not been clearly understood how the mechanisms of speech works. However, it can be said with confidence that the posterior parts of the speech areas seem to be concerned with understanding of speech and the formulation of thoughts, i.e., the embodiment of thought in proper syntactical and grammatical form and with correct form and usage of words. The more anterior parts seem to be concerned with the expression and communication of oral and written language. With the advent of neuro-imaging techniques, further research entails that the complex distributed representation are involved in brain which require more sophisticated experimental procedures for its study like PET, ERP's, etc.

Sociolinguistics: Sociolinguistics studies the ways in which language interacts with society. It is the study of the way in which language structure changes in response to its different social functions and definitions of what these functions are. It takes into account factors like social background of listener and speaker, relationship between speaker and listener and content and manner of interaction, maintaining that they are crucial to an understanding of both the structure and function of the language used in that situation. As the usage of language varies from place to place (dialect), language usage varies among social classes; and it is these sociolects that sociolinguistics study.

The study of language variation is concerned with social constraints determining language in its contextual environment. Code-switching is the term given to the use of different varieties of language in different social situations. Sociolinguistics also study language change- how it changes over time in analyzing structural features over time.

One of the ultimate goals of sociolinguistics is that of identifying some of the more universal social features involved in people's choice of language and along with this of showing how their choice is manifested in terms of language, dialect, variety, style, variant, etc.

As emphasis is placed on language use- direct observation or video recording is needed for sociolinguistic emphasis of language.

Clinical Linguistics: Crystal (1984) defines Clinical linguistics as the application of the theories, methods and findings of Linguistics to the study of those situations where language handicaps are diagnosed and treated.

Clinical linguistics gradually emerged as a coherent sub-discipline of applied linguistics. It emerged in large measure as a result of the pioneering work of David Crystal. Linguistics is known to play a major role in the study of communication disorders. Some areas of clinical linguistics include clinical phonetics, clinical phonology, and clinical pragmatics.

Clinical linguistics is the application of theoretical and descriptive linguistics to speech and language pathologies and remediation (Perkins and Howard (1995). Crystal defined as the application of theories, methods and findings of linguistics (including phonetics) to the study of those situations where language handicaps are diagnosed and treated. In other words, clinical linguistics is seen as an applied discipline which is only ultimately justified if it can be shown to contribute to remedial progress. The applications of linguistics to other activities serving particular purposes in the world are collectively known as applied linguistics. Clinical linguistics is a branch of applied linguistics.

Crystal (1984) and Grunwell (1985b,1993) argues that the careful and systematic description of the client's communicative behaviour provides a means of assessing that behaviour in relation to linguistic and developmental areas. They suggest that clinical linguistic analysis can reveal the systematic and communicative status of the client's linguistic patters in their own right, regardless of considerations of target norms. They further suggest that the descriptive and analytical processes should aid differential diagnosis and categorization of the client's behaviours according to different identifiable types of linguistic deficit and disorder. The information derived from analysis should also facilitate the formulation of specific treatment aims and strategies. Careful analysis carried out at different points during the assessment and management process allows identification and evaluation of changes in the client's communicative behaviour over time. Thus, clinical linguistic analysis and description have an important role and developing role both inside and outside the treatment room.

Developments in various areas of linguistic theory include:

(a) ***Phonetics and Phonology***—the assessment and treatment of phonological disorder have been firmly grounded on segmental linear models of phonology. Another development in theoretical phonetics and phonology which is yet to have a significant impact on speech pathology is the growing interest in models that seek to unite the areas of phonetics and phonology to produce more unified accounts of the ways in which the two areas interrelate and can inform each other. This inturn may have implications for phonological disorders and its relation to disorders of articulation and phonetics.

(b) ***Grammar***—the most influential theory of grammar is Chomsky's theory of Universal Grammar. Using this model it has been argued, for eg. that the fact that English speaking individuals with Broca's aphasia often omit noun and verb inflections, whereas, Italian speaking individuals with Broca's aphasia never do so can be explained by attributing to each group a different initial setting for the stem parameter (Leonard and Frome Loeb, 1988). Grodzinsky (1990) and Tait and Shillock (1993) characterize agrammatism in similar terms and Frome Loeb and Leonard (1988) likewise describe specific language impairment in children as a failure to set pragmatics appropriately.

(c) ***Pragmatics***—Pragmatics is playing an important role in language pathology. Eg. speech act theory (Lucas, 1980), discourse analysis (Joanette and Brownell, 1990) and conversation analysis (Lesser and Millroy, 1993)

(d) *Cognitive Neuropsychology*—one area of psycholinguistics that many speech language therapists have recently found useful in clinical work- particularly in assessment and treatment of aphasia is cognitive neuropsychology. Cognitive neuropsychology models the psychological processes that underlies language production and comprehension and focuses on processing in individuals, rather than, attempting to identify properties of language that are universal.

Clinical linguistics' contribution to speech language therapy has been increasingly recognized. Besides ongoing developments in theory and practice in areas such as phonology and grammar, developments in pragmatics and conversation analysis, together with rapid expansions in theory and application of cognitive neuropsychology, all provide speech language therapists with valuable new frameworks for clinical assessment and analysis. There is an assumption that the speech language therapist should be able to do all the necessary clinical linguistic analysis and assessment incorporating an appropriate level of theoretical knowledge and practical detail across all client groups and disorders and across all areas of linguistics.

Scope of Clinical linguistics: Crystal, D (1984) and Grunwell (1985, 93) focusing on the application of Clinical linguistics, have summarized that:

The careful and systematic description of client's communicative behavior provides a means of assessing that behavior in relation to linguistic and where appropriate developmental norms.

- The clinical linguistic analysis can reveal the systematic and communicative status of the client's linguistic patterns.
- Descriptive and analytic processes of linguistics should aid in differential diagnosis and categorization of the client's behaviors. This differential diagnosis and categorization is according to the different identifiable types of the linguistic deficit and disorder.

- This in turn facilitates in the formulation of specific treatment aim and strategies.
- And also careful analysis at different points during assessment and management process allows the identification and evaluation of changes in the client's communicative behavior.

A range of people do Clinical linguistics in various forms and for various purposes. This range includes Academic linguists at one end and practicing Speech language pathologists on the other end. Linguists are interested in theoretical aspects of communication disorders. They have a role in academic involvement with an SLP training course, in teaching linguistics and its clinical applications to SLP students and carrying out research in the area. They are interested in the ways in which aspects of communication disorders can be described and/or explained using linguistic frameworks and concepts and in how communication disorders can provide information to the study of language in general.

SLPs are professionally qualified to provide appropriate management for clients with communication disorders, Clinical linguistics forms a part of their broader professional knowledge base. The primary aim of their linguistic knowledge is for the effective assessment, description and management of a wide range of multifaceted disorders. For SLPs Clinical linguistics have provided a new dimension of viewing each client as a potentially unique case and thus the necessity of making full and detailed descriptions of individual patterns of skills and deficits, rather than falling back on broad diagnostic categories which prove superficial and misleading. Clinical linguistics will be the central focus in making an assessment of the client's communicative behaviour.

The process of making an assessment and carrying out linguistic analysis of client's communicative behaviours in the initial stages of client care and management is time consuming. But they are fundamental necessities, which actually save time in the long term by leading to more finely targeted and effective management. For this there is a strong need of automatic analysis techniques-techniques of analysis using microprocessors, techniques of remediation using interactive instrumentation.

Other Applications of Linguistics

(a) Linguistics and Anthropology: The subject matter of linguistics is 'language' which is man's prime area of communication and that of anthropology is 'man'. The range of research activities of linguistic anthropologist is broad. Practical applications of research activities of linguistic anthropologies are many, like preparing foreign language text books, preparing school grammar.

(b) Computational Linguistics: This is also called mathematical linguistics, statistical linguistics or mechano-linguistics. It deals with application of computer in linguistics field. These include:

- Computer oriented studies in morphology and syntax made popular for techniques like 'predictive analyses'.
- Computer is not only used for collecting and manipulating language and linguistic data, but also a medium for the communication of language and linguistic data. It is used in machine translation and retrieval of linguistic data.
- It is useful in teaching purposes.
- It helps in comparative study of language

(c) Linguistics and instruction in the Native Languages: Linguistics plays an important role in giving instruction in native language. Linguistics has been recently used in the English language text books, reading, spelling materials. The results of the discipline have been applied by linguists. Eg. For reading and spelling, linguists have looked to the correspondence between phonemes and graphic representation. The knowledge of language which linguists provide can be seen to aid the teacher in coping with many of the language problems that arise.

(d) Linguistics and Teaching Foreign Language: There are limitations to the old translation and direct methods of language learning. The linguistic approach to language teaching involves learning or teaching a set of rules to the learner, which enables to implement rules and come out with or generate new sentences on his/her own.

Principles and Theories of Linguistics and their Clinical Relevance

Ferdinand de Saussure (1857-1913) made the first major contribution to our current understanding of what language is and he is widely recognized as the founder of modern linguistics.

In 1957, Noam Chomsky published *Syntactic Structures,* which is said to have revolutionized the study of linguistics. The theories of Saussure and Chomsky are not incompatible; however both concepts of language have profound implications for the remediation of language disabilities.

Theory of Language–Saussure: *Speech circuit*— According to this theory, speech communication act involve at least two people - speaker and listener. The act can be divided into three distinctions.

(*a*) Psychological phenomena: (concepts and sound patterns–language)–The speaker has an idea/ concept, which triggers a sound pattern in the brain, sound pattern here refers to the words which are in 'think-state' and not the articulation. The association of concept and sound pattern can be seen to occur within the brain, therefore is a psychological phenomena.

(*b*) Physiological phenomena: (speaking and hearing) – After the psychological phenomena, the brain sends impulses to the speech organs and the speaker utters appropriate word. This second stage, involving brain, nerves, chemicals and muscles, is physiological.

(*c*) Physical phenomena: (speech sound waves)–Once the word is uttered, the speech sound waves travel through air and reaches the listener's ear, this is purely physical.

Once it reaches the listener's ear the same three processes occur in the reverse order. At this stage the listener can either choose to respond to the message, in which case the whole cycle is started again.

The psychological phenomena (the combination of the concepts and the sound patterns- which Saussure termed as 'Linguistic signs') form the language. Saussure asserted that the notion of the linguistic sign and the facts that surround it, are fundamental to the understanding of the true nature of language. These issues are important also in understanding of language disordered individuals and their remediation.

• *The two parts of the Linguistic sign–concept and sound patterns – are inseparable:*

In language disorders, there can be difficulty in either matching sound patterns to the known concept or appreciating concepts to which their language are matched.

• *Both parts of the linguistic sign are totally arbitrary:*

Arbitrariness of sound patterns- There is no reason why, in English, an apple for example, should not be known as an *apfel, pomme, mela*, it just happens that, in English, *apple* is the sound pattern which matches the concept *round, firm, fleshy fruit of the Rosaceous tree.* This can explain the nature of the problem for the children who confuse opposite terms for instance. In English the concept *hot* and *cold*, exist as two ends of a heat continuum. *Hot-* sound pattern matches the +heat end and *Cold-* sound pattern matches with –heat end, as a product of chance or accident. So language disabled individuals experience difficulty in maintaining a spontaneous connection between each concept and its corresponding sound pattern.

Arbitrariness of concepts–There is no intrinsic reason for acknowledging the existence of a concept and for assigning a sound pattern to it. In some instances linguistic divisions reflect the social needs of the community. For example, whereas in

English, there is one linguistic sign *snow*, Eskimos have twelve different linguistic sings. That is presumably because; snow holds more significance for Eskimos and therefore they are attuned to noticing the fine variations of its substance which we do not necessarily perceive.

The linguistic signs which we use may seem natural and logical to us, but how world look to a child or an adult with brain damage is not the same. Their perceptions of time, space, touch, taste, color, emotion, quality, quantity is not clear. In some cases, individuals with language disorder have difficulty in remembering words (sound patterns), or have little appreciation of concepts. Thus language therapy should involve teaching concepts using practical, non-verbal methods prior to teaching sound patterns.

• *Linguistic signs do not exist in isolation but are part of a system.*

Each sign has its place in an interrelated network of other signs and it forms this system that each sign gains meaning. For example, In English, red has meaning in the context of other terms in the color spectrum. It is that color, which is not blue, yellow, orange, green and so on. In the absence of the rest of the color terms then, red has no meaning at all.

Jonathan Culler (1976)–Hypothetical example: A language teacher tries to teach a non- English speaking student 'brown' by presenting him with hundred brown objects of different types and spends several hours in teaching that each object is 'brown'. On testing the student does not appear to have grasped the concept of brown, this is because, he has not been taught to distinguish between brown and other colors.

Syantagmatic and Paradigmatic Relations: To appreciate the above principle of linguistics it is necessary to examine the ways in which linguistic signs link to form a system. Saussure distinguished two major types of relationship which exist between linguistic elements.

Consider the relationship which exists between opposing (or alternative) elements, Eg: in the sentence *This tea is hot.*

Hot may be replaced with *cold* or *tepid* or *scorching*. *Tea* can be replaced by *coffee* or *water* or *drink; this* may be replaced by *my* or *your* or Aunt *Lucy's*; and *is* may be replaced by *was* or *should be* or *isn't*, and so on. Making any of these changes would of course alter the meaning of the sentence but it would still make sense. The point is that there are connections between, *hot, cold, tepid,* and *scorching* as there are between *tea, coffee, water* and *drink*. Saussure called the relations which exist between such elements *associative* but they are now commonly referred to as Paradigmatic. So, Paradigmatic relations refers to, the set of relationships which a linguistic unit has, with other units in specific context. In other words, words that have something in common are associated in the memory, resulting in groups marked by diverse relations.

The other major relationship is one which exists when linguistic elements are combined with one another. The sequential characteristics of speech, seen as a string of units are usually arranged in a linear order. The relationships between the constituents in a string are referred to as "Syantagmatic relations". Eg: In the sentence, *we can come tomorrow*, the words are arranged in a linear order i.e., the word *we* is correlated with *can, can* with *come*, and so on.

If we return to the problem of the child who confuses opposite terms, we can see that it is one of paradigmatic relations (*The tea is hot/cold*). One approach to remediating this problem might be to teach the two opposite terms together and introduce the child to say, *hot* objects and *cold* objects so that the child feels the difference between them and learn hot and cold.

If the child has difficulty to remember which sound patterns match which concepts, an alternate approach would be to take one term at a time and teach terms which are syntagmatically related to it for example, *hot/fire/danger/burn/hurt; hot/sun/summer/holiday/beach/swim/tan*

The notions of Paradigmatic and Syantagmatic relations lead to *Structuralist* view of language i.e., language is a structured network of interrelated signs but in addition consists of different levels. At each level the units contrast and combine with one another to form the larger units of the next level (sounds'! parts of words/words'! parts of sentences/sentences'! discourse). This view helps us to analyze where exactly the problem lies in the language and decide upon the priorities for therapy.

Synchrony and Diachrony: This distinction refers to the main temporal dimensions of linguistic investigation. It is introduced by Saussure. In synchronic linguistics, languages are studied at a theoretical point of time, a 'state'. E.g.: The language of 18th century or of the present day. In diachronic linguistics, languages are studied from the point of view of their historical development. E.g.: the changes which have taken place between Old and Modern English can be classified and described in terms of grammar, vocabulary, pronunciation, etc.

Clinical implication of diachronic linguistics is that it provides information about normal development and decay of language in a person. This can provide a perspective for remedial work. Carrying out synchronic linguistic analysis is equally important because, to be able to compare the two linguistic states, we have to be aware of what the two states are.

Chomsky's Contribution to Language Theory

Two major aspects of his theories which have clinical relevance are:

(*a*) Investigation in the nature of rules which govern language, i.e., development of the theory of **deep** and **surface** structures

(*b*) Distinction between **competence** and **performance** which is similar to Saussure's distinction of *Langue and Parole.*

The starting point of the theory is the creativity of language i.e., it does not consist of a finite number of possible sentences which are learned and repeated by speakers of that language. Rather, the possible combinations of words are finite and the language users can understand and produce an infinite variety of combinations. That is to say, we can create an infinite number of sentences from a finite set of rules — the grammar of language — and it is the grammar of language that we store.

Deep and Surface Structures: Chomsky developed Transformational Generative Grammar, which leads to the concepts of deep and surface structure. Phrase structure (PS) rules are rules which govern the sentence structure and generate deep structure of sentences. Deep structures are the structures of sentences which embodies meaning. Deep structure sentences are active, affirmative and declarative in nature. Transformations may be applied to deep structures to provide various surface structures. The idea of deep and surface structure captures the interrelatedness of meaning between active and passive sentences. And also accounts for our ability to acknowledge two interpretations of ambiguous sentences.

Linguistic Competence and Performance: *Linguistic Competence* – It is the individual's knowledge of grammar of the native language, which is represented in the mind or brain. Linguistic competence as described by Chomsky in *intuitive*, due to the facts that, we are able to use language whether or not we are aware of the fact that it can be analyzed into noun phrases and verb phrases. We are able to make judgments about the grammaticality of sentences without necessarily knowing why some are ungrammatical or how we know that they are. We use our grammatical knowledge only when we are required to do so, otherwise it is just there and we use it without even being aware that we do.

Performance–It is the use of language. It is the actual use of sentences in concrete situations. For better understanding of the distinction between linguistic competence and performance, consider vocabulary. Each of us have a passive vocabulary—the words which we understand and an active vocabulary — the words which we use when speaking. The full extent of our passive vocabulary is part of our linguistic competence. We do not make use of all that vocabulary in performance. Further performance is subject to many psychological variables such as memory, attention, fatigue, emotional status and so on. Errors of performance due to the effect of variables can be hesitations, false starts, repetitions, and unfinished sentences, and should not be confused as errors of competence. Thus performance does not necessarily reflect competence.

The important point for speech language pathologist is that inferences of linguistic competence should not be drawn with mere observations of performance. All humans produce languages which contains errors, so while making a diagnosis the clinician should know which errors are within normal limits and which constitutes a language disorder. Once a language disorder is diagnosed, a further decision has to be made regarding which errors are performance errors and which reflect underlying competence defects. If the errors are of performance types the implication is that the psychological variables such as memory, attention needs to be worked upon. And if the errors are of linguistic competence then management should focus on teaching specific rules of language. In practice, it is difficult to separate linguistic competence and performance, so clinicians have to plan for management of both the psychological processes.

CHAPTER

2

Phonetics and Phonology

Concept, Acquisition/Development, Disorder and their Clinical Relevance

Phonetics

Phonetics is a branch of linguistics that comprises the study of the sounds of human speech. It is concerned with the physical properties of speech sounds (phones), and the processes of their physiological production, auditory reception, and neurophysiological perception.

Phonetics was studied as early as 2500 years ago in ancient India, with Panini's account of the place and manner of articulation of consonants in his 5th century BC treatise on Sanskrit. The major Indic alphabet today orders their consonants according to PâGini's classification.

Subfields of Phonetics

Phonetics as a research discipline has three main branches:

- Articulatory phonetics is concerned with the articulation of speech: The position, shape, and movement of articulators or speech organs, such as the lips, tongue, and vocal folds.
- Acoustic phonetics is concerned with acoustic of speech: The properties of the sound waves, such as their frequency and harmonics.
- Auditory phonetics is concerned with speech perception: How sound is received by the inner ear and perceived by the brain.

Phoneme, Phone and Allophone

In human language a *phoneme* is the smallest posited structural unit that distinguishes meaning, though they may or may not carry semantic content themselves. In theoretical terms, phonemes are not the physical segments themselves, but cognitive abstractions or categorizations of them.

In effect, a phoneme is a group of slightly different sounds which are all perceived to have the same function by speakers of the language in question. An example of a phoneme is the/ k/sound in the words kit and krill. (In transcription, phonemes are placed between slashes, as here.) Even though most native speakers don't notice, in most dialects, the ks in each of these words are actually pronounced differently: they are different speech sounds, or phones (which, in transcription, are placed in square brackets). In our example, the/k/in kit is aspirated, [kʰ], while the/k/in krill is not, [k]. The reason why these different sounds are nonetheless considered to belong to the same phoneme in English is that if an English-speaker used one instead of the other, the meaning of the word would not change: saying [kʰ] in krill might sound odd, but the word would still be recognised. By contrast, some other sounds could be substituted which would cause a change in meaning, producing words like frill (substituting/ ʃ /), grill (substituting/g/) and shrill (substituting/ ʃ /). These other sounds (/f/,/g/and/ ʃ /) are, in English, different phonemes. In some languages, however, [kʰ] and [k] are different phonemes, and are perceived as such by the speakers of those languages. Thus, in Icelandic,/kʰ/is the first sound of kátur 'cheerful', while/k/is the first sound of gátur 'riddles'.

In many languages, each letter in the spelling system represents one phoneme. However, in English spelling there is a very poor match between spelling and phonemes. For example, the two letters sh represent the single phoneme/ ʃ, while the letters k and c can both represent the phoneme/k/ (as in kit and cat).

Phone is a speech sound or gesture considered a physical event without regard to its place in the phonology of a language. It is a speech segment, which possesses distinct physical or perceptual properties. In other words, it is a physical realization of phoneme.

Every phoneme has multiple variation realizations depending on the context. These are called as *Allophones*, which are the phones that belong to the same phoneme, such as [t] and [t^h] for English/t/, are called allophones. A common test to determine whether two phones are allophones or separate phonemes rely on finding minimal pairs: words that differ by only the phones in question. For example, the words tip and dip illustrate that [t] and [d] are separate phonemes,/ t/and/d/, in English, whereas the lack of such a contrast in Korean (/t^hata/is pronounced [t^hada], for example) indicates that in this language they are allophones of a phoneme/t/. A sound which is an allophone in one language may be a phoneme in another language and vice versa as we have seen earlier.

Consonant

In articulatory phonetics, a consonant is a speech sound that is articulated with complete or partial closure of the upper vocal tract, the upper vocal tract being defined as that part of the vocal tract that lies above the larynx.

Each consonant can be distinguished by several features:

The *manner of articulation* is the method that the consonant is articulated, such as nasal (through the nose), stop (complete obstruction of air), or approximant (vowel like).

The *place of articulation* is where in the vocal tract the obstruction of the consonant occurs, and which speech organs are involved. Places include bilabial (both lips), alveolar (tongue against the gum ridge), and velar (tongue against soft palate). Additionally, there may be a simultaneous narrowing at another place of articulation, such as palatalisation or pharygealisation.

The *phonation* of a consonant is how the vocal cords vibrate during the articulation. When the vocal cords vibrate fully, the consonant is called voiced; when they do not vibrate at all, it's voiceless.

The *voice onset time* (VOT) indicates the timing of the phonation. Aspiration is a feature of VOT. ?

The *airstream mechanism* is how the air moving through the vocal tract is powered. Most languages have exclusively pulmonic egressive consonants, which use the lungs and diaphragm, but ejectives, clicks and implosives use different mechanisms.

The *length* is how long the obstruction of a consonant lasts. This feature is borderline distinctive in English, as in "wholly" [hoʊlli] vs. "holy" [hoʊli], but cases are limited to morpheme boundaries.

The *articulatory force* is how much muscular energy is involved. This has been proposed many times, but no distinction relying exclusively on force has ever been demonstrated.

All English consonants can be classified by a combination of these features.

Classification of Consonants

Place of articulation: In articulatory phonetics, the place of articulation (also point of articulation) of a consonant is the point of contact, where an obstruction occurs in the vocal tract between an active (moving) articulator (typically some part of the tongue) and a passive (stationary) articulator (typically some part of the roof of the mouth). Along with the manner of articulation and phonation, this gives the consonant its distinctive sound.

A place of articulation is defined as both the active and passive articulators. For instance, the active lower lip may contact either a passive upper lip (bilabial, like [m]) or the upper teeth (labiodental, like [f]). The hard palate may be contacted by either the front or the back of the tongue. If the front of the tongue is used, the place is called retroflex; if back of the tongue ("dorsum") is used, the place is called "dorsal-palatal", or more commonly, just palatal.

There are five basic active articulators: the lip ("labial consonanat"), the flexible front of the tongue ("coronal consonant"), the middle/back of the tongue ("dorsal consonant"), the root of the tongue together with the epiglottis ("radical consonant"), and the larynx ("laryngeal consonant"). These articulators can act independently of each other, and two or more may work together in what is called coarticulation (will be discussed later).

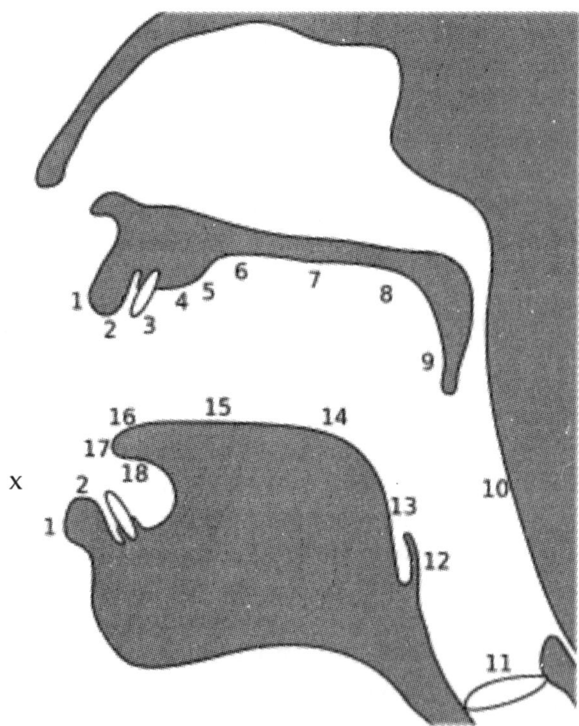

Places of articulation (passive and active):

1. Exo-labial, 2. Endo-labial, 3. Dental, 4. Alveolar, 5. Post-alveolar, 6. Pre-palatal, 7. Palatal, 8. Velar, 9. Uvular, 10. Pharyngeal, 11. Glottal, 12. Epiglottal, 13. Radical, 14. Postero-dorsal, 15. Antero-dorsal, 16. Laminal, 17. Apical, 18. Sub-apical

The passive articulation, on the other hand, is a continuum without many clear-cut boundaries. The places linguolabial and interdental, interdental and dental, dental and alveolar, alveolar and palatal, palatal and velar, velar and uvular merge into one another, and a consonant may be pronounced somewhere between the named places.

Consonants that have the same place of articulation, such as the alveolar sounds — n, t, d, s, z, l – in English, are said to be homorganic.

List of places where the obstruction may occur:

- Bilabial: between the lips
- Labiodental: between the lower lip and the upper teeth
- Linguolabial: between the front of the tongue and the upper lip
- Dental: between the front of the tongue and the top teeth
- Alveolar: between the front of the tongue and the ridge behind the gums (the alveolus)
- Post alveolar: between the front of the tongue and the space behind the alveolar ridge
- Retroflex: in "true" retroflexes, the tongue curls back so the underside touches the palate
- Palatal: between the middle of the tongue and the hard palate
- Velar: between the back of the tongue and the soft palate (the velum)
- Uvular: between the back of the tongue and the uvula (which hangs down in the back of the mouth)

  (All of the above may be nasalized, and most may be lateralized.)
- Pharyngeal: between the root of the tongue and the back of the throat (the pharynx)
- Glottal: at the glottis.

- Nasals and laterals consonants: In nasals, the velum is lowered to allow air to pass through the nose (technically a place, but generally considered as a manner of articulation). In laterals, the air is released past the tongue sides and teeth rather than over the tip of the tongue. English has only one lateral, /l/, but many languages have more than one, e.g. Spanish written "l" vs. "ll"; Hindi with dental, palatal, and retroflex laterals; and numerous Native American languages with not only lateral approximants, but also lateral fricatives and affricates.

Co-articulation

Some languages have consonants with two simultaneous places of articulation, called co-articulation. When these are doubly articulated, the articulators must be independently movable, and therefore there may only be one each from the categories labial, coronal, dorsal, and radical. (The glottis controls phonation and sometimes the airstream, and is not considered an articulator.)

However, more commonly there is a secondary articulator of an approximantic nature, in which case both articulations can be similar, such as labialized labials, palatalized velars, etc.

Some common co-articulations include:

- Labialization: rounding the lips while producing the obstruction, as in [kʷ] and English/w/.
- Palatalization: raising the body of the tongue toward the hard palate while producing the obstruction, as in Russian/tʲ/.
- Velarization: raising the back of the tongue toward the soft palate (velum), as in the English dark l, [lʸ] or [ɫ].
- Pharyngealization: constriction of the throat (pharynx), such as Arabic "emphatic" [tˤ].

- Doubly articulated stop: a stop produced simultaneously with another stop, such as labial-velar consonants like [kap], found throughout West and Central Africa. There are also labial-alveolar consonant [tap dab nam], found as distinct consonants only in a single language in New Guinea, which also contrasts labial-postalveolar stops.

Manner of articulation: Manner of articulation describes how the tongue, lips, jaw, and other speech organs are involved in making a sound make contact. Often the concept is only used for the production of consonants. For anyplace of articulation, there may be several manners, and therefore several homorganic consonants.

One parameter of manner is stricture, that is, how closely the speech organs approach one another. Parameters other than stricture are those involved in the ar sounds (taps and trills), and the sibilancy of fricatives. Often nasality and laterality are included in manner, but phoneticians such as Peter Ladefoged consider them to be independent.

- Plosive or oral stop, where there is complete occlusion (blockage) of both the oral and nasal cavities of the vocal tract, and therefore no air flow. Examples include English/p t k/(voiceless) and/b d g/(voiced). If the consonant is voiced, the voicing is the only sound made during occlusion; if it is voiceless, a plosive is completely silent. What we hear as a/p/or/k/is the effect that the onset of the occlusion has on the preceding vowel, and well as the release burst and its effect on the following vowel. The shape and position of the tongue (the place of articulation) determine the resonant cavity that gives different plosives their characteristic sounds. All languages have plosives.
- Nasal stop, usually shortened to nasal, where there is complete occlusion of the oral cavity, and the air passes instead through the nose. The shape and position of the tongue determine the resonant cavity that gives different nasal stops their characteristic sounds.

Examples include English/m, n/. Nearly all languages have nasals, the only exceptions being in the area of Puget Sound and a single language on Bouganville Island.

- Fricatives, sometimes called spirant, where there is continuous frication (turbulent and noisy airflow) at the place of articulation. Examples include English/f, s/(voiceless),/v, z/(voiced), etc. Most languages have fricatives, though many have only a/s/. However, the Indigenous Australian languages are almost completely devoid of fricatives of any kind.
- Sibilants are a type of fricative where the airflow is guided by a groove in the tongue toward the teeth, creating a high-pitched and very distinctive sound. These are by far the most common fricatives. Fricatives at coronal (front of tongue) places of articulation are usually, though not always, sibilants. English sibilants include/s/and/z/.
- Lateral fricatives are a rare type of fricative, where the frication occurs on one or both sides of the edge of the tongue. The "ll" of Welsh and the "hl" of Zulu are lateral fricatives.
- Affricate, which begins like a plosive, but this releases into a fricative rather than having a separate release of its own. The English letters "ch" and "j" represent affricates. Affricates are quite common around the world, though less common than fricatives.
- Flap, often called a tap, is a momentary closure of the oral cavity. The "tt" of "utter" and the "dd" of "udder" are pronounced as a flap in North American English. Many linguists distinguish taps from flaps, but there is no consensus on what the difference might be. No language relies on such a difference. There are also lateral flaps.
- Trill, in which the articulator (usually the tip of the tongue) is held in place, and the airstream causes it to

vibrate. The double "r" of "perro" is a trill. Trills and flaps, where there are one or more brief occlusions, constitute a class of consonant called rhotics.

- Approximant, where there is very little obstruction. Examples include English/w/and/r/. In some languages, such as Spanish, there are sounds which seem to fall between fricative and approximant.

One use of the word semivowel is a type of approximant, pronounced like a vowel but with the tongue closer to the roof of the mouth, so that there is slight turbulence. In English,/w/is the semivowel equivalent of the vowel/u/, and/j/(spelled "y") is the semivowel equivalent of the vowel/ i/in this usage. Other descriptions use semivowel for vowel-like sounds that are not syllabic, but do not have the increased stricture of approximants. These are found as elements in diphthongs. The word may also be used to cover both concepts.

Lateral approximants, usually shortened to lateral, are a type of approximant pronounced with the side of the tongue. English/l/is a lateral. Together with the rhotics, which have similar behavior in many languages, these forms a class of consonant called liquids.

Broader Classifications

Manners of articulation with substantial obstruction of the airflow (plosives, fricatives, affricates) are called obstruents. These are prototypically voiceless, but voiced obstruents are extremely common as well. Manners without such obstruction (nasals, liquids, approximants, and also vowels) are called sonorants because they are nearly always voiced. Voiceless sonorants are uncommon, but are found in Welsh and Classical Greek (the spelling "rh"), in Tibetan (the "lh" of Lhasa), and the "wh" in those dialects of English which distinguish "which" from "witch".

Sonorants may also be called resonants, and some linguists prefer that term, restricting the word 'sonorant' to non-vocoid resonants (that is, nasals and liquids, but not vowels or semi-vowels). Another common distinction is between stops (plosives and nasals) and continuants (all else); affricates are considered to be both, because they are sequences of stop plus fricative.

Other Airstream Initiations

All of these manners of articulation are pronounced with an airstream mechanism called pulmonic egressive, meaning that the air flows outward, and is powered by the lungs (actually the ribs and diaphragm). Other airstream mechanisms are possible. Sounds that rely on some of these include:

Ejectives, which are glottalic egressive. That is, the airstream is powered by an upward movement of the glottis rather than by the lungs or diaphragm. Plosives, affricates, and occasionally fricatives may occur as ejectives. All ejectives are voiceless.

Implosives, which are glottalic ingressive. Here the glottis moves downward, but the lungs may be used simultaneously (to provide voicing), and in some languages no air may actually flow into the mouth. Implosive oral stops are not uncommon, but implosive affricates and fricatives are rare. Voiceless implosives are also rare.

Clicks, which are velaric ingressive. Here the back of the tongue is used to create a vacuum in the mouth, causing air to rush in when the forward occlusion (tongue or lips) is released. Clicks may be oral or nasal, stop or affricate, central or lateral, voiced or voiceless. They are extremely rare in normal words outside Southern Africa. However, English has a click in its "tsk tsk" (or "tut tut") sound, and another is used to say "giddy up" to a horse.

Voicing: Voice or voicing is a term used in phonetics and phonology to characterize speech sounds, with sounds described as either voiceless (unvoiced) or voiced. The term, however, is used to refer to two separate concepts. Voicing can refer to the articulatory process in which the vocal cords vibrate. This is its primary use in phonetics to describe phones, which are particular speech sounds. It can also refer to a classification of speech sounds that tend to be associated with vocal cord vibration but need not actually be voiced at the articulatory level. This is the term's primary use in phonology when describing phonemes, or in phonetics when describing phones.

At the articulatory level, a voiced sound is one in which the vocal cords vibrate, and a voiceless sound is one in which they do not. Voicing is the difference between the pairs of sounds that are associated with the English letters "s" and "z". The two sounds are symbolically written [s] and [z] to distinguish them from the English letters, which have several possible pronunciations depending on context. If one places the fingers on the voice box (ie the location of the Adam's apple in the upper throat), one can feel a vibration when one pronounces zzzz, but not when one pronounces ssss. In European languages such as English, vowels and other sonorants (consonants such as m, n, l, and r) are modally voiced.

When used to classify speech sounds, voiced and unvoiced are merely labels used to group phones and phonemes together for the purposes of classification. We return to this below.

The distinction between the articulatory use of voice and the phonological use rests on the distinction between phone and phoneme. The difference is best illustrated by a rough example. Words are composed of phonemes. The English word "pods" is made up of a sequence of phonemes, represented symbolically as "/padz/", or the sequence of/ p/,/a/,/d/, and/z/. Each letter is an abstract symbol for a phoneme. This is a part of our grammatical knowledge.

Consonant phonemes are classified as either voiced or voiceless. Some voiced phonemes of English are/b,d,g,v,z/. Each of these obstruents has an unvoiced counterpart,/ p,t,k,f,s/. The classification is useful for describing phonological processes such as vowel lengthening that occurs before voiced consonants but not before unvoiced consonants or vowel quality changes (i.e. the sound of the vowel) in some dialects of English that occur before unvoiced but not voiced consonants.

However, phonemes are not sounds. Rather, phonemes are, in turn, converted to phones before being spoken. The/ z/phoneme, for instance, can be pronounced as the [s] phone or the [z] phone, depending on context, and so the sequence of phones for "pods" might be [pads] or [padz]. The different type of brackets indicates that these are symbols for phones now. As described above, while the [z] phone has articulatory voicing, the [s] phone does not. It is hard to directly observe the difference between [pods] and [podz] because of the voicing in the preceding [d], but one can readily see that both pronunciations are common using digital audio tools.

Vowel

In phonetics, a vowel is a sound in spoken language, pronounced with an open vocal tract so that there is no build-up of air pressure at any point above the glottis. This contrasts with consonants, such as English sh! [ʃ:], where there is a constriction or closure at some point along the vocal tract. A vowel is also understood to be syllabic: an equivalent open but non-syllabic sound is called a semivowel.

In all languages, vowels form the nucleus or peak of syllables, whereas consonants form the onset and (in languages which have them) coda. However, some languages also allow other sounds to form the nucleus of a syllable, such as the syllabic l in the English word table [tej.bl)] (the stroke under the l indicates that it is syllabic; the dot separates syllables), or the r in Serbian vrt [vr)t] "garden".

We might note the conflict between the phonetic definition of 'vowel' (a sound produced with no constriction in the vocal tract) and the phonological definition (a sound that forms the peak of a syllable). The approximants [j] and [w] illustrate this conflict: both are produced without much of a constriction in the vocal tract (so phonetically they seem to be vowel-like), but they occur on the edge of syllables, such as at the beginning of the English words 'yes' and 'wet' (which suggests that phonologically they are consonants). The American linguist Kenneth Pike suggested the terms 'vocoid' for a phonetic vowel and 'vowel' for a phonological vowel, so using this terminology, [j] and [w] are classified as vocoids but not vowels.

Classification of Vowels

The articulatory features that distinguish different vowel sounds are said to determine the vowel's quality. Daniel Jones developed the cardinal vowel system to describe vowels in terms of the three common features height (vertical dimension), backness (horizontal dimension) and roundedness (lip position). These three parameters are indicated in the schematic IPA vowel diagram on the right. There are however still more possible features of vowel quality, such as the velum position (nasality), type of vocal fold vibration (phonation), and tongue root position. The vowels can be classified on the basis of their respective qualities.

Tongue Height: Vowel height is named for the vertical position of the tongue relative to either the roof of the mouth or the aperture of the jaw. In high vowels, such as [i] and [u], the tongue is positioned high in the mouth, whereas in low vowels, such as [a], the tongue is positioned low in the mouth. The IPA prefers the terms close vowel and open vowel, respectively, which describes the jaw as being relatively open or closed. However, vowel height is an acoustic rather than articulatory quality, and is defined today not in terms of tongue height, or jaw openness, but according to the relative frequency of the first formant (F1). The higher the F1 value, the lower (more open) the vowel; height is thus inversely correlated to F1.

The International Phonetic Alphabet identifies seven different vowel heights:

- close vowel (high vowel)

- near-close vowel
- close-mid vowel
- mid vowel
- open-mid vowel
- near-open vowel
- open vowel (low vowel)

True mid vowels do not contrasts with both close-mid and open-mid in any language and the letters [e ø d o] are typically used for either close-mid or mid vowels.

Although English contrasts all six contrasting heights in its vowels, these are interdependent with differences in backness, and many are parts of diphthongs. It appears that some varieties of German have five contrasting vowel heights independently of length or other parameters. The Bavarian dialect of Amstetten has thirteen long vowels, reported to distinguish four heights (close, close-mid, mid, and near-open) each among the front unrounded, front rounded, and back rounded vowels, plus an open central vowel:/i e [" æ"/,/y ø œ" v"/,/u o T" R"/,/a/. Otherwise, the usual limit on the number of contrasting vowel heights is four.

The parameter of vowel height appears to be the primary feature of vowels cross-linguistically in that all languages use height contrastively. No other parameter, such as front-back or rounded-unrounded (see below), is used in all languages. Some languages have vertical vowel systems in which, at least at a phonemic level, only height is used to distinguish vowels.

Backness of the Tongue: Vowel backness is named for the position of the tongue during the articulation of a vowel relative to the back of the mouth. In front vowels, such as [i], the tongue is positioned forward in the mouth, whereas in back vowels, such as [u], the tongue is positioned towards the back of the mouth. However, vowels are defined as back or front not according to actual articulation, but according to the relative frequency of the second formant (F2). The higher the F2 value, the fronter the vowel; backness is thus inversely correlated to F2.

The International Phonetic Alphabet identifies five different degrees of vowel backness:

- front vowel
- near-front vowel
- central vowel
- near-back vowel
- back vowel

Although English has vowels at all five degrees of backness, there is no known language that distinguishes all five without additional differences in height or rounding.

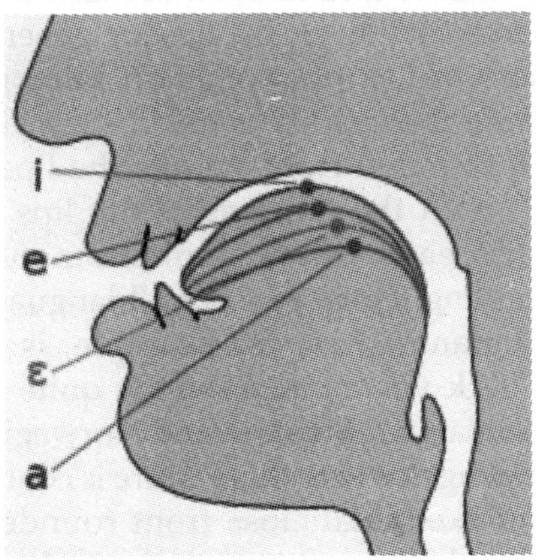

Source: www.wikipedia.com.

Tongue positions of cardinal front vowels with highest point indicated. The position of the highest point is used to determine vowel height and backness.

Roundedness (lip orification): Roundedness refers to whether the lips are rounded or not. In most languages, roundedness is a reinforcing feature of mid to high back vowels, and is not distinctive. Usually the higher a back vowel is, the more intense the rounding. However, some languages treat roundedness and backness separately, such as French and German (with front rounded vowels), most Uralic languages (Estonian has a rounding contrast for/o/and front vowels), Turkic languages (with an unrounded/u/),

Vietnamese (with back unrounded vowels), and Korean (with a contrast in both front and back vowels).

Nonetheless, even in languages such as German and Vietnamese, there is usually some phonetic correlation between rounding and backness: front rounded vowels tend to be less front than front unrounded vowels, and back unrounded vowels tend to be less back than back rounded vowels. That is, the placement of unrounded vowels to the left of rounded vowels on the IPA vowel chart is reflective of their typical position.

Different kinds of labialization are also possible. In mid to high rounded back vowels the lips are generally protruded ("pursed") outward, a phenomenon known as exolabial rounding because the insides of the lips are visible, whereas in mid to high rounded front vowels the lips are generally "compressed", with the margins of the lips pulled in and drawn towards each other, a phenomenon known as endolabial rounding. However, not all languages follow this pattern. The Japanese/u/, for example, is an endolabial (compressed) back vowel, and sounds quite different from an English exolabial/u/. Swedish and Norwegian are the only two known languages where this feature is contrastive, having both endo- and exo-labial close front rounded vowels and close central rounded vowels, respectively. In many phonetic treatments, both are considered types of rounding, but some phoneticians do not believe that these are subsets of a single phenomenon of rounding, and prefer instead the three independent terms rounded (exolabial), compressed (endolabial), and spread (unrounded).

Classifications based on Other Qualities*—Nasalization:* Nasalization refers to whether some of the air escapes through the nose. In nasal vowels, the velum is lowered, and some air travels through the nasal cavity as well as the mouth. An oral vowel is a vowel in which all air escapes through the mouth. French, Polish and Portuguese contrast nasal and oral vowels.

Phonation: Voicing describes whether the vocal cords are vibrating during the articulation of a vowel. Most languages only have voiced vowels, but several Native American languages, such as Cheyenne and Totonac, contrast voiced and devoiced vowels. Vowels are devoiced in whispered speech. In Japanese and Quebec French, vowels that are between voiceless consonants are often devoiced.

Modal voice, creaky voice, and breathy voice (murmured vowels) are phonation types that are used contrastively in some languages. Often, these co-occur with tone or stress distinctions; in the Mon language, vowels pronounced in the high tone are also produced with creaky voice. In cases like this, it can be unclear whether it is the tone, the voicing type, or the pairing of the two that is being used for phonemic contrast. This combination of phonetic cues (i.e. phonation, tone, stress) is known as register or register complex.

Tongue root retraction: Advanced tongue root (ATR) is a feature common across much of Africa. The contrast between advanced and retracted tongue root resembles the tense/lax contrast acoustically, but they are articulated differently. ATR vowels involve noticeable tension in the vocal tract.

Secondary narrowing in the vocal tract: Pharyngealized vowels occur in some languages; Sedang uses this contrast, as do the Tungusic languages. Pharyngealisation is similar in articulation to retracted tongue root, but is acoustically distinct.

A stronger degree of pharyngealisation occurs in the Northeast Caucasian languages and the Khoisan languages. These might be called epiglottalized, since the primary constriction is at the tip of the epiglottis.

The greatest degree of pharyngealisation is found in the strident vowels of the Khoisan languages, where the larynx is raised, and the pharynx constricted, so that either the epiglottis or the arytenoid cartilages vibrate instead of the vocal cords.

Note that the terms pharyngealized, epiglottalized, strident, and sphincteric are sometimes used interchangeably.

Syllable

A syllable is a unit of organization for a sequence of speech sounds. For example, the word water is composed of two syllables: wa and ter. A syllable is typically made up of a syllable nucleus (most often a vowel) with optional initial and final margins (typically, consonants).Syllables are often considered the phonological "building blocks" of words. They can influence the rhythm of a language, its prosody, its poetic meter, its stress patterns, etc.

Syllablic writing began several hundred years before the first letter. The earliest recorded syllables are on tablets written around 2800 BC in the Sumerian city of Ur. This shift from pictograms to syllables has been called 'the most important advance in the history of writing'.

A word that consists of a single syllable (like English cat) is called a monosyllable (such a word is monosyllabic); while a word consisting of two syllables (like monkey) is called a disyllable (such a word is disyllabic). A word consisting of three syllables (such as indigent) is called a trisyllable (the adjective form is trisyllabic). A word consisting of more than three syllables (such as intelligence) is called a polysyllable (and could be described as polysyllabic), although this term is often used to describe words of two syllables or more.

Syllable Structure

The general structure of a syllable consists of the following segments:

- Onset (obligatory in some languages, optional or even restricted in others)
- Rhyme
- Nucleus (obligatory in all languages)
- Coda (optional in some languages, highly restricted or prohibited in others)

In some theories of phonology, these syllable structures are displayed as tree diagram (similar to the trees found in some types of syntax). Not all phonologists agree that syllables have internal structure; in fact, some phonologists doubt the existence of the syllable as a theoretical entity.

The syllable nucleus is typically a sonorant, usually making a vowel sound, in the form of a monophthong, diphthong or triphthong, but sometimes sonorant consonants like [l] or [r]. The syllable onset is the sound or sounds occurring before the nucleus, and the syllable coda (literally 'tail') is the sound or sounds that follow the nucleus. The term rhyme covers the nucleus plus coda. In the one-syllable English word cat, the nucleus is a, the onset c, the coda t, and the rime at. This syllable can be abstracted as a consonant-vowel-consonant syllable, abbreviated CVC.

Generally, every syllable requires a nucleus. Onsets are extremely common, and some languages require all syllables to have an onset. (That is, a CVC syllable like cat is possible, but a VC syllable such as at is not.) A coda-less syllable of the form V, CV, CCV, etc. is called an open syllable, while a syllable that has a coda (VC, CVC, CVCC, etc.) is called a closed syllable (or checked syllable). All languages allow open syllables, but some, such as Hawaiian, do not have closed syllables.

Syllabification

Syllabification is the separation of a word into syllables, whether spoken or written. In most languages, the actually spoken syllables are the basis of syllabification in writing too. However, due to the very weak correspondence between sounds and letters in the spelling of modern English, for example, written syllabification in English has to be based mostly on etymological i.e. morphological instead of phonetic principles. English "written" syllables therefore do not correspond to the actually spoken syllables of the living language.

(Syllabification may also refer to the process of a consonant becoming a syllable nucleus.)

Syllabic Consonants and Non-syllabic Vowels

Consonants and vowels correspond to distinct parts of a syllable: The most sonorous part of the syllable (that is, the part that's easiest to sing), called the syllabic peak or nucleus, is typically a vowel, while the less sonorous margins (called the onset and coda) are typically consonants. Such syllables may be abbreviated CV, V, and CVC, where C stands for consonant and V stands for vowel. This can be argued to be the only pattern found in most of the world's languages, and perhaps the primary pattern in all of them. However, the distinction between consonant and vowel is not always clear cut: there are syllabic consonants and non-syllabic vowels in many of the world's languages.

One blurry area is in segments variously called semivowels, semi consonants, or glides. On the one side, there is vowel-like segments which are not in themselves syllabic, but which form diphthong, as part of the syllable nucleus, as the i in English boil ['B ɔɪ̯ L]. On the other, there are approximants, which behave like consonants in forming onsets, but are articulated very much like vowels, as the y in English yes ['jɛs]. Some phonologists model these as both being the vowel/i/, so that the English word bit would phonemically be/bit/, beet would be/ bii̯t /, and yield would be phonemically/ i̯ii̯ld /. Similarly, foot would be/fut/, food would be/ fuu̯d /, wood would be/ u̯ud /, and wooed would be/ u̯uu̯d /. However, there is a (perhaps allophonic) difference in articulation between these segments, with the [j] in ['jɛs] yes and ['jiʲld] yield and the [w] of ['wuʷd] wooed having more constriction and a more definite place of articulation than the [ɪ] in ['B ɔɪ̯ L] boil or ['bɪt] bit or the [ʊ] of ['fʊt].

Diphthong

A diphthong, (also gliding vowel) is a contour vowel—that is, a unitary vowel that changes quality during its pronunciation, or "glides", with a smooth movement of the tongue from one articulation to another, as in the English words eye, boy, and cow. This contrasts with "pure" vowels, or monophthongs, where the tongue is held still, as in the English word papa.

Diphthongs often form when separate vowels are run together in rapid speech. However, there are also unitary diphthongs, as in the English examples above, which are heard by listeners as single vowel sounds (phonemes).

In the International Phonetic Alphabet, pure vowels are transcribed with one letter, as in English "sum" [sŒm]. Diphthongs are transcribed with two letters, as in English "eye" [aj/] or "same" [sej/m]. The two vowel symbols are chosen to represent the beginning and ending positions of the tongue, though this can be only approximate. The diacritic < > is placed under the less prominent component to show that it is part of a diphthong rather than a separate vowel, though it is sometimes left off in languages such as English, where there is not likely to be any confusion. (That is, in precise transcription, [ai] represents two vowels in hiatus, as found for example in Hawaiian and in the English word "naïve". It would not be a diphthong, for instance, in the English word, "knives").

Types of Diphthongs

Falling (or descending) diphthongs start with a vowel quality of higher prominence (higher pitch or louder) and end in a semivowel with less prominence, like [aj/] in "eye", while rising (or ascending) diphthongs begin with a less prominent semivowel and end with a more prominent full vowel, like [j/a] in "yard". The less prominent component in the diphthong may also be transcribed as an approximant, thus [aj] in "eye" and [ja] in "yard". However, when the diphthong is analysed as a single phoneme, both elements are often transcribed with vowel letters (/aj//,/j/a/). Note also that semivowels and approximants are not equivalent in all treatments, and in the English and Italian languages, among others, many phoneticians do not consider rising combinations to be diphthongs, but rather sequences of approximant and vowel. There are many languages (such as Romanian) that contrast one or more rising diphthongs with similar sequences of a glide and a vowel in their phonetic inventory.

In closing diphthongs, the second element is closer than the first (e.g. [ai]); in opening diphthongs, more open (e.g. [ia]). Closing diphthongs tend to be falling ([ai̯]), and opening diphthongs are generally rising (i̯a), because open vowels are more sonorous and therefore tend to be more prominent. However, exceptions to this rule are not rare in the world's languages. In Finnish, for instance, the opening diphthongs/ ie̯ /and/ uo̯ /are true falling diphthongs, since they begin louder and with higher pitch and fall in prominence during the diphthong.

A centering diphthong is one that begins with a more peripheral vowel and ends with a more central one, such as [ɪə̯], [ɛə̯], and [ʊə̯] in Received Pronunciation or [iə̯] and [uə̯] in Irish. Many centering diphthongs are also opening diphthongs (iə̯], [uə̯).

Some languages contrast short and long diphthongs, the latter usually being described as having a long first element. Languages that contrast three quantities in diphthongs are extremely rare, but not unheard of: Northern Sami is known to contrast long, short and finally stressed diphthongs, the last of which are distinguished by a long second element.

While there are a number of similarities, diphthongs are not the same as a combination of a vowel and a semivowel or glide. Most importantly, diphthongs are contained in the syllable nucleus while a semivowel or glide is restricted to the syllable boundaries (either the onset or the coda). This often manifests itself phonetically by a greater degree of constriction; though this phonetic distinction is not always clear. The English word yes, for example, consists of a palatal glide followed by a monophthong rather than a rising diphthong.

Supra-segmentals

In linguistics, prosody is the rhythm, stress, and intonation of connected speech (as opposed to smaller elements like syllables or words). Prosody may reflect various features of the speaker or the utterance: the emotional state of a speaker; whether an utterance is a statement, a question, or a command; whether the speaker is being ironic or sarcastic; emphasis, contrast, and focus; or other elements of language that may not be encoded by grammar or choice of vocabulary.

Pitch represents the perceived fundamental frequency of a sound. Pitch means how high or low a note is and is one of the five main elements of music. It is one of the three major auditory attributes of sounds along with loudness and timbre. When the actual fundamental frequency can be precisely determined through physical measurement, it may differ from the perceived pitch because of overtones, also known as partials, harmonic or otherwise, in the sound. The human auditory perception system may also have trouble distinguishing frequency differences between notes under certain circumstances. According to ANSI acoustical terminology, it is the auditory attribute of sound according to which sounds can be ordered on a scale from low to high.

In linguistics, *stress* is the relative emphasis that may be given to certain syllable in a word. The term is also used for similar patterns of phonetic prominence inside syllables. The word accent is sometimes also used with this sense.

In linguistics *tone* is variation of pitch while speaking which is used to distinguish words (word level). In other words, tone is the use of pitch in language to distinguish lexical or grammatical meaning—that is, to distinguish or inflect words. All languages use pitch to express emotional and other paralinguistic information, and to convey emphasis, contrast, and other such features in what is called *intonation*, but not all languages use tones to distinguish words or their inflections, analogously to consonants and vowels. Such tonal phonemes are sometimes called *tonemes*.On the other hand, intonation is variation of pitch while speaking which is not used to distinguish words (pitch variation at sentence level). Intonation and stress are two main elements of linguistic prosody.

All languages use pitch semantically, that is, as intonation, for instance for emphasis, to convey surprise or irony, or to pose a question. Tonal languages such as Chinese and Hausa use pitch to distinguish words in addition to intonation. Rising intonation means the pitch of the voice increases over time; falling intonation means that the pitch decreases with time. A dipping intonation falls and then rises, whereas a peaking intonation rises and then falls.

So far, we have discussed about Phonetics, now we shall discuss about Phonology. Let us try to find out whether there is any relationship between these two terms or not.

Phonology

Phonology is the system of rules, representations, and principles governing the distribution/arrangement of sounds. It is the systematic use of sound to encode meaning in any spoken human language, or the field of linguistics studying this use.

Is there any relationship between Phonetics and Phonology?

In contrast to phonetics, phonology is the study of language-specific systems and patterns of sound and gesture, relating such concerns with other levels and aspects of language. While phonology is grounded in phonetics, it has emerged as a distinct area of linguistics, dealing with abstract systems of sounds and gestural units (e.g., phoneme, features, mora, etc.) and their variants (e.g., allophones), the distinctive properties (features) which form the basis of meaningful contrast between these units, and their classification into natural classes based on shared behaviour and phonological processes. Phonetics tends to deal more with the physical properties of sounds and the physiological aspects of speech production and perception. It deals less with how sounds are patterned to encode meaning in language (though overlap in theorizing, research and clinical applications are possible.

Just as a language has syntax and vocabulary, it also has phonology in the sense of a sound system. When describing the formal area of study, the term typically describes linguistics analysis either beneath the word (e.g., syllable, onset and rime, phoneme, articulatory gesture, articulatory feature, mora, etc.) or to units at all levels of language that are thought to structure sound for conveying linguistic meaning.

It is viewed as the subfield of linguistics that deals with the sound systems of languages. Whereas phonetics is about the physical production, acoustic transmission and perception of the sounds of speech, phonology describes the way sounds function within a given language or across languages to encode meaning. The term 'phonology' was used in the linguistics of a greater part of the 20th century as a cover term uniting phonemics and phonetics. Current phonology can interface with disciplines such as psycholinguistics and speech perception, resulting in specific areas like articulatory or laboratory phonology.

Sounds vary considerably based on context. This variation is not arbitrary but follows a predictable pattern which needs to be figured out. In spite of all this complexity children learn phonology of their native language quiet easily.

Types of Phonology

The two basic types include:

(1) Segmental/linear phonology

(2) Non-segmental/non-linear phonology

Segmental/linear Phonology

These are the phonological theories based on the understanding that all speech segments are arranged in a sequential order. It deals with sound segments. Basic characteristics include:

(*a*) Emphasis on linear, sequential arrangement of sound segments.

(*b*) Assumption that each discrete segment consists of a bundle of distinctive features.

(*c*) Assumption that a common set of distinctive features is attributable to all sound segments according to a binary + and – system.

(*d*) Assumption that all sound segments have all equal value and all distinctive features are equal, thus, no one sound segment has control over other units.

Phonological rules generated apply only to segmental level and to those changes that occur in distinctive features.

Limitations:

(1) These are type of Phonologies that fails to analyze, recognize and describe the larger linguistic units like suprasegmentals.

(2) Also doesn't account for the possibility of hierarchical interaction between segments and other linguistic units.

Segmental phonology is further divided into:

(1) Natural phonology

(2) Generative phonology

Natural Phonology and its clinical implications: Natural Phonology was a theory based on the publications of its proponent David Stampe in 1969 and (more explicitly) in 1979. In this view, phonology is based on a set of universal phonological processes which interact with one another; which ones are active and which are suppressed are language-specific. Rather than acting on segments, phonological processes act on distinctive features within prosodic groups. Prosodic groups can be as small as a part of a syllable or as large as an entire utterance. Phonological processes are unordered with respect to each other and apply simultaneously (though the output of one process may be the input to another). The second-most prominent Natural Phonologist is Stampe's wife, Patricia Donegan; there are many Natural Phonologists in Europe, though also a few others in the U.S., such as Geoffrey Pullum. The principles of Natural Phonology were extended to morphology by Wolfgang U. Dressler, who founded Natural Morphology.

Natural phonology is a natural theory, in that it presents language as a natural reflection of the needs, capacities and world of its users, rather than as a merely conational institution. [Donegan and Stamps, 1979]:

- It incorporates features of naturalness theories and specially designed to explain the development of the child's phonological system.
- It postulates that the patterns of speech are governed by innate, universal set of phonological processes.
- It assumes that, the child's innate phonological system continuously revised in the direction of the adult phonological system.

Stampe (1969), proposed 3 mechanisms to account for their changes:

(1) Limitation

(2) Ordering

(3) Suppression

(1) Limitations: Occurs when difference between the child's and the adult's system become limited to only specific standard classes or standard sequences.

Ex: Initially the child might substitute , natural standards for marked ones.

Ex: Stops for fricatives.

Later, all fricatives substitutes will become limited to fricatives only.

(2) Ordering: Occurs when substitutions that appeared unordered and random become more organized.

(3) Suppression: It occurs when previously used phonological processes are not used any more.

Clinical Implications:

- It is used in the study of the normal developmental process.

- It is used in the assessment of the disordered phonological system, by comparing with the normal development and helps to classify the process into different types like persisting phonological process, chronological mismatch etc.
- Treatment based on this theory emphasizes suppression of the phonological process in order to increase the complexity of the child's phonological pattern

Generative Phonology and its clinical implications: It represents the applications of principles of generative or transformational grammar to phonology. It assumes two levels of representation, an abstract underlying form called phonological representation and its modified surface form called phonetic representation. Phonological rules are used to demonstrate the relationship between the two. Distinctive features are also central to the concept of generative phonology. Generative phonology is an attempt to understand and explain the said patterns of language. In this theory, inherent idea is that a phonological description is dependent on information from other linguistic level i.e. morphological or syntactic level rules influences phonological descriptions.

Ex: National→Nationality

Noble→Nobility

Mobile→Mobility

Here a phonological rule (derivation) is applied on the phonological representation of the root word or lever to establish surface level phonetic representation.

- Phonological rules are also used to describe the pronunciation pattern that is not related to morphological changes.
- Distinctive feature are often employed while formulating phonological rules, according to the classification of segments into natural classes, similar to that in language.

- Generative phonology uses markedness, to explain the acquisition/phonological development.

Clinical Implications:

(1) Helps to study or analyze the phonological systems of language and also phonological development in children.

(2) Its application to phonological development in children has been done by Smith(1973)

(3) Helps to analyze the phonological development in children with disordered phonological systems, by comparing the child's phonological system to the adult's pattern. It analyzes errors in terms of substitutions and deletions.

(4) The generative marked ness offers insight into the acquisition of sound features and possibly, the type of substitutions that may be seen in the speech of children with disordered phonological system.

i.e. children with phonological disorders have a tendency to substitute more natural/unmarked classes of segments for marked ones.

Nonsegmental/Nonlinear Phonologies/Multilineared /Multitiered Phonology

These are a group of phonological theories understanding segments as governed by more complex linguistic dimensions. It deals with suprasegmental feature.

Here complex linguistic dimensions, for eg. Stress, intonation, metrical and rhythmic linguistic factors may control segmental conditions and explain the influence of larger linguistic entities on sound segments.

In this type of phonology, a hierarchy of factors is hypothesized to effect the segmental units i.e here the features are ranked one above the other.

(1) Syllable structure could affect the segmental level.

Ex: *jumping→jumpin, window→widow*

Child deletes the final consonant in multisyllabic words.

Here the number of syllabus determines the segmental features.

Nonlinear phonologies rank syllable structure above the level of sound segments.

(2) Stress determines segmental realizations.

Ex: Banana→na–na

Potato→te-to }Here unstressed syllable is deleted.

Nonlinear phonologies are able to describe that how the stress governs the segmental features/segments, i.e. one level of unit is governed by another.

There are many different types of nonlinear phonology which include:

Autosegmental phonology and its clinical implication: Autosegmental phonology is the name of a framework of phonological analysis proposed by John Goldsmith in his PhD Thesis in 1976 at the Massachusetts Institute of Technology (MIT). As a theory of phonological representation, autosegmental phonology developed a formal account of ideas that had been sketched in earlier work by several linguists, notably Bernard Bloch (1948), Charles Hockett (1955) and J.R.Firth (1948). On such a view, phonological representations consist of more than one linear sequence of segments; each linear sequence constitutes a separate tier. The co-registration of elements (or autosegments) on one tier with those on another is represented by association lines. There is a close relationship between analysis of segments into distinctive features and an autosegmental analysis; each feature in a language appears on exactly one tier. The working hypothesis of autosegmental analysis is that a large part of phonological generalizations can be interpreted as a restructuring or reorganization of the autosegments in a representation. Clear examples of the usefulness of autosegmental analysis came in early work from the detailed study of Africantone languages, as well as the study of vowel and nasal harmony systems. A few years later, John McCarthy proposed an important development by showing that the vocalism and consonantism of Arabic could be analyzed autosegmentally.

As a theory of the dynamic of phonological representations, autosegmental phonology includes a Well-formedness Condition on association lines (each element on one tier that "may" be associated to an element on another tier "must" be associated to such an element, and association lines do not cross) plus an instruction as to what to do in case of a violation of the Well-formedness Condition: add or delete the minimum number of association lines in order to maximally satisfy it. Many of the most interesting predictions of the autosegmental model derive from the automatic effects of the Well-formedness Condition and their independence of language-particular rules.

Phonological phenomena are no longer seen as operating on one linear sequence of segments, called phonemes or feature combinations, but rather as involving some parallel sequences of features which reside on multiple tiers. Augosegmental phonology later evolved into Feature Geometry, which became the standard theory of representation for the theories of the organization of phonology as different as Lexical Phonology and Optimality Theory.

Autosegmental phonology accounts for tone phenomena in languages in which segmental features interact with varying tones. Autosegmental representations are fundamentally different from conventional segmental representations in that features can be represented on one tier and segments on another tier i.e another parallel tier, resulting in a multilayered representation. And it helps to describe the relationships like, a single feature may be associated with one or more segments or possibly even no segment and also, a single segment may be associated with a single feature, a linear sequence of features, or even no feature.

Autosegmental relationships between segments and features:

(X→Segment and F→Feature)

(1) One to one:

X }also conventional phonology
|
[+F]

(2) One to many (Assimilation):

(3) Many to One (Contour Tones):

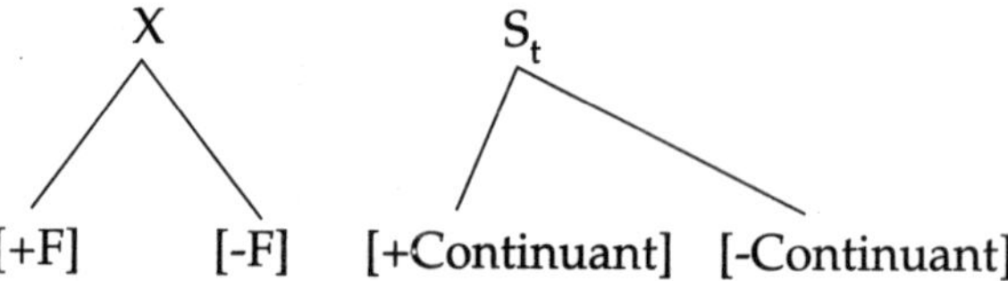

(4) One to One (Floating Feature):

[+F]

(5) None to One (Featureless Segment):

X

Here a particular feature behaves independently of other feature or segments. In tonal phenomena, the features and segments act independent of each other.

Autosegmental representations also explain contour tones in some languages. Contour tones are:

(1) Rising

(2) Falling

Within the autosegmental phonology, contour tones can be derived from a linear sequence of two different level tones, both of which are associated with the same vowel. Autosegmental representation of contour tones:

Rising Tone Falling

V V

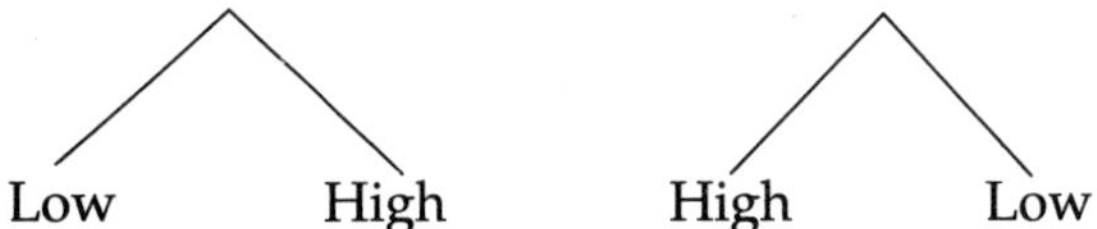

Where as in conventional segmental theories, each of these tones requires a different feature such as [+High tone] or [+ Rising tone].

It also accounts for feature spreading, in which the feature of one segment spreads to the adjacent segment i.e., "assimilation" process.

Clinical implication:

- It can be used to analyze error pattern like initial consonant deletion or cluster reduction.
- Features spreading can be used to teach co articulating conditions in therapy, Leonard and Brown, (84) and Pollock and Churaty (88), have used autosegmental principles to analyze disordered phonological system.

Metrical Phonology and its clinical implication: Metrical phonology is a phonological theory concerned with organizing segments into groups of relative prominence. Segments are organized into syllables, syllables into metrical feet, feet into phonological words, and words into larger units.

This is a theoretical construct propounded by Liebermann (1975), that extends hierarchical analysis procedures to stress and syllable boundaries. It extended a hierarchical based analysis to stress.

This organization is represented formally by metrical trees and grids.

Example (metrical tree):

Here is an example of a metrical tree of the word *metricality:*

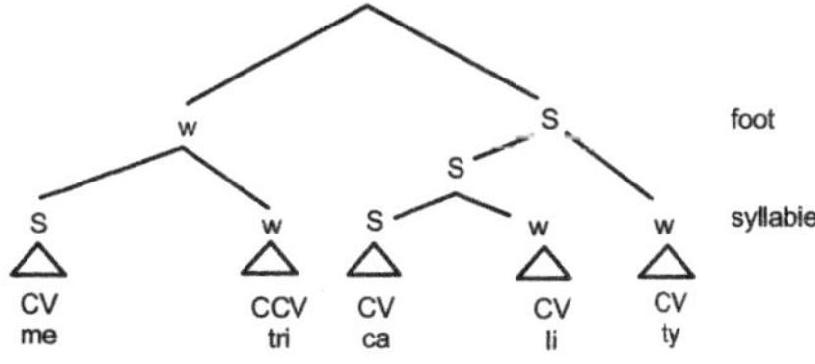

On the word and foot level, s and w indicate relative stress. The w indicates weaker prominence, and the s indicates relative stronger prominence.

The internal syllable structure in the above figure has been omitted and is represented by triangles. Within the syllable, **s** and **w** refer to stronger and weaker degrees of sonorance, not stress, and **s** corresponds to the syllable nucleus, which is the most sonorant segment in a syllable.

In metrical trees, the strongest unit of the word is the one that is dominated by **s** all the way up the tree.

Example (metrical grid):

Here is an example of a metrical grid of the word *metricality:*

Stress within feet and words can be represented as a metrical grid:

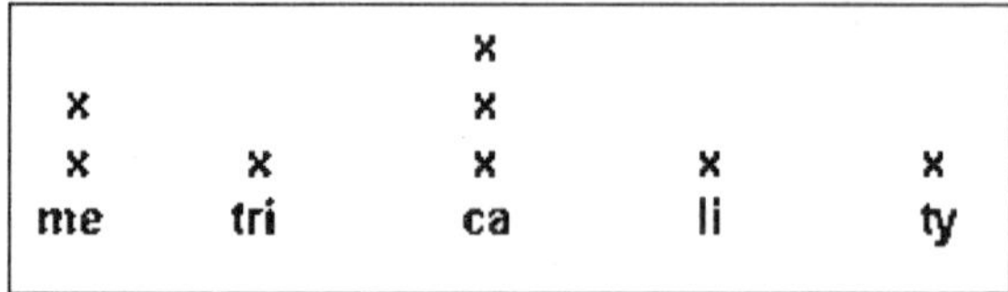

In a grid, the most prominent unit is the one that is dominated by the most number of **x**'s.

Clinical implication:

(*a*) Can be used to analyze an error pattern like where a child deletes the unstressed syllables, in 2-syllable and 3-syllable words.

(*b*) Kehoe (2001) has documented how a metrical approach can form the basis for an analysis of multisyllabic word productions.

(*c*) Velleman and Shriberg (1999), have used metical phonology to analyze the speech of children with developmental apraxia of speech, which have abnormal stress.

Feature Geometry and its clinical implication: It is a nonlinear theory which has adopted the tiered/hierarchical representation of features from autosegmental phonology. It attempts to explain why some features (not others) are affected by as similar process (known as spreading or linking of features) while others are affected by neutralization or deletion processes (known as delinking):

Ex: Spreading :-(gnk) for duck

Delinking (d^) for [duck]

It theorizes that segments are composed of multitiered hierarchical organized features. (Here specific nodes that can dominate other features and link various level of representation are designated.)

Clinical implication: It gives information about the child's underlying process/representation; i.e. in the example: - Spreading :-(gnk) for duck; Delinking (d^) for [duck] gives information about:

(a) Dorsal place node, i.e. about |k| and |g|; also g/d;

(b) Informs that child has articulatory constraints i.e. Prevents realization of final consonants; if articulatory constraints are eliminated, thus child's g/d substitution (backing) can be eliminated.

Optimality theory and its clinical implication: In a course at the LSA summer institute in 1991, Alan Prince and Paul Smolensky developed Optimality theory—an overall architecture for phonology according to which languages choose a pronunciation of a word that best satisfies a list of constraints which is ordered by importance: a lower-ranked constraint can be violated when the violation is necessary in order to obey a higher-ranked constraint. The approach was soon extended to morphology by John McCarthy and Alan Prince, and has become the dominant trend in phonology. Though this usually goes unacknowledged, Optimality Theory was strongly influenced by Natural Phonology; both view phonology in terms of constraints on speakers and their production, though these constraints are formalized in very different ways.

Optimality Theory (OT) is a linguistic model proposing that the observed forms of language arise from the interaction between conflicting constraints. There are three basic components of the theory:

1. GEN generates the list of possible outputs, or candidates,
2. CON provides the criteria, violable constraints, used to decide between candidates, and
3. EVAL chooses the optimal candidate.

Optimality theory assumes that these components are universal. Differences in grammars reflect different rankings of the universal constraint set, CON. Language acquisition can be described as the process of adjusting the ranking of these constraints.

Optimality theory is usually considered a development of generative grammar, which shares its focus on the investigation of universal principles, linguistic typology and language acquisition. Optimality theory is often called a connectionist theory of language, because it has its roots in neural network research, though the relationship is now largely of historical interest.

(*a*) It was originally developed to explain the differences that occur between languages.

(*b*) It proposes a universal grammar and states that constraint characterizes universals.

According to the OT, *constraints* are a means of:

(1) Characterizing universal patterns that occur across languages.

(2) Demonstrating variations of patterns that occur between languages i.e.

Eg.: In general American English, a word can begin with three consonants, but not with more than four consonants in a row; for example, *Street.*

In Hawaiian language, it allows not more than 1 consonant in a row; ex; *Kanaka*-man.

Therefore, Hawaiian has more constraint than English in terms of number of consonants in a row.

(3) Demonstrating markedness indicated by constraint violations.

Based on this, following are the typical properties of a syllable:

- Syllables begin with consonants □ ONSET; ex: away, cat
- Syllables have one vowel □ PEAK; ex: no two vowels usually
- Syllables end with a vowel □ NOCODA; ex: hat, clock
- Syllables have at most one consonant at an edge ? COMPLEX; ex: clocks.

Optimality theory ranks order the constraints on the basis of violation i, e, from rarely violated to the most violated rule:

PEAK > ONSET > NOCODA > COMPLEX.

Clinical implication:

- According to this theory the child acquires unmarked constraints first and then the marked constraints and thus helps to understand the normal developmental process.
- In children with phonological disorder, they have unique constraint ranking. So, we need to identify the ranking than account for the error pattern and then re-rank the constraint, so that they are more in line with the input.
- Barlow (2001) and Dinnesen and O'Connor (2001), demonstrated that this theory can be used to analyze the child's speech and arrive at treatment.

Minimal Pairs

We know that a phoneme is the basic speech sound which is used for distinguishing or contrasting one word from another. Eg:/s/and/z/are phonemes of English as they are used for distinguishing between the words 'sip' and 'zip'. The words 'sip' and 'zip' are minimal pairs because the words differ in exactly one sound in the same place in the word.

Transcription of Segments

Transcription (or phonetic notation) is the visual system of symbolization of the sounds occurring in spoken human language. The most common type of phonetic transcription uses a phonetic alphabet (such as the International Phonetic Alphabet).

The International Phonetic Alphabet (IPA) is one of the most popular and well-known phonetic alphabets. It was originally created by primarily British language teachers, with later efforts from European phoneticians and linguists. It has changed from its earlier intention as a tool of foreign language pedagogy to a practical alphabet of linguists. It is currently becoming the most often seen alphabet in the field of phonetics.

The International Phonetic Association recommends that a phonetic transcription should be enclosed in square brackets "[ ]". A transcription that specifically denotes only phonological contrasts may be enclosed in slashes "/ /" instead. If one is in doubt, it is best to use brackets, for by setting off a transcription with slashes one makes a theoretical claim that every symbol within is phonemically contrastive for the language being transcribed.

For phonetic transcriptions, there is flexibility in how closely sounds may be transcribed. A transcription that gives only a basic idea of the sounds of a language in the broadest terms is called a broad transcription; in some cases this may be equivalent to a phonemic transcription (only without any theoretical claims). A close transcription, indicating precise details of the sounds, is called a narrow transcription. These are not binary choices, but the ends of a continuum, with many possibilities in between. All are enclosed in brackets.

To avoid confusion with IPA symbols, it may be desirable to specify when native orthography is being used, so that, for example, the English word jet is not read as "yet". This is done with angle brackets or chevrons: <jet>. It is also common to italicize such words, but the chevrons indicate specifically that they are in the original language's orthography, and not in English transliteration.

Narrow and Broad Transcription

Phonetic transcription may aim to transcribe the phonology of a language, or it may wish to go further and specify the precise phonetic realisation. In all systems of transcription we may therefore distinguish between broad transcription and narrow transcription. Broad transcription indicates only the more noticeable phonetic features of an utterance, whereas narrow transcription encodes more information about the phonetic variations of the specific allophones in the utterance. The difference between broad and narrow is a continuum. One particular form of a broad transcription is a phonemic transcription, which disregards all allophonic difference.

For example, one particular pronunciation of the English word little may be transcribed using the IPA as/Èljtl)/or [Èljtk)]; the broad, phonemic transcription, placed between slashes, indicates merely that the word ends with phoneme/ l/, but the narrow, allophonic transcription, placed between square brackets, indicates that this final/l/([l]) is dark.

The advantage of the narrow transcription is that it can help learners to get exactly the right sound, and allows linguists to make detailed analyses of language variation. The disadvantage is that a narrow transcription is rarely representative of all speakers of a language. Most Americans and Australians would pronounce the/t/of little as a tap [τ]. Many people in England would say/t/as ["] (a glottal stop) and/or the second/l/as [w]. A further disadvantage in less technical contexts is that narrow transcription involves a larger number of symbols which may be unfamiliar to non-specialists.

The advantage of the broad transcription is that it allows statements to be made which apply right across a relatively diverse language community. It is thus more appropriate for the pronunciation data in foreign language dictionaries, which may discuss allophones in the preface but rarely give them for each entry. A rule of thumb in many linguistics contexts is therefore to use a narrow transcription when it is necessary for the point being made, but a broad transcription whenever possible.

THE INTERNATIONAL PHONETIC ALPHABET (2005)

CONSONANTS (PULMONIC)

	LABIAL		CORONAL				DORSAL			RADICAL		LARYNGEAL
	Bilabial	Labio-dental	Dental	Alveolar	Palato-alveolar	Retroflex	Palatal	Velar	Uvular	Pharyngeal	Epi-glottal	Glottal
Nasal	m	ɱ		n		ɳ	ɲ	ŋ	ɴ			
Plosive	p b	ȹ ȸ		t d		ʈ ɖ	c ɟ	k ɡ	q ɢ		ʡ	ʔ
Fricative	ɸ β	f v	θ ð	s z	ʃ ʒ	ʂ ʐ	ç ʝ	x ɣ	χ ʁ	ħ ʕ	ʜ ʢ	h ɦ
Approximant		ʋ		ɹ		ɻ	j	ɰ				
Trill	ʙ			r					ʀ			
Tap, Flap		ⱱ		ɾ		ɽ						
Lateral fricative				ɬ ɮ								
Lateral approximant				l		ɭ	ʎ	ʟ				
Lateral flap				ɺ								

Where symbols appear in pairs, the one to the right represents a modally voiced consonant, except for murmured ɦ. Shaded areas denote articulations judged to be impossible. Light grey letters are unofficial extensions of the IPA.

CONSONANTS (NON-PULMONIC)

Anterior click releases (require posterior stops)	Voiced implosives	Ejectives
ʘ Bilabial fricated	ɓ Bilabial	ʼ Examples:
ǀ Laminal alveolar fricated ("dental")	ɗ Dental or alveolar	pʼ Bilabial
ǃ Apical (post)alveolar abrupt ("retroflex")	ʄ Palatal	tʼ Dental or alveolar
ǂ Laminal postalveolar abrupt ("palatal")	ɠ Velar	kʼ Velar
ǁ Lateral alveolar fricated ("lateral")	ʛ Uvular	sʼ Alveolar fricative

CONSONANTS (CO-ARTICULATED)

ʍ Voiceless labialized velar approximant

w Voiced labialized velar approximant

ɥ Voiced labialized palatal approximant

ɕ Voiceless palatalized postalveolar (alveolo-palatal) fricative

ʑ Voiced palatalized postalveolar (alveolo-palatal) fricative

ɧ Simultaneous x and ʃ (disputed)

k͡p t͡s Affricates and double articulations may be joined by a tie bar

VOWELS

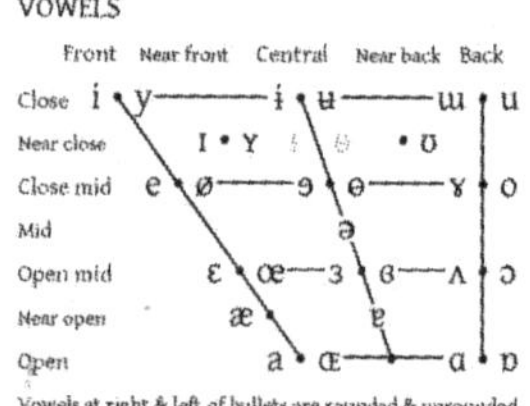

Vowels at right & left of bullets are rounded & unrounded.

SUPRASEGMENTALS

ˈ Primary stress

ˌ Secondary stress

ˑ Extra stress [ˌfoʊnəˈtɪʃən]

eː Long

eˑ Half-long

e Short

ĕ Extra-short

. Syllable break

‿ Linking (no break)

INTONATION

| Minor (foot) break

‖ Major (intonation) break

↗ Global rise

↘ Global fall

TONE

Level tones

e̋ ˥ Top

é ˦ High

ē ˧ Mid

è ˨ Low

ȅ ˩ Bottom

Tone terracing

ꜛ Upstep

ꜜ Downstep

Contour-tone examples:

ě ˩˥ Rising

ê ˥˩ Falling

e᷄ ˧˥ High rising

e᷅ ˩˧ Low rising

e᷇ ˥˧ High falling

e᷆ ˧˩ Low falling

e᷈ ˧˦˧ Peaking

e᷉ ˧˨˧ Dipping

DIACRITICS

Diacritics may be placed above a symbol with a descender, as ŋ̊. Other IPA symbols may appear as diacritics to represent phonetic detail: tˢ (fricative release), bʱ (breathy voice), ˀa (glottal onset), ᵊ (epenthetic schwa), oʷ (diphthongization).

SYLLABICITY & RELEASES		PHONATION		PRIMARY ARTICULATION		SECONDARY ARTICULATION			
n̩ ɹ̩	Syllabic	n̥ d̥	Voiceless or Slack voice	t̪ b̪	Dental	tʷ dʷ	Labialized	ɔ̹ x̹	More rounded
e̯ ʊ̯	Non-syllabic	s̬ d̬	Modal voice or Stiff voice	t̺ d̺	Apical	tʲ dʲ	Palatalized	ɔ̜ xʷ̜	Less rounded
tʰ ʰt	(Pre)aspirated	n̤ a̤	Breathy voice	t̻ d̻	Laminal	tˠ dˠ	Velarized	ẽ z̃	Nasalized
dⁿ	Nasal release	n̰ a̰	Creaky voice	u̟ t̟	Advanced	tˤ dˤ	Pharyngealized	ɚ ɝ	Rhoticity
dˡ	Lateral release		Strident	i̠ t̠	Retracted	ɫ z̴	Velarized or pharyngealized	e̘ o̘	Advanced tongue root
t̚	No audible release	n̼ d̼	Linguolabial	ä ɟ̈	Centralized	ɯ̽	Mid-centralized	e̙ o̙	Retracted tongue root
e̞ β̞	Lowered (β̞ is a bilabial approximant)			e̝ ɹ̝	Raised (ɹ̝ is a voiced alveolar non-sibilant fricative, r̝ a fricative trill)				

Source: www.wikipedia.com

Extended IPA

The Extensions to the IPA are extensions of the International Phonetic Alphabet and were designed for disordered speech. However, some of the symbols (especially diacritics) are occasionally used for transcribing normal speech as well.

The Extended IPA for speech pathology has added additional bracket notations. Parentheses are used to indicate mouthing (silent articulation), as in (ʃ ::), a silent sign to hush; parentheses are also used to indicate silent pauses, for example (...). Double parentheses indicate obscured or unintelligible sound, as in ((2 syll.)), two audible but unidentifiable syllables. Curly brackets with Italian musical terms are used to mark prosodic notation, such as [{falsetto h[lp falsetto}].

Extended IPA letters

EXTENDED IPA LETTERS AND DIACRITICS

ʩ	Velopharyngeal fricative (occurs with a cleft palate)	s͋	Velopharyngeal frication
ʭ	Bidental percussive (gnashing teeth)	n̪͆ h̪͆	Interdental or bidental
v̼	Dentolabial	b̪	Labiodental
ʬ	Bilabial percussive (smacking lips)	kʋ	Labiodentalized
b͇ ŋ͇	Alveolar or alveolarized	tʶ	Uvularized
s͍	Labial spreading	xᵓ	Open-rounded labialization
¡	Sublaminal lower alveolar click (sucking tongue)	ǃ¡	Alveolar & sublaminal click ('click clack')
ʪ	ɬ͡s Voiceless centro-lateral alveolar fricative (a lisp)	ʫ	ɮ͡z Voiced centro-lateral alveolar fricative (a lisp)
s͔	Laterally offset left	s͕	Laterally offset right
p↓	Ingressive airflow	!↑	Egressive airflow
n͋ v͋	Nareal fricative	n͊	Denasal (as with a head cold)
p⁼	Unaspirated	a̤	Whispery phonation
v͈	Strong articulation	v͉	Weak articulation
aᶣ	Faucalized (stretched throat 'yawn')	a!	Harsh (ventricular or 'pressed' voice, as when lifting weights)
s͎	Whistled articulation	s‼	Ventricular (uses the false vocal cords)
θ͢s	Slurred (sliding) articulation	t\t\t	Stuttered (reiterated articulation)

Parentheses and offset may be used with diacritics to indicate degree and timing:

z̥ partially devoiced, z̥ initial partial devoicing, ̬z prevoiced, z̬ postvoiced;

s̬ partially voiced, s̬ final partial voicing, a̰ creaky offglide

The letters and diacritics of the ExtIPA

fŋ	Velopharyngeal fricative (often occurs with a cleft palate)
ls	Voiceless central-plus-lateral alveolar fricative, [ɬ͡s] (a lisp)
lz	Voiced central-plus-lateral alveolar fricative, [ɮ͡z] (a lisp)
ʬ	Bilabial percussive (smacking lips)
ʭ	Bidental percussive (gnashing teeth)
¡	Sublaminal lower alveolar click (sucking tongue)

Source: www.wikipedia.com

The last symbol may be used with the alveolar click for [!¡], a combined alveolar and sublaminal click or "cluck-click".

Extended IPA diacritics:

The ExtIPA has widened the use of some of the regular IPA symbols, such as ʰp for pre-aspiration, tʁ for uvularization, or s̼ for a linguolabial sibilant, as well as adding some new ones. Some of the ExtIPA diacritics are occasionally used for non-disordered speech as well.

One modification is the use of subscript parentheses around the phonation diacritics to indicate partial phonation; a single parenthesis at the left or right of the voicing indicates that it is partially phonated at the beginning or end of the segment. For example, (s̬) is a partially voiced [s], (s̬ shows partial initial voicing, and s̬) partial final voicing; also (z̥) is a partially devoiced [z], (z̥ shows partial initial devoicing, and (z̥) partial final devoicing. These conventions may be convenient for representing various voice onset times.

Phonation diacritics may also be prefixed or suffixed rather than placed directly under the segment to represent relative timing. For instance, z̬ is a pre-voiced [z], z̬ a post-voiced [z], and a̰ is an [a] with a creaky off glide.

Other Ext IPA diacritics are:

Essive airflow	Airstream mechanism		
p↓	Ingressive airflow	!↑	Egressive airflow
	Phonation		
p⁼	Unaspirated	ạ	Whispery phonation
aᴴ	Faucalized voice (stretched pharynx, as in a yawn)	a!	Harsh voice, ('pressed voice'; involves thefalse vocal cords, as when lifting a load)
ʰp	Pre-aspiration	a!!	Ventricular vibration
	Nasalization		
ñṽ	Nasal fricative or frication	m̃	Denasal (as with a headcold)
	Articulatory strength		
f H	Strong articulation	v	Weak articulation
	Articulation		
v̪	Dentolabial	n h	Interdental or bidental
s̳ f̳	Alveolar(ized)	s t	Whistled
	Secondary articulation		
s̬	Labial spreading	3ᶱ	Open-rounded labialization
kᵛ	Labiodentalized	s̃	Velopharyangeal friction
	Timing		
s̳θ̳	Slurred/sliding articulation	p\p\p	Stutter (reiterated articulation)

Source: www.wikipedia.com.

In addition to these symbols, a subscript < or > indicates that an articulation is laterally offset to the left or right.

Prosodic notation

The Ext IPA also makes use of Italian musical notation for the tempo and dynamics of connected speech. These are subscripted on the insides of a {brace} notation that indicates that they are comments on the prosody.

Pauses are indicated with periods or numbers inside parentheses.

(.)	Short pause	(..) Medium pause	(...)	Long pause	(1.2) 1.2-second pause
f	Loud speech ('forte')	[{$_{f}$laʊd$_{f}$}]	*ff*	Louder speech ('fortissimo')	[{$_{ff}$laʊdə$_{ff}$}]
p	Quiet speech ('piano')	[{$_{p}$kwalət$_{p}$}]	*pp*	Quieter speech ('pianissimo')	[{$_{pp}$kwalətə$_{pp}$}]
allegro	Fast speech	[{allegro fa:st allegro}]	*lento*	Slow speech	[{lento sloʊ lento}]

crescendo, *rallentando*, and other musical terms may also be used.

Source: www.wikipedia.com.

Distinctive Feature

In linguistics, a distinctive feature is the most basic unit of phonological structure that may be analyzed in phonological theory. Distinctive features are grouped into categories according to the natural classes of segments they describe: major class features, laryngeal features, manner features, and place features. These feature categories in turn are further specified on the basis of the phonetic properties of the segments in question. Since the inception of the phonological analysis of distinctive features in the 1950's, features traditionally have been specified by assigning them binary values to signify that the segment being described by the feature either possesses that phonetic property or it does not. Therefore, a positive value, [+], denotes the presence of a feature, while a negative value, [-], indicates its absence.

However, in recent developments to the theory of distinctive features, phonologists have proposed the existence of single-valued features. These features, called univalent features, can only describe the classes of segments that are said to possess those features, and not the classes that are without them.

Major Class Features: The features that represent the major classes of sounds:

1. [+/- consonantal] Consonantal segments are produced with an audible constriction in the vocal tract, like plosives, affricates, fricatives, nasals, laterals and [r]. Vowels, glides and laryngeal segments are not consonantal.
2. [+/- sonorant] This feature describes the type of oral constriction that can occur in the vocal tract. [+son] designates the vowels and sonorant consonants, which are produced without the imbalance of air pressure in the vocal tract that might cause turbulence. [-son] alternatively describes the obstruents, articulated with a noticeable turbulence caused by an imbalance of air pressure in the vocal tract.
3. [+/- syllabic] Syllabic segments may function as the nucleus of a syllable, while their counterparts, the [-syll] segments, may not.

Laryngeal Features: The features that specify the glottal states of sounds.

1. [+/- voice] This feature indicates whether vibration of the vocal folds occurs with the articulation of the segment.
2. [+/- spread glottis] Used to indicate the aspiration of a segment, this feature denotes the openness of the glottis. For [+sg] the vocal folds are spread apart wide enoughfor frication to occur; for [-sg] there is not the same friction-inducing spreading.
3. [+/- constricted glottis] The constricted glottis features denotes the degree of closure of the glottis. [+cg] implies that the vocal folds are held closely together,

enough so that air cannot pass through momentarily. [-cg] implies the opposite.

Manner Features: The features that specify the manner of articulation:

1. [+/- continuant] Continuant features describe the passage of air through the vocal tract. [+cont] segments are produced without any significant obstruction in the tract, and so air passes through in a continuous stream. [-cont] segments on the other hand have such an obstruction, and so occlude the air flow at some point of articulation.
2. [+/- nasal] This feature describes the position of the velum. [+nasal] segments are produced by lowering the velum so that air can pass through the nasal tract. [- nasal] segments conversely are produced with a raised velum, blocking the passages of air to the nasal tract and shunting it to the oral tract.
3. [+/- strident] The strident feature applies to obstruents only and refers to a type of friction that is noisier that usual. This is caused by high energy white noise.
4. [+/- lateral] This feature designates the shape and positioning of the tongue with respect to the oral tract. [+lat] segments are produced as the center of the tongue rises to contact the roof of the mouth, thereby blocking air from flowing centrally through the oral tract and instead forcing more lateral flow along the lowered side(s) of the tongue.
5. [+/- delayed release] This feature distinguishes stops from affricates. Affricates are designated [+dr].

Place Features: The features that specify the place of articulation:

[Labial] Labial segments are articulated with the lips:

1. [+/- round] [+round] are produced with lip rounding. [-round] are not.

[Coronal] Coronal sounds are articulated with the tip and/or blade of the tongue:

1. [+/- anterior] Anterior segments are articulated with the tip or blade of the tongue at or in front of the alveolar ridge.
2. [+/- distributed] For [+dist] segments the tongue is extended for some distance in the mouth.

[Dorsal] Dorsal sounds are articulated by raising the dorsum of the tongue. All vowels are DORSAL sounds:

1. [+/- high] [+high] segments raise the dorsum close to the palate. [-high] segments do not.
2. [+/- low] [+low] segments bunch the dorsum to a position low in the mouth.
3. [+/- back] [+back] segments are produced with the tongue dorsum bunched and retracted slightly to the back of the mouth. [-back] segments are bunched and extended slightly forward.
4. [+/- tense] This feature (mainly) applies to the position of the root of the tongue when articulating vowels. [+tense] vowels have an advanced tongue root. In fact, this feature is often referred to as advanced tongue root, though there is a debate on whether tense and ATR are same or different features.

[Radical] Radical sounds are articulated with the root of the tongue.

Clinical Application of Distinctive Feature Theory

- Distinctive feature systems were developed as a means of analyzing phonemes and entire phoneme systems of languages. Each phoneme of the particular system was assessed to determine if the distinctive feature was present (+) or absent (-).
- Therapeutic implications follow logically, i.e., if the child can be taught to differentiate between the presence and absence of these differentiating distinctive features, the aberrant sound productions should be easily remediated. Treatment of one phonemic opposition with specific distinctive features

should lead to the norm production of other phonemic oppositions with the same distinctive feature oppositions. This would be a means of treating more than one phoneme in a time-efficient manner.

- The concept of naturalness and markedness became a relevant clinical issue when it was observed that children with phonological disorder have a tendency to substitute more unmarked, natural classes of segments for marked ones.

  Naturalness: it designates two sound aspects:

  - The relative simplicity of a sound production, and
  - Its high frequency of occurrence in languages.

  In other words, more natural sounds are those that are considered easier to produce and occur in many languages.

  Markedness: refers to sounds that are relatively more difficult to produce and are found less frequently in languages.

Distinctive Feature (DF) Approaches used in Therapy

DF approach is designed to capitalize on patterns (features) of commonalities among error productions. Although features are taught in sounds, feature analysis and remediation represent an endeavor to correct several sounds simultaneously by teaching a feature in one target sound with the assumption that it will generalize to other sounds containing the target feature. Let us see some of them:

Blache (1989) published a distinctive feature approach to remediation of phonological delay. This approach is organized into four basic steps:

Step 1. Discussion of words: In this step, clinician should determine whether or not the child knows the meaning of lexical items to be used in therapy. Once a minimal pair contrast has been selected to teach a distinctive feature, it is important to determine if the child understands both lexical items in the word-pair.

Step 2. Discrimination testing and training: The child is tested to determine if he or she can perceive the feature contrast.

Step 3. Production training: Child will be instructed to say the word and the clinician points to the picture of the word the client pronounced. The client should always be able to correctly pronounce one word of the pair but may not be able to pronounce the other member of the word-pair; thus, a correct production of an error sound may not be required at this stage. Production training continues until the client can use target feature in a correct production of a target sound.

Step 4. Carryover training: Once the child is able to pronounce the target word, the word is placed longer and more complex linguistics environments.

Weiner and Bankson (1978): designed to teach (+) friction in a child who substitutes stops for fricatives.

(*i*) Introduction of the concept of "dripping" sounds (stops) and "flowing" sounds (fricatives).

(*ii*) Identification of words that begin with dripping as compared to flowing sounds.

(*iii*) Imitation of words containing fricatives in the initial position, with such fricatives emphasized through duration of initial sound (e.g., *f-f-f-fish*). Following his or her production, the client was required to judge whether the word began with dripping or flowing sound. Feedback was provided for both production and identification.

(*iv*) Repetition of step 3 without exaggeration of the word-initial fricative.

(*v*) Presentation of a 20-item picture-naming task in which each item began with a fricative.

Mc. Reynolds and Bennet (1972): They described instructional procedures designed to teach a feature contrast that was absent in a child's productive repertoire.

Phase I. Production focused on nonsense syllables, which contained the target feature in initial position. E.g., + continuant, (*f*a).

Phase II. Production focused on nonsense syllables, which contained the target feature in final position. E.g., +continuant, (a*f*).

Costello and Onstine's Program:

They extended Mc Reynolds program. Designed to teach/ t/verses/θ/and/t/versus

/s/. It has 9 phases:

Phase I. Sound established in isolation.

Phase I. Production practice in CV syllables i.e., production of target sound in CV contexts.

Phase III. Production practice in VC syllables.

Phase IV and V. Production practice in words. Imitation of/t/,/s/in releasing or initial position of words.

Phase VI and VII. Production practice in phrases and sentences.

Phase VIII and IX. Production precise in connected in speech.

Distinctive Features in Developmental Phonology

Distinctive features are used in explanation of certain phenomena in applied phonology. An area that has been active with this inquiry is Child's phonology. The obvious advantage of the use of distinctive feature in child substitutions is the power of the generalization that occurs with different sounds.

Research Support: Mc. Reynolds and Bennet (1972) reported that all three of their subjects reflected distinctive feature generalization from the exemplar sounds to other sounds, although the amount of feature generalization varied across subjects. Similarly, Weiner and Bankson (1978) reported that their subject generalized [+ frication] to non-trained items. Costello and Onstine (1976) reported that their distinctive feature instructional approach was successful in teaching a subject to generalize the [+ continuant] feature. These data support the finding that feature generalization is seen with distinctive feature approaches to remediation.

Pollack and Rees (1972) showed that distinctive feature theory or approach can be used effectively in children with defective articulation.Feeney, M. P., (1990) used distinctive feature scoring technique for the purpose of improving test reliability and found that distinctive feature scoring may provide a more effective means of differentiating among listeners with high frequency sensorineural hearing loss than traditional scoring.Mc. Reynolds and Bennet (1972) observed from their study that generalization of trained features across phonemes in which the feature had been in error.

Phonotactics

Phonotactics is a branch of phonology that deals with restrictions in a language on the permissible combinations of phonemes. Phonotactics defines permissible syllable structure, consonant cluster, and vowel sequences by means of phonotactical constraints.

Phonotactic constraints are language specific. For example, in Japanese, consonant clusters like/st/are not allowed, although they are in English. Similarly, the sounds/kn/and/an/are not permitted at the beginning of a word in Modern English but are in German and Dutch, and were permitted in Old and Middle English.

English Phonotactics

The English syllable (and word) twelfths/tw[lfès/is divided into the onset/tw/, the nucleus/[/, and the coda/lfès/, and it can thus be described as CCVCCCC (C = consonant, V = vowel). On this basis it is possible to form rules for which representations of phoneme classes may fill the cluster. For instance, English allows at most three consonants in an onset, but among native words under standard accents, phonemes in a three-consonantal onset are limited to the following scheme:

/s/+ pulmonic + approximant:

/s/+/m/+/j/

/s/+/t/+/j .I/

/s/+/p/+/j .I l/

/s/+/k/+/j .I l w/

This constraint can be observed in the pronunciation of the word blue: originally, the vowel of blue was identical to the vowel of cue, approximately [iw]. In most dialects of English, [iw] shifted to [ju:]. Theoretically, this would produce **[blju:]. The cluster [blj], however, infringes the constraint for three-consonantal onsets in English. Therefore, the pronunciation has been reduced to [blu:] by elision of the [j].

Principles and Practices of Phonemic Analysis

Phonemic analysis is motivated by the following considerations:

1. A need to overcome the massive detail that narrow description provides.
2. A practical need to create alphabetic systems appropriate for a given language.
3. A belief that people have psychologically real notion of the sounds of their language, in a fashion that corresponds to phonemes and not phones.
4. A recognition that there are constancies across dialects that involve objects more abstract than sounds; these objects are phonemes.

Principle of Contrastive Distribution

The best test of whether two phones might be realizations of the same phoneme is the minimal pair test. If we can find two words that are different words and which are identical, except that one contains phone X and another phone Y in the same position, then they constitute a minimal pair with regard to X and Y and X and Y cannot be allophones of the same phoneme. If the two sounds can make a minimal pair, they are considered as two separate phonemes of that language. Conditions to be satisfied by words to be minimal pairs are:

- There must be minimal difference. (eg: get and rate are not minimal pairs)
- The difference must be the result of substitution. (eg: bat-bats cant be a minimal pair)
- The minimal difference must change the meaning.(pin-phin not a minimal pair)

Principles of Complimentary Distribution

Sounds that occur in complimentary distribution are allophones of the same phoneme. In complimentary distribution, the distributions of two sounds are such that they occur in mutually exclusive environments. That is, when one occurs other cannot.

Principle of Phonetic Similarity

It states that the phonetically entirely dissimilar sounds are to be treated as phonemes. Allophones of phonemes are phonetically similar, but that doesn't mean that all phonetically similar sounds are allophones. [/p/and/ph/are allophones in English but in Hindi they are separate phonemes.].

Principle of Free Variation

Two sounds can occur in the same place without changing the meaning (they are in free variation); these sounds are to be treated as allophones of the same phoneme.

Eg: In African, do:g- girl ; zo:g-girl

Thus/d/and/z/are in free variation and they are allophones.

Principle of Pattern Congruity

It states that sounds occur in a pattern in any language. If there is no minimal pair for two given sounds, then they can be established as phonemes if the feature that differentiates one from the other is phonemic.

Eg: In Assamese,

/pal/	to bring up
/dan/	donation
/bat/	way
/tal/	palm fruit
/gal/	cheek
/kali/	yesterday
/khali/	empty
/bhat/	cooked rice
/thal/	plate
/dhan/	paddy
/ph«l/	fruit
/bagh/	tiger

If we consider/g/and/gh/

1. First principle of minimal pairs doesn't apply.
2. Second principle can be applied, but the feature (frication) that differentiates the 2 sounds is phonemic. When such is the case there is no reason why/g/and/gh/cannot be separate phonemes. Hence based on this principle we can establish that these two sounds [/g/and/gh/] are two separate phonemes in Assamese.

Principle of Economy

It states that while analyzing the sounds into phonemes and allophones one has to look into economic aspect. One should check the allophonic variants in a proper way. E.g.: A given language has 50 sounds. All are not phonemes. One linguist says that there are 40 phonemes. The other says there are 42 phonemes. The linguist who says that there are lesser phonemes is a better linguist because s/he has analyzed the sounds in a proper way. In other words, s/he has looked into all the possibilities to identify various allophonic variants of the language in question.

Application of Phonemic Analysis in Speech-language Pathology

The knowledge of phonemic analysis is important to a speech-language pathologist as the cases that approach them are multi-lingual and the language might not always be a known one. If the SLP knows the phonemes he/she can make the therapy plans so as to teach the client the less difficult words. So, he/she will teach the phonemes first and then their allophones. They might face the following situations:

- Where the child substitutes the sound. [eg:/l/for/r/ in/ri:d/]

  The kid might not be able to perceive the sound so he fails to produce it. The child perceives the different sound but he tends to produce both in the same manner.

- The child perceives the difference and can articulate/ l/and/r/but he may not produce the sounds correctly in all environments.

  For therapy, perception, articulation and contrastive functions should be taught firstly.

Phonological Processes

Assimilation

Assimilation is a common phonological process by which the phonetics of a speech segment becomes more like that of another segment in a word (or at a word boundary). A common example of assimilation would be "don't be silly" where the/n/and/t/in "don't" become/m/and/p/, where said naturally in many accents and discourse styles ("dombe silly"). Assimilation can be synchronic being an active process in a language at a given point in time or diachronic being a historical sound change.

There are four configurations found in assimilations: the increase in phonetic similarity may be between adjacent segments or between segments separated by one or more intervening segments; and the changes may be in reference to a preceding segment, or to a following one. Although all four occur, changes in regard to a following adjacent segment account for virtually all assimilatory changes (and most of the regular ones). Also, assimilations to an adjacent segment are vastly more frequent than assimilations to a non-adjacent one. (These radical asymmetries might contain hints about the mechanisms involved, but they are unobvious.)

If a sound changes with reference to a following segment, it is traditionally called "regressive assimilation"; changes with reference to a preceding segment are traditionally called "progressive". Many find these terms confusing, as they seem to mean the opposite of the intended meaning. Accordingly, a variety of alternative terms have arisen—not all of which avoid the problem of the traditional terms. Regressive assimilation is also known as right-to-left, leading or anticipatory assimilation. Progressive assimilation is also known as left-to-right or perseveratory or preservative, lagging or lag assimilation. The terms anticipatory and lag will be used here.

Very occasionally two sounds (invariably adjacent) may influence one another in reciprocal assimilation. When such a change results in a single segment with some of the features of both components, it is known as coalescence or fusion.

Some authorities distinguish between partial and complete assimilation, i.e., between assimilatory changes in which there remains some phonetic difference between the segments involved, and those in which all differences are obliterated. There is no theoretical advantage to such a classification, as one of the following examples will show.

Tonal languages may exhibit tone assimilation (tonal umlaut, in effect), while sign languages also exhibit assimilation when the characteristics of neighbouring phonemes may be mixed.

Dissimilation

In phonology, particularly within historical linguistics, dissimilation is a phenomenon whereby similar consonant or vowel sounds in a word becomes less similar. For example, when one/r/sound occurs before another in the middle of a word in rhotic dialects of English, the first tends to drop out, as in "beserk" for berserk, "supprise" for surprise, "paticular" for particular, and "govenor" for governor (note this doesn't affect the pronunciation of government, which has only one/ r/).

Metathesis

Metathesis is a sound change that alters the order of phonemes in a word. The most common instance of metathesis is the reversal of the order of two adjacent phonemes, such as "comfterble" for comfortable (in rhotic dialects such as American English). Many languages have words that show this phenomenon, and some use it as a regular part of their grammar (e.g.Fur). The process of metathesis has altered the shape of many familiar words in the English language, too. What is sound before and after metathesis depends on assumption of language ancestry if protowords cannot be attested.

Metathesis in English

Metathesis is responsible for the most common types of speech errors, such as children acquiring spaghetti as pasghetti. The pronunciation of ask as/'æks/goes back to Old English days, when ascian and axian/acsian were both in use. Some other frequent English pronunciations that display metathesis are:

/'æks/for ask (possibly the most common metathesis in English)

/'æstərɪks/for asterics

/'kælvəri/for cavalry

/'kʌmftərbəl/for comfortable

/'fəɪljdʒ/for foliage

/ɪntər'dju:s/for introduce

/ɪntrəgəl/for integral

/'nju:kjələr/for nuclear (though this likely emerged by analogy with words such as "particular," "binocular," etc.)

/'pʌrti/for pretty

/'rɛvələnt/for relevant

The process has shaped many English words historically. Bird in English was once bryd, horse was hros, wasp is also recorded as wæps and hasp, hæps. The discrepancy between the spelling of iron and the usual pronunciation (/'aɪ.ərn/, as if spelled "eyern") is the result of metathesis.

Lenition

Lenition is a kind of consonant mutation that appears in many languages. Along with assimilation, it is one of the primary sources of historical change of languages. Lenition means 'softening' or 'weakening' (from Latin lenis = weak), and it refers to the change of a consonant considered 'stronger' into one considered 'weaker' (or fortis → lenis).

Elision is the omission of one or more sounds (such as a vowel, a consonant, or a whole syllable) in a word or phrase, producing a result that is easier for the speaker to pronounce. Sometimes, sounds may be elided for euphonic effect. Elision is normally unintentional, but it may be deliberate. The result may be impressionistically described as "slurred" or "muted."

An example of deliberate elision occurs in Latin poetry as a stylistic device. Under certain circumstances, such as one word ending in a vowel and the following word beginning in a vowel, the words may be elided together. Elision was a common device in the works of Catullus. For example, the opening line of Catullus 3 is: Lugete, O Veneres Cupidinesque, but would be read as Lugeto Veneres Cupidinesque.

The elided form of a word or phrase may become a standard alternative for the full form, if used often enough. In English, this is called a contraction, such as can't from cannot. Contraction differs from elision in that contractions are set forms that have morphologized, but elisions are not.

A synonym for elision is syncope, though the latter term is most often associated with the elision of vowels between consonants (e.g., Latin tabula → Spanish tabla). Another form of elision is aphesis, which means elision at the beginning of a word (generally of an unstressed vowel).

The opposite of elision is epenthesis, whereby sounds are inserted into a word to ease pronunciation.

The omission of a word from a phrase or sentence is not elision but ellipsis or, more accurately, elliptical construction.

Examples of elision in English

comfortable:	/'kʌqf⌊t⌊b⌊l/	→ /'kʌmft⌊b⌊l/
fifth:	/fɪfθ/	→ /'fɪθ/
him:	/hɪm/	→ /ɪm/
laboratory:	/læ'b ɑr⌊t ɑri/	→ /'læbr⌊t ɑri/(American English),/l⌊'b ɑr⌊tri/ (British English)
temperature:	/'tɛmp⌊r⌊tʃ⌊/	→/'tɛmp⌊tʃ⌊/,/ 'tɛmpr⌊tʃ⌊/
vegetable:	/'vɛdʒ•t⌊b⌊l/	→ /'vɛdʒt⌊b⌊l/

Haplology

Haplology is defined as the elimination of a syllable when two consecutive identical or similar syllables occur. Linguists sometimes jokingly refer to the phenomenon as "haplogy" (subjecting the word "haplology" to haplology).

Conditions,

(1) Syllables are both medial; and

(2) The structure of the two syllables is similar.

Example,

Basque: sagarrardo > sagardo 'apple cider'

English (colloquial):

- Engla land > England
- particularly > particuly
- pierced-ear earrings > pierced earrings
- probably > probly

Vowel Harmony

Vowel harmony is a type of long-distance assimilatory phonological process involving vowels in some languages. In languages with vowel harmony, there are constraints on what vowels may be found near each other.

Harmony processes are "long-distance" in the sense that the assimilation involves sounds that are separated by intervening segments (usually consonant segments). In other words, harmony refers to the assimilation of sounds that are not adjacent to each other. For example, a vowel at the beginning of a word can trigger assimilation in a vowel at the end of a word. The assimilation sometimes occurs across the entire word.

The vowel that causes the vowel assimilation is frequently termed the trigger while the vowels that assimilate (or harmonize) are termed targets. In most languages, the vowel triggers lie within the root of a word while the affixes added to the roots contains the targets. This may be seen in the Hungarian dative suffix:

Root	*Dative*	*Gloss*
város	város-nak	"city"
öröm	öröm-nek	"joy"

The dative suffix has two different forms -nak/-nek. The -nak form appears after the root with back vowels (a and o are both back vowels). The -nek form appears after the root with front vowels (ö and e are front vowels).

Another example: Turkish araba (car) pluralises to arabalar but tren (train) pluralises to trenler.

Harmony assimilation may spread either from the beginning of the word to the end or from the end to the beginning. Progressive harmony (a.k.a. left-to-right harmony) proceeds from beginning to end; regressive harmony (a.k.a. right-to-left harmony) proceeds from end to beginning. Languages that have both prefixes and suffixes often have both progressive and regressive harmony. Languages that primarily have prefixes (and no suffixes) usually have only regressive harmony—and vice versa for primarily suffixing languages.

(Some more processes will be studied later in the chapter).

Phonological Acquisition/Development

It refers to the development of speech sound form and function within the language system. Phonological development implies the acquisition of a functional sound system intricately connected to the child's overall growth in language.

Phonological acquisition is mainly explained by "Natural Phonology". Stampe (1979) regarded that all children embark on the development of their phonological systems from the same beginnings i.e. from the very beginning; the child's perceptual understanding of the phonemic system mirrors that of adults. In addition, this view presents children as passively suppressing these phonological processes whereas others consider children as actively involved in the development of their phonological systems (Eg: Kiparsky and Menn, 1977).

Stages of Acquisition

Phonological acquisition occurs in 2 stages (Stark, 1986):

(1) Prelinguistic stage-before the first word.

(2) Linguistic stage-starts from the appearance of the first word.

Prelinguistic Stages

Stage 1: Reflexive crying and vegetative sounds (0- 2months)

- This stage is characterized by reflexive vocalizations (cries, coughs, grunts etc reflecting physical state) and vegetative sounds associated with activities like feeding.

- Vocalizations resemble vowels, but are quasi-resonant since oral resonance is limited (nasalized vowel).

***Stage* 2**: Cooing and laughter (2-4 months)

- Produced during comfortable states
- Sounds produced are acoustically similar to back vowels and CV or VC syllables
- Early comfort sounds have quasi-resonant nuclei. Also, syllables sequences are considered primitive here due to the irregular timing in the opening and closing of the consonantal and vocalic segments.
- From 12 weeks there will be a decrease in the frequency of crying, disappearance of primitive vegetative sounds and by 16 weeks, sustained laughter appears.

Stage 3: Vocal play or Exploration-Expansion (4-6 months)

- Period of vocal play in which child gains better control of laryngeal and articulatory mechanisms and thus longer segments with extreme variations in pitch and loudness.
- Vowels have better oral resonance and hence termed fully resonant nuclei and demonstrate more variation in tongue height and position.
- Marginal babbling appears.

***Stage* 4**: Canonical babbling (6 months and later)

- Collective term for reduplicated and non-reduplicative/variegated babbling.
- Reduplicated babbling: marked by similar strings of consonants. Eg: mama
- Non- reduplicated babbling: demonstrates variations of both consonants and vowels from syllable to syllable. Eg: bat.

- Stoel-Gammmon et al., 1989 suggest that both reduplicated and variegated forms extend through entire babbling period.

In the beginning, babbling is used in a self-stimulatory manner and not to communicate. Toward the end of this stage, babbling may be used in ritual imitation games with adults. The child's segmental production towards the end of canonical babbling stage is not true words and consonants, but referred to as vocoids and contoids respectively (Pike, 1943). From 13-14 months of age, there was continued predominance of vocoids; i.e. front and central vocoids were favoured over high and back vocoids. The most frequent contoids were/h/ ,/b/,/d/,/m/,/t/,/g/and/w/and suggests that only limited set of phones are babbled (Locke, 1990). With respect to syllable shapes, open syllables (Eg: V, CV, VCV, CVCV) were more frequent than closed syllables (KentandBauer, 1985).

***Stage** 5*: Jargon stage (10 months and older)

- This form of babbling, also called conversational babble or modulated babble, overlaps with first meaningful words.
- It is characterized by strings of babbled utterances that are modulated primarily by intonation, rhythm and pausing (Crystal, 1986).
- It sounds as if the child is actually attempting sentences but without actual words.

Babbling and its relationship to later language development: Jacobson's discontinuity hypothesis denounced any link between babbling and later language development. However, several researchers have suggested that both the quantity and diversity of vocalizations do indeed play a role in later language development and so, we can predict later language ability by analyzing babbling.

Prosodic Feature Development: The infants utilizes patterns of prosodic behaviour primarily intonation, rhythm and pausing (Crystal, 1986) at approximately 6 months of age i.e. in canonical babbling stage. Acoustic analysis shows that falling pitch is the most common intonation contour for the first tear of life. Prosodic patterns continue to diversify toward the end of the babbling period to such a degree that names like expressive jargon and prelinguistic jargon have been applied to them. These strings of babbles typically end in a manner characteristic adult intonation patterns (Jargon stage).Adult like intonational patterns are noted prior to the appearance of first word and the onset of stress patterns occur before the age of 2.The entire prosodic feature development doesn't complete till the age of 12years.

Transition from babbling to meaningful speech: This is the actual beginning of the development of articulation and phonological skills. There is considerable overlap between the 2 stages (babbling and meaningful speech) and hence difficult to differentiate the two. Transition is a gradual process and is characterized by

1. primarily monosyllabic utterances
2. Frequent use of consonants, followed by nasals and fricatives.
3. bilabial and apical productions
4. rare use of consonant clusters
5. Frequent use of central, mid-front and low front vowels.

In spite of all the similarities, distinctions between babbling and 1st words are:

1. A large diversity existed between children's productions in each of the areas investigated (phonetic tendencies, consonant and vowel inventories and word selection). More the words acquired, the more this diversity seemed to diminish.
2. Voiced stops used in babbling but not in words eg:/ g/
3. Vowels produced during babbling were used as substitute for other vowel productions in words. The high-front vowel/i/was a frequent substitute.

4. Productions were context dependent. Eg: high front vowels occurred frequently following alveolar; high back vowels following velars and central vowels after consonants.

Linguistic Stage

The first fifty words: the 1st word is defined as an entity of the relatively stable form that is produced consistently by the child in a particular context and is recognizably related to the adult like word form of a particular language.

Eg: If child says/ba/consistently in the context of being shown a ball, this form would qualify as being shown a ball; this form would qualify as a word. But/dodo/for the same context does not qualify as a word form. These "invented words" used consistently but without a recognizable adult model are called as protowords, phonetically consistent forms, vocables and quasi-words by various authors.

The first fifty words stage begins at approximately 1 year and ends at approximately 18-24 months when child can string 2 words together. At this point, the comprehension vocabulary is around 200 words although expression is 50 words. This fact has an effect on the development of semantic meaning as well as on the phonological system. During this period, children are not just learning sounds, which are then used to make up words but, rather, they seem to learn word units that happen to contain particular sets of sounds. Ingram (1976) called this a pre-systematic stage in which contrastive words rather than contrastive phonemes are required. The pre-systematic stage can be related to Cruttenden's (1981) item learning and systematic learning stages of early phonological development. In item learning, the child 1st acquires word forms as unanalyzed units as productional wholes. Only later, characteristically after the first fifty word stage does system learning occur, during which the child acquires the phoneme principal that apply to the phonological system in question. The early portion of the item learning stage is called as holophrastic period, the span of the time during which the child uses one word to indicate a complete idea. Eg; a child might say 'juice' to convey the information 'I want more juice'.

Segmental Form Development

Several authors noted phonetic variability and a limitation of syllable structures and sound segments during the first 50 words stage. Phonetic variability refers to the unstable pronunciations if the child's first 50 words.

First limitation of the syllable structure is that certain syllable types (CV, VC, CVC) predominate when CVCV syllable are present, they are w.r.t sound segment limitations in this stage, the 1st consonants are followed by/t/and later/k/, fricatives are present only after the respective homorganic stops have been acquired and the first vowel is or/a/., followed by/u/and/or/i/.

Clinical Application: SLP's follow a developmental model in therapy i.e. sounds developed earlier are targeted before those that are acquires later. Stoel Gammon's (1985) data support techniques utilized in therapy.

1. Sounds first appear in the word in initial position. In therapy, a newly acquired sound is typically placed in the word initial position.
2. Anterior stops and nasals are acquired earlier. These sounds are very early and hence should be in the speech of children. Even most children with phonological disorders have them in their consonant inventories.

Certain interesting results often are not employed in therapy:

1. The liquid/r/nearly always appeared in word final position: words like more and bear might be easier than red or rope for a child with/r/difficulties.
2. Word initial inventories contained voiced stops first; word final inventories contained voiceless stops first. According to this, child with/k/and/g/problems

might benefit from first working on/g/in word initial position before/k/in word final position.

Individual Acquisition Patterns:

Phonological acquisition may vary across children based on 2 factors:

1. *Salience factor*: is defines as a child's active selection in early word productions of words containing sounds that are important or remarkable (salient) to the child.
2. *Avoidance factor*: is defined as the avoidance of words that do not contain sounds within a child's inventory.

Prosodic Feature Development

An important aspect of communication during the first fifty word stage is prosodic variation. Pitch variations could be used to indicate differences in meaning. A Prosodic features associated with intentional communication include:

10-12 months: 1st word, naming, labelling.

Begin with falling contour only. Flat or level contour usually accompanied by variations such as falsettos or variations in duration or loudness.

13-15 months: Requesting, attention, getting, curiosity, surprise, recognition, insistence, greeting.

- Rising contour and high falling contour. Eg./da/ increase/da/

Prior to 18 months: Playful anticipation, emphatic stress.

- High falling and high rising falling contour.

Around 18 months: Warnings playfulness.

- Falling rising contour and rising falling contours.

Intonational changes develop prior to stress. Contrastive stress is first evidenced only at the beginning of the 2 word stage (approx 1.6 years).

Preschool Child

This stage stresses information on the phonological development from 24 months – 6 years. It is during this time that the largest growth within the phonological system takes place.

From 18-24/30 months of age, the child's expressive vocabulary grows up to 150-300 while the receptive vocabulary is around 1200 words. The transition from one-word utterances to 2 word sentences occurs at this time.

By 5 years of age expressive vocabulary has expanded to approximately 2200 words while receptive vocabulary is around 9600 words. Almost all of the basic grammatical forms of the language such as questions, negative statements dependents clauses and compound sentences are now present as well. At this stage, the child knows how to use language to communicate in an effective manner.

Segmental form development: 1. Vowels: children show the acquisition of/a/,/i/,/I/and/^/at 18 months if criterion is set at 70% accuracy for with virtually no production errors. In general, vowels are mastered at the age of 3.

2. Consonants: Acquisition period varies according to the various authors.

Templin (1957) classified consonantal acquisition in the initial, medial and final position and reported the following.

By 3 yrs- m, n, p, f, w, h

3.6 yrs-j

4 yrs – k, b, d, g, r.

4.5 yrs – s, ...

6yrs – t, l, v.

7 yrs – z , dz.

It has been hypothesized that phonological idioms or regression occurs as the child attempts to master other complexities of language. Both items refer to accurate sound productions that are later replaced by inaccurate ones, when trying to deal with more complex morphosyntactic or semantic structures.

Child Language Acquisition and Phonological Process

Lowe (1996) describes a phonological process as a systematic sound change that affects classes of sounds or sound sequences and results in a simplification of production.

The term Phonological Process (PP) is most frequently used to describe the patterned modifications of the adult model by normally developing children when the child's motor capacities do not yet allow their norm realization. Clinically, this term is also used to describe the sound error patterns used by children diagnosed with a phonological disorder. Phonological processes are innate and universal.

Phonological process is categorized as 3 broad types:

(1) Syllable structure process

(2) Substitution process

(3) Assimilating process

Syllable Structure Process

It describes the sound changes that modify the syllabic structure of words as the child attempts to produce the adult target.

(*a*) Unstressed syllable/weak syllable deletion: omission of syllable with at least stress from a polysyllabic word. It suppresses by 4 years of age.

(*b*) Reduplication/doubling: common process in the 1st word stage i.e. 12-18 months. E.g. Total reduplication: dada for dog, Partial reduplication: didi for dog.

(*c*) Final consonant deletion: disappears by the age 3. Eg:/bu/for books,/h/for hand.

(*d*) Diminutization: Earlier process. Eg:/kpi/for cup,/d^ali/for doll.

(*e*) Epenthesis: Insertion of an unstressed vowel (usually schwa//) between two consonants. Normal till 2.5 – 8 years./spun/for spoon,/b_b/for back. Can occur after final voiced stop (Stoel-Gammmon and Dunn, 1985).

(*f*) Initial consonant deletion: Not a naturally occurring process. Eg:/on/for phone/indou/for window.

(*g*) Cluster reduction: Suppressed by around 5 years but can go upto 8-9 years.

E.g. total cluster reduction://for/flag/

Partial cluster reduction:/tap/for stop.

Cluster substitution:/bwed/for/bread/.

Substitution Process

In this process, one class of sound is substituted for another.

(*a*) Stopping:/p t/for fat,/d b/for job.

Age of suppression varies for different stops.

(*b*) Fronting: Suppression by around 3.5 years.

E.g. velar fronting:/tap/for cap, palatal fronting:/su/ for shoe.

(*c*) Gliding of liquids/fricatives: Seen between 5-7 years. Eg:/wuk/for wok,/lop/for soap.

(*d*) Labialization: suppressed by 6 years. Eg:/f m/for thumb.

(*e*) Alveolarization: suppressed by 5 years. Eg:/s m/for thumb.

(*f*) Deaffrication: suppressed by 4 years. Eg:/ter/for chair.

(*g*) Affrication: suppressed by 3 years. Eg./t i/for she.

(*h*) Denasalization: suppressed by 2 years. Eg:/bob/for mom.

(*i*) Deplatalization: suppressed by 4.6 years. Eg:/t k/for check.

(*j*) Vowelization/Vocalization: suppresses by 4.6 years. Eg:/tebo/for table.

(*k*) Voicing: suppressed by 6 years. Eg: du/two, gi/key

(*l*) Devoicing: suppressed by 5 years. Eg: coat/goat.

(*m*) Derhotacization: suppressed by 4 years. Eg:/w d/for red.

Assimilatory Process/Harmony Process

Refers to the phenomenon by which one sound changes to become more like another sound, particularly its neighbouring sound. Normal if seen from 1.5 – 2 years and considered a danger sign for disordered phonological system if persists beyond 3 years of age.

(*a*) Labial assimilation:/p b/for pen

(*b*) Velar assimilation:/kng/for cup

(*c*) Nasal assimilation:/non/for nose.

(*d*) Alveolar assimilation:/dod/for ten.

(*e*) Prevocalic voicing:/d n/for ten.

(*f*) Post-vocalic devoicing:/t k/for tug.

It can also be total/partial.

Clinical Application of Phonological Process

1. Assessment procedures using Phonological Process consists of controlling the target word to child's production and several tests are developed based on the PP like Assessment of Phonological Processes (Hodson, 1986), Natural Processes Analysis (Shribergand Kwiatkowski, 1980) etc.
2. The process is listed and the frequency of occurrence of individual process along with the relative age of suppression plays a role in targeting a process for therapy.
3. To be considered a target for therapy, PP should have a frequency of occurrence. Eg 20% according to Hudson and Paden, 1991.
4. Helps identify the idiosyncratic processes in phonological disordered population.
5. A treatment approach based on the PP holds the premise that remediation of a process can influence all of the sounds that are similarly affected through generalization. For example, if a child has the process of fricative stopping, then targeting only the/f/and/

s/, we can expect the generalization to other fricatives without specific treatment.

Templin (1957): Processes that are expected to disappear by 3 years – USD, FCD, Reduplication, Diminutization, Velar fronting, consonant assimilation, pre-vocalic voicing.

Processes persisting beyond 3 years: Epenthesis, gliding, vocalization, stopping, depalatalization and cluster reduction.

Prosodic Feature Development during Pre-school age

Use of contrastive stress is an important development this stage.The child is now able to integrate prosody of 2 words into one tone-unit. A "tone-unit" or a "sense group" is an organizational unit imposed on prosodic data (Crystal, 1956) and it conveys meaning beyond that of verbal production only.

Initially, pauses are of greater duration in this stage and it gradually reduces to give away to unifying rhythmic relations.

Eg: Daddy (pause) eat

Daddy (pause shortens) eat

Daddy eat (no pause, both stresses)

Daddy eat (first word stressed).

The School Age

The phonological inventory is nearly complete but all the phonological features are not mastered at this time.

Later developing sounds with approximately age of mastery.

s, z – 7.5 – 9 yrs

r - 7.5 – 8 yrs.

v, - 6-7 yrs

z – 6-7 yrs

In the range of 8-9 years age, reduction 2 consonants clusters to a single element were seen in pl, gl, sl, tw, tr, dr, sw, fr, sm, sn, st, sk. From 5-9 years,/br/and/r/shows greater cluster reduction.

Epenthesis occurs up to 8-9 years of age.

In addition, interconnections between learning to speak and learning to read develop. A strong correlation between phonological development, especially segmentation skills and later reading achievement has been found. Metaphonological skills (conscious awareness of sounds within that particular language) are also related to reading. It enables the child to combine sounds to form words.

Although it is not clear whether metaphonological skills are precursors of emerging literacy or the result of developing reading skills to reading skills2 factors remain

1. Metaphonology is related to reading performance
2. These skills develop at the time when most children start to read i.e between 5-6 years.

Phonological Abilities of school children with poor reading skills has confirmed the following metaphonological difficulties:

1. *Phonological awareness*: Poor readers have difficulty analyzing words into syllables and sounds.
2. *Memory storage of phonetic coding*: Poor readers are less efficient at creating and maintaining the necessary phonological code for storing verbal information: Poor phonological awareness.
3. *Phonetic perception in recreating a phonological code*: On repetition, poor readers exhibit clearly greater difficulties if background noise is introduces or if words to be read are larger and less familiar

   Studies have shown that speech sound difficulties beyond 5-6 years of age are risk factors for poor phonological awareness and poor reading skills.

Prosodic Feature Development

Little evidence is available for school-age period. In general, development of contrastive stress continues and prosodic features mostly take up grammatical function i.e. to signal grammatical contrasts.

Phonological Disorder/Disability

'Developmental Phonological Disorders, also known as phonological disability or phonological disorders, are a group of language disorders that affect children's ability to develop easily understood speech by the time they are four years old, and, in some cases, their ability to learn to read and spell. Therefore, Phonological disorders involve a difficulty in learning and organizing all the sounds needed for clear speech, reading and spelling' (Bowen, 1998).

As well, in the literature they are referred to as: phonomotor disability (Folkins and Bleile, 1990), syntactic phonological syndrome (Howell and Dean, 1991), phonological disorder (Dean, Howell, Hill and Waters, 1990; Fey, 1992; Kamhi, 1992; Stackhouse, 1993), and expressive phonological impairment (Bird, Bishop and Freeman, 1995).

Dodd (1993) distinguished three distinct types of phonological disorder (excluding articulation disorders): delayed phonological acquisition, inconsistent deviant disorder, and consistent deviant disorder. He describes that children with delay are those who use normal developmental processes that are inappropriate for their chronological age and the one with deviance are those who use some processes which do not occur among the normally developing children.

Grunwell and Russell (1990) also posited at least three types, related to (1) form: the inventory and contrastive system (2) function: the variability in the realization of adult contrasts, and (3) phonotactics.

Characteristics of Children with Disordered Phonology

- It is said that even the normal children use unusual phonological patterns less frequently, but the children with phonological disorder use unusual patterns more frequently and less systematically as reported.

- Leonard et al.(1987) tested normally developing children and children with phonological disorder on words which contained consonants which were produced correctly by the child mostly (in phonology words),on the words which contained consonants which were attempted by the child many times but not produced correctly (attempted words) and on the words which contained consonants to which the child was exposed for the first time (out of phonology words).The results indicated that,
  - Normally developing children produced unusual patterns more on out of phonology words i.e.45%, and lesser i.e. 20.2% on attempted words, whereas,
  - Children with disordered phonology produced errors on all types of words with no significant difference.
- Studies have shown that the children with phonological disorder when compared to the normal children, use sounds which are absent in their native language .The English speaking children uses ingressive alveolar fricatives as given by Ingram and Terselic (1983); lateral fricatives by Fey (1985) and alveolar fricatives by Edwards (1980).
- Failure to use developmentally expected speech sounds that are appropriate for age and dialect (e.g., errors in sound production, use, representation, or organization such as, but not limited to, substitutions of one sound for another [use of/t/for target/k/ sound] or omissions of sounds such as final consonants).

The difficulties in speech sound production interfere with academic or occupational achievement or with social communication.

Some children with developmental phonological disorders have other speech and language difficulties such as immature grammar and syntax, stuttering or word-retrieval difficulties. However, many of them just have a 'pure' developmental phonological disorder, involving:

- A problem with speech clarity in the preschool years, with no subsequent reading and spelling problems, or
- A problem with speech clarity in the pre-school years, and, in the early school years, difficulty learning to read, and difficulties with reading comprehension, or
- Speech and reading problems as described above, plus difficulty with spelling, or
- Speech and spelling problems (i.e., no reading difficulties), or
- Speech clarity problems in the pre-school years, and difficulties with written expression in primary school.

Phonologically disabled children will be able to produce lengthy utterances which are grammatically structured and appropriate to context, but they have problem only in pronunciation of words.

The cause of phonological disorder in children is largely unknown. It has been suggested that this disorder has a genetic component due to the large proportion of children who have relatives with some type of similar disorder. However there is no available data to support these observations.

Children with phonological disorders use phonological processes differently than do normally developing children. Grunwell (1987) provides the following 5 classifications which serve as diagnostic indicators:

(1) ***Persisting normal processes:*** these are normal phonological processes that remain in a child's pronunciation patterns long after the age at which they would be expected to have been suppressed. Eg: Prevocalic voicing being present after 4 years,though it normally suppreses by 3 years of age.

(2) ***Chronological mismatch:*** refers to the cooccurrence of some of the earliest normal simplifying processes together with patterns characteristic of later stages of phonological development. Eg: velar fronting and development of word initial clusters present in the speech of a 4 year old.

(3) ***Systematic sound preference:*** occurs when one type of consonant (single phonetic realization) is used for a large range of phonemes. It results in massive reduction pf phonological contrasts and is seen when both normal development processes and idiosyncratic processes co- occur. Eg: a child substituting/d/for s, z, sh, ch and all initial consonant blends (Weiner, 1981).

(4) ***Unusual or idiosyncratic processes:*** it is characterized by patterns that are uncommon in the speech of normally developing children or those that are seen in the speech of individual children with phonological disorder.

Some idiosyncratic processes seen in children with phonological disorders are:

(*a*) Initial consonant deletion. Eg: ack for back
(*b*) Backing of stops. Eg:kap for tap
(*c*) Backing of fricatives. Eg: shun for sun
(*d*) Glottal replacements. Eg: n for gun
(*e*) Denasalizations. Eg: bob for mom
(*f*) Fricatives replacing stops. Eg: sin for tin
(*g*) Stops replacing glides. Eg: dawn for yawn
(*h*) Metathesis. Eg: corol for color
(*i*) Migration. Eg: usb for bus
(*j*) Affrication. Eg: ig for dig
(*k*) Unusual cluster reduction. Eg: ross for cross
(*l*) Unusual substitution processes. Eg: rock for flock
(*m*) Centralization of vowels. Eg: b d for b d

(5) Variable use of processes: occurs when more than one simplifying process routinely operates with the same type of structure, so that the child's realizations are variable and unpredictable: /bai/for pie,/po/for pour. This variability is potentially progressive in that it entails the possible development of target contrast. Variability is abnormal when it is not potentially progressive. Eg:/leik/for rake,/wing/for ring.

A phonological disorder is different from phonetic or articulation disorder:

Phonetic Disorder	Phonological Disorder
Phonetic error	Phonemic error
Problems in speech sound production	Problems in language specific function of phonemes.
Difficulties with speech sound form	Difficulties with phoneme function
Disturbance in relatively peripheral motor processes that result in speech	Disturbances represent an impairment of representation or organization within a language system
Do not impact language areas like morphology, syntax and semantics.	Phoneme difficulties may impact language areas like morphology, syntax and semantics.

CHAPTER

3

Morphology and Syntax (Grammar)

Concept, Acquisition/Development, Disorder and their Clinical relevance

Grammar

Linguistic communications are channelled mainly through our senses of sound and sight. Linguists identify different aspects of language. The components of language occur simultaneously through the continuous stream of sounds and symbols produced as we speak. The major linguistic aspects of language are traditionally identified as Grammar (its structure), Semantics (its meaning) and Pragmatics (its social use). These same components have been referred to as Form, Content and Use, respectively (Bloom and Lahey, 1978). Grammar is the central component of language. It mediates between the system of sounds or of written symbols, on the one hand and the system of meaning on the other. The word *grammar* derives from Greek, through Latin, from the word 'gamma' meaning 'letter' and 'ars' meaning 'craft to' meaning the 'craft to letters'.

The Grammatical Aspect of Language

Grammar is a systematic study and description of a language. It can also be defined as the set of rules and examples dealing with the syntax (word order) and morphology (word parts) of a standard language. In its most basic sense, grammar refers to the conventional rules for arranging the symbols of language in sequences that convey the intended meaning.

According to Denver (1978), "grammar represents the patterns of behaviour that occur over and over". As such, grammar is comprised of morphological and syntactic elements.

For Saussure, "Grammar is a question of a complex and systematic object concerning the interplay of coexisting values. Grammar studies language as a system of means of expression.

Properties of Grammar

Grammar should have the following properties:

1. It should be finite.
2. It should predict an infinite number of sentences.
3. It should be describable in purely formal terms without reliance on meaning.

Function of Grammar

One main function of grammar is it helps preserving a language and its rules. That is grammar prevents any change in the language through time and by influence of any other language and its speakers.

Types of Grammar

1. Prescriptive verses descriptive grammar.

This distinction might be illustrated by the contrast between "telling you how to talk" versus "describing how you talk". Prescriptive grammar is a set of rules that specifies how a language should be spoken. It refers to the notion that there is one correct way of speaking a language. This suggests the rules that the speakers of a language must follow to be considered proper speakers of the language. Prescriptive grammar prescribes what is traditionally correct.

Descriptive grammar refers to the linguistic process of identifying and describing the regularities that occur naturally in a language. It attempts to capture the current language patterns that have resulted from the social and cultural forces that influence a language.

2. Intuitive verses Formal grammar

The distinction between intuitive and formal grammar might be most easily thought of as the difference between the grammar in our heads and grammar linguists put down on paper. Intuitive grammar refers to the underlying knowledge speakers demonstrate by using and understanding their native language. When confronted with correct and incorrect sentences in their language, most speakers can instantly identify which are grammatical and which are not instinctively, but we may still be unable to express the specific rules that pertain to the instances that are ungrammatical. In contrast a formal grammar is the written summary of the hypothetical rules that describes the regularities in a language.

David Crystal lists six Types of Grammar

1. Descriptive Grammar

An approach that describes the grammatical constructions used in a language without making any evaluative judgments about their standing in society.

2. Pedagogical Grammar

A book specifically designed for teaching a foreign language, or for developing an awareness of the mother tongue. These are widely used in schools, so much so that many people have only one meaning for the term grammar – A Grammar Book.

3. Prescriptive Grammar

A manual that focuses on constructions where usage is divided, and lays down rules governing the socially correct use of language.

4. Reference Grammar

A grammatical description that tries to be as comprehensible as possible, so that it can act as a reference book for those interested in establishing grammatical facts

5. Theoretical Grammar

An approach that goes beyond the study of individual languages, to determine what constructs are needed in order to do any kind of grammatical analysis and how these can be applied consistently in the investigating of linguistic universals.

6. Traditional Grammar

A term often used to summarize the range of attitudes and methods found in the period of grammatical study before the advent of linguistic science.

Morphology

Morphology is the branch of linguistics that studies patterns of word formation within and across languages, and attempts to formulate rules that model the knowledge of the speakers of those languages. In short, morphology is the study of the form of words. Morphology and grammar are two aspects of grammar. The Greek word 'morph' means 'form' and 'logos' mean 'word'.

Morphological Units

Word

A word is the smallest free form (an item that may be uttered in isolation with semantic or pragmatic content) in a language, in contrast to a morpheme which is the smallest unit of meaning. A word may consist of only one morpheme (e.g. Cat) but a single morpheme may not be able to exist as a free form (e.g. the English plural morpheme -s).

Typically a word will consist of a root or stem and zero or more affixes. Words can be combined to create other units of language such as phrases, clauses, and sentences. A word consisting of two or more stems joined together form a compound. A word combined with an already existing word or parts of a word form a portmanteau.

Depending on the language, words can be difficult to identify or decipher. Dictionaries take upon themselves the task of categorizing a language's lexicon into lemmas. These can be taken as an indication of what constitutes a "word" in the opinion of the authors.

Word Boundaries

In spoken language, the distinction of individual words is usually given by rhythm or accent, but short words are often run together. Spoken French has some of the features of a polysynthetic language: il y est allé ("He went there") is pronounced [ilj[tale]. Since the majority of the world's languages are not written, the scientific determination of word boundaries becomes important.

There are five ways to determine where the word boundaries of spoken language should be placed:

Potential pause: A speaker is told to repeat a given sentence slowly, allowing for pauses. The speaker will tend to insert pauses at the word boundaries. However, this method is not foolproof: the speaker could easily break up polysyllabic words.

Indivisibility: A speaker is told to say a sentence out loud, and then is told to say the sentence again with extra words added to it. Thus, I have lived in this village for ten years might become I and my family have lived in this little village for about ten or so years. These extra words will tend to be added in the word boundaries of the original sentence. However, some languages have infixes, which are put inside a word. Similarly, some have separable affixes; in the German sentence "Ich komme gut zu Hause an," the verb ankommen is separated.

Minimal free forms: This concept was proposed by Leonard Bloomfield in 1926. Words are thought of as the smallest meaningful unit of speech that can stand by themselves. This correlates phonemes (units of sound) to lexemes (units of meaning). However, some written words are not minimal free forms, as they make no sense by themselves (for example, the and of).

Phonetic boundaries: Some languages have particular rules of pronunciation that make it easy to spot where a word boundary should be. For example, in a language that regularly stresses the last syllable of a word, a word boundary is likely to fall after each stressed syllable. Another example can be seen in a language that has vowel harmony (like Turkish): the vowels within a given word share the same quality, so a word boundary is likely to occur whenever the vowel quality changes. Nevertheless, not all languages have such convenient phonetic rules, and even those that do present the occasional exceptions.

Semantic units: Much like the above mentioned minimal free forms, this method breaks down a sentence into its smallest semantic units. However, language often contains words that have little semantic value (and often play a more grammatical role), or semantic units that are compound words.

A further criterion: Pragmatics: The idea of a lexical item being considered, a word should also adjust to pragmatic criteria. The word "hello", for example, does not exist outside of the realm of greetings being difficult to assign a meaning out of it. This is a little more complex if we consider "how do you do?" is it a word, a phrase, or an idiom? In practice, linguists apply a mixture of all these methods to determine the word boundaries of any given sentence. Even with the careful application of these methods, the exact definition of a word is often still very elusive. There are some words that seem very general, but may truly have a technical definition, such as the word "soon," usually meaning within a week.

Root

The root is the primary lexical unit of a word, which carries the most significant aspects of semantic content and cannot be reduced into smaller constituents. Content words in nearly all languages contain, and may consist only of, root morphemes. However, sometimes the term "root" is also used to describe the word minus its inflectional endings, but with its lexical endings in place. For example, chatters has the inflectional root or lemma chatter, but the lexical root chat. Inflectional roots are often called stems, and a root in the stricter sense may be thought of as a mono-morphemic stem.

The traditional definition allows roots to be either free morphemes or bound morphemes. Root morphemes are essential for affixation and compounds. However, in polysynthetic languages with very high levels of inflectional morphology, the term "root" is generally synonymous with "free morpheme". Many such languages have a very restricted number of morphemes that can stand alone as a word: Yup'ik, for instance, has no more than two thousand.

The root of a word is a unit of meaning (morpheme) and, as such, it is an abstraction, though it can usually be represented in writing as a word would be. For example, it can be said that the root of the English verb form running is run, or the root of the Spanish superlative adjective amplísimo is ampl-, since those words are clearly derived from the root forms by simple suffixes that do not alter the roots in any way. In particular, English has very little inflection, and hence a tendency to have words that are identical to their roots. But more complicated inflection, as well as other processes, can obscure the root; for example, the root of mice is mouse (still a valid word), and the root of interrupt is, arguably, rupt, which is not a word in English and only appears in derivational forms (such as disrupt, corrupt, rupture, etc.). The root rupt is written as if it was a word, but it's not.

This distinction between the word as a unit of speech and the root as a unit of meaning is even more important in the case of languages where roots have many different forms when used in actual words, as is the case in Semitic languages. In these, roots are formed by consonants alone, and different words (belonging to different parts of speech) are derived from the same root by inserting vowels. For example, in Hebrew, the root gdl represents the idea of largeness, and from it we have gadol and gdola (masculine and feminine forms of the adjective "big"), gadal "he grew", higdil "he magnified" and magdelet "magnifier", along with many other words such as godel "size" and migdal "tower".

Stem

In linguistics, a stem (sometimes also theme) is the part of a word that is common to all its inflected variants. Stems are often roots, e.g. atomic, its root is atom, but its stem is atom·ic. A stem can be morphologically complex, as seen with compound words (cf. the compound nouns meat ball or bottle opener) or words with derivational morphemes (cf. the derived verbs black-en or standard-ize). Thus, the stem of the complex English noun photographer is photo·graph·er, but not photo. For another example, the root of the English verb form destabilized is stabil-, a form of stable that does not occur alone; the stem is de·stabil·ize, which includes the derivational affixes de- and -ize, but not the inflectional past tense suffix -(e)d. That is, a stem is that part of a word that inflectional affixes attach to.

The exact use of the word 'stem' depends on the morphology of the language is question. In Athabaskan linguistics, for example, a verb stem is a root that cannot appear on its own, and that carries the tone of the word. Athabaskan verbs typically have two stems in this analysis, each preceded by prefixes.

Affix

An affix is a morpheme that is attached to a word stem to form a new word. Affixes may be derivational, like English -ness and pre-, or inflectional, like English plural -s and past tense -ed. They are bound morphemes by definition; prefixes and suffixes may be separable affixes. Affixation is, thus, the linguistic process speakers use to form new words (neologisms) by adding sounds (affixes) at the beginning (prefixation), the middle (infixation) or the end (suffixation) of words.

Positional categories of affixes: Affixes are divided into several categories, depending on their position with reference to the stem. Prefix (bound morpheme before the root) and suffix (bound morpheme after the root) are extremely common terms. Infix and circumfix are less so, as they are not important in most of the languages. The other terms are uncommon:

Categories of Affixes

Affix	Example	Schema	Description
Prefix	un-do	prefix-stem	Appears at the front of a stem
Suffix/Postfix	look-ing	stem-suffix	Appears at the back of a stem
Infix	saxo‹ma›phone	st‹infix›em	Appears within a stem — common in Borneo-Philippines languages
Circumfix	a›scatter‹ed	circumfix› stem‹ circumfix	One portion appears at the front of a stem, and the other at the rear
Interfix	speed-o-meter	stem_a-interfix-stem_b	Links two stems together in a compound
Duplifix	teeny~weeny	stem~duplifix	Incorporates a reduplicated portion of a stem (may occur in front, at the rear, or within the stem)
Transfix	Maltese: k‹i›t‹e›b "he wrote" (compare root ktb "write")	s‹transfix› te‹transfix›m	A discontinuous affix that interleaves within a discontinuous stem
Simulfix	mouse ? mice		Changes a segment of a stem
Suprafix	produce (noun) produce (verb)		Changes a supra-segmental phoneme of a stem
Disfix	Alabama: tipli "break up" (compare root tipasli "break")	stm	The elision of a portion of a stem

Source: www.wikipedia.com.

The function of the suffix is both grammatical and semantic. A suffix is a letter or letters added to the end of a base word to change its meaning. Some suffixes specifically form nouns, such as age in mileage,*-hood* in *childhood.*

There are two types of suffixes, those that start with a vowel and those that start with a consonant. So we can refer to a suffix as a *vowel suffixes* or a *consonant suffix*, classifying it by the first letter of the suffix.

Suffixing rules:

There are four suffixing rules:

(*a*) ***Add rule:*** Many suffixes can just be added to the base word without any trouble, as in , for example, trains, dancer and absolutely

(*b*) ***Doubling rule:*** Double the final consonant of the base word, as in stopper, hugged, robbed, sloppy

The advanced doubling rule- can be applied in longer words. If the base word has two syllables or more, you need to identify the stressed syllable in the word.

If the stress is on the last syllable of the base word, then treat that syllable as if it were a one-syllable word and double the middle consonant.

For example: re - *fer* + ing = *referring*

If the stress is on the first syllable, do not double the final consonant

E.g. ***tar*** – get + ed = targeted

Second rule – there is an extra suffixing rule which applies to British English, but not to American English. If the base word ends in the letter l, it is doubled before a vowel suffix

	British English	American English
E.g. travel + ing =	travelling	traveling

(*c*) The drop the e rule–In this rule drop the final e of a word if you are adding a vowel suffix.

E.g. dance + ing = dancing.

There are few exceptional words in which the e is not dropped.

E.g. e may be needed to soften a c or a g as in traceable and spongeable, or to make distinction with another word which would otherwise be identical, as in singing/singeing, and dying/dyeing.

(*d*) ***The change rule***–this the most complex rule if the base word ends in the letter y, and if there is a consonant before the y , for the most part you change the y to I and add the suffix. E.g. try + ed = tried.

Prefixes:

The prefix changes the meaning of the word.

E.g. Popular becomes unpopular.

Prefixes can be divided into two kinds,

Consonant prefixes	-	E.g. in- , un-, con-, which ends in a consonant
Vowel prefixes	-	E.g. re- , pre-, pro-, which end in a vowel

Prefixing rules

There are two prefixing rules

(a) Add rule: Prefixes ending in a vowel can just be added onto the beginning of the base words.Eg. resit, react, presume, preempt, produce, proactive.

Many of the consonants also the same rule can be applied. E.g. unwise, disobey, superstructure.

(b) Change rule: Some of the consonant prefixes, particularly those of Latin origin, change their last letter of the base word. Eg. in + legal = illegal, ob + fer = offer.

The prefixes ad- , con- , in- , ob- , sub-, dis-, ex- may all change their final letter.

E.g. con + lect = collect, in + mortal = immortal, ex + fect = effect

However, when in or con precedes a p as in in + prove or con + pel is pronounced like m and so it has become assimilated so we say and write as impossible, compel.

Morphemes, Morph and Allomorph

Morph

A morph is a phonological string (of phonemes) that cannot be broken down into smaller constituents that have a lexico-grammatical function. In some sense it corresponds to a word form. It is the physical representation of morphemes.

Morphemes

Morpheme is a minimal unit of meaning or grammatical function. That is, Morpheme is the smallest unit of grammar. E.g. in the word *unkind,* two morphemes are there: *un-* and *kind,* unhappiness – 3 morphemes *un-, happy* and *-ness.*

Allomorph

An allomorph is a term for a variant form of a morpheme. The concept occurs when a unit of meaning can vary in sound (phonologically) without changing meaning. It is used in linguistics to explain the comprehension of variations in sound for a specific morpheme.

One of the largest sources of complexity in morphology is that one to one correspondence between meaning and form scarcely applies to every case in the language. In English word form pairs like ox/oxen, goose/geese, and sheep/sheep, where the difference between singular and plural is signalled in a way that departs from the regular pattern, or is not signalled at all. Even cases considered "regular", with the final –s, are not so simple; the –s in *dogs* is not pronounced in the same way as the –s in cats, and in a plural like dishes; an "extra" vowel appears before the –s. These cases where the same distinction is affected by alternative forms of a word are called *allomorphy.*

Allomorphy in English suffixes:

English has several morphemes that vary in sound but not in meaning. Examples include the past tense and the plural morphemes.

For example, in English, a past tense morpheme is *-ed*. It occurs in several allomorphs depending on its phonological environment, assimilating voicing of the previous segment or inserting a schwa when following an alveolar stop:

- as/Ld/or/ɪd/in verbs whose stem ends with the alveolar stops/t/or/d/, such as 'hunted'/hʌntLd/or 'banded'/bændLd/
- as/t/in verbs whose stem ends with voiceless phonemes other than/t/, such as 'fished'/fjʃt/
- as/d/in verbs whose stem ends voiced phonemes other than/d/, such as 'buzzed'/bʌzd/

Notice the "other than" restrictions above. This is a common fact about allomorphy: if the allomorphy conditions are ordered from most restrictive (in this case, after an alveolar stop) to least restrictive, then the first matching case usually "wins". Thus, the above conditions could be re-written as follows:

- as/Yd/or/ɪd/when the stem ends with the alveolar stops/t/or/d/
- as/t/when the stem ends with voiceless phonemes
- as/d/in verbs

The fact that the/t/allomorph does not appear after stem-final/t/, despite the fact that the latter is voiceless, is then explained by the fact that/Ld/appears in that environment, together with the fact that the environments are ordered. Likewise, the fact that the/d/allomorph does not appear after stem-final/d/is because the earlier clause for the/Ld/ allomorph takes priority; and the fact that the/d/allomorph does not appear after stem-final voiceless phonemes is because the preceding clause for the/t/takes priority.

Irregular past tense forms, such as "broke" or "was/were", can be seen as still more specific cases (since they are confined to certain lexical items, like the verb "break"), which therefore take priority over the general cases listed above.

Free and Bound Morphemes

Free morphemes are which can stand by themselves e.g. open tour etc. Bound morphemes are those which cannot normally stand alone, but which are typically attached to another form e.g. re-, -ist, -ed, -s. All affixes are bound morphemes. When free morphemes are used with sound morphemes, the basic word form involved is technically known as stem E.g. carelessness:

Care	less	ness
Stem	suffix	suffix
(Free)	(Bound)	(Bound)

There are a number of English words in which the element which seem to be the 'stem' is not, in fact, a free morpheme. In words like receive, reduce, repeat, we can recognize the bound morpheme re-, but the elements – ceive, -duce, and – peat are clearly not free morphemes. –ceive and –duce are 'bound stem'.

The set of affixes which fall into the 'bound' category can be divided into two types. One is derivational morphemes. These are used to make new words in the language and are often used to make words of a different grammatical category from the stem. This addition of the derivational morphemes changes the adjective 'good' to the noun 'goodness'. The noun *care* can become the adjective, *careful* or *careless* via the derivational morphemes –ful or –less. A list of derivational morphemes will include suffixes and prefixes.

The second set of sound morphemes contains what is called inflectional morphemes. It is used to indicate aspects of grammatical function of a word. It indicates if a word is singular or plural, past tense or not, comparative or possessive from English has only inflectional forum.

- Tom's sister
- Likes to play
- Laughing
- Liked

- Taken
- Loudest
- Quieter

All inflectional morphemes listed here are suffixes.

Noun + - s, -s

Verb + -s, -ing, -ed, -ch

Adjective+ -est, -er

The possessive sometimes occur as –s' (those boys' bags) and post participle as –ed (they have finished).

Inflectional and Derivational Morphemes

An inflectional morpheme never changes the grammatical category of a word. Both old and older are adjectives. The –er inflection simply creates a different version of the adjective.

Derivational morphemes can change the grammatical category of a word. The word *teach* becomes the noun *teacher* if we add the derivational morpheme *–er.*

So the suffix form –er can be an inflectional morpheme as part of an adjective and also a distinct derivational morpheme as part of a noun. Just because the (-er) look the same does not mean they do the same kind of work.

Differences between inflection and derivation:

- Inflection produces different forms of the same lexeme, whereas derivation results in the formation of new lexemes. In other words, inflection has a grammatical function whereas, derivation has a lexical function.
- Derivational affixes may be class changing or class maintaining; but in English, as many other languages, inflectional affixes are always class changing. E.g., *write* becomes- *writes, written, wrote,* etc. (inflectional changes); *write* becomes- *writer* (derivational).
- In words, in which both inflectional and derivational affixes are present, the derivational affix occurs closer to the root than the inflectional affix.

Principle, Practice and Application of Morphemic Analysis in Clinical Situation

There are six principles propounded by Eugene A. Nida (1946) which we may apply in isolating and identifying morphemes. None of the principles is complete in itself; each is supplementary to the basic definition and must be considered so. If each were interpreted as being exclusive of all situations not specifically noted in the principle, the statement would be contradictory.

Principle 1

Forms which have a common semantic distinctiveness and an identical phonemic form in all their occurrences constitute a single morpheme.

The Meaning of Principle 1

Principle 1 means that such a form as –er added to the verb in such construction as worker, dancer, runner, walker, and flier is a morpheme. It always has the same phonetic form, and essentially the same meaning, namely, that of 'the doer of the action' (also called 'agentative'). The principles used the phrase "common semantic distinctiveness" as a way of indicating that the meaning which is common to all the occurrences of the suffix –er contrasts with (or is distinctively set off from) meaning of all the similar forms.

Example:

Worker- work/er

Dancer- walk/er

-er added to verbs in such a way that it always has same meaning, namely, that of 'the doer of the action' (also called 'agentative')

However, in English there is another suffixal morpheme with the form –er in comparative adjectives such as

Smaller –small/er

Deeper –deep/er

Here, -er depicts the comparative adjective.

So, though they have the similar phonemic structure but there is no common semantic distinction, we may say that. They are two different morphemes.

Principle 2

Forms which have common semantic distinctiveness but which differ in phonemic form (i.e. the phonemes) may constitute a morpheme provided the distribution of formal difference is phonologically definable.

The Meaning of Principle 2

It means that when we discover forms with some common semantic distinctiveness but with different phonemes or arrangement of phonemes, we can still put these various forms together as a single morpheme provided we can discover phonological conditions which "govern" the occurrence of such phonologically different forms.

Example:

Intolerable –in/tolerable, Indecent –in/decent

Impossible –im/possible, Impractical –im/practical

The forms in- and im- bear a partial phonetic- semantic resemblance and the positions in which they occur are determined by the type of consonant following. Before alveolar sound such as't' and'd', the alveolar nasal 'n' occurs e.g. intangible, indecent. Before a bilabial sound such as p, the bilabial nasal occurs e.g. impracticable, impersonal. We may say that the form of word to which prefix is added "determines" the form of prefix. This is just another way of saying that the distribution (i.e. positions of occurrence) of in- and im- can be defined by the phonological characteristics of the form in which they occur.

Principle 3

Forms which have common semantic distinctiveness but which differ in phonemic form in such a way that their distribution cannot be phonologically defined constitute a single morpheme if the forms are in complementary distribution.

The Meaning of Principle 3

"Common semantic distinctiveness" is here identical in meaning and application with this phrase as it is used in the development in principle 1and 2.

The clause "but which differ in phonemic form in such a way that their distribution cannot be phonologically defined" means that the difference of the form cannot be treated under principle 2, whereby we reconcile such formal contrasts by determining the phonological distribution.

"complementary distribution means that difference of form are paralleled by differences of distribution, for example, let us assume that a morpheme has three allomorphs and that these allomorphs occur with stem A through Jin such a way that not more than one allomorph ever occurs with a single stem, e.g. A1, B1, C3, D2, E1, F3, G2, H1, I3, J2. In accordance with this type of distribution, we may sat that the allomorphs 1, 2, 3 are in complementary distribution with stem A through J.

E.g. boxes, boys, lips

All of them are plural forms of noun in English and the suffixes used are/-∂z ~ - z ~ -s/(predominantly used pattern) but there are other ways of forming the plural e.g. ox/en. Here, form/-∂n/is in complementary distribution with plural markers/-∂z ~ - z ~ -s/and share common semantic distinctiveness. So we can say that/(-∂z ~ - z ~ -s) ∞ -∂n/are the allomorphs of the same morpheme

'~' indicates complementation based on phonological environment

'∞' indicates complementation based on morphological environment

E.g. Impossible, Intolerable

Here negative prefixes are/in-~im/but other form of negative prefix can be/un-/in untouchable. We can say that/(in-~im) ∞-un/are allomorphs of the same morpheme.

Principle 4

An overt formal difference in a structural series constitutes a morpheme if in any member of such a series; the overt formal difference and a zero structural difference are the only significant features for distinguishing a minimal unit of phonetic-semantic distinctiveness.

The meaning of principle 4

An overt formal difference means a contrast which is indicated by differences in phonemes or in the order of phonemes. e.g. The distinction between foot/fut/and feet/fiyt/is an overt difference, since it consists in a difference of phonemes. The contrast between the singular sheep and plural sheep consists of zero and is covert.

A member of a structural series may occur with a zero structural difference and an overt formal difference. For example, feet/fiyt/as the plural of foot/fut/has a structural zero similar to the zero occurring with sheep/siyp/as the plural of sheep/siyp/.This zero consists in a significant absence of the suffix/ez/,which occurs in the vast majority of plural formations. The overt difference between foot and feet is the replacement of/u/by/iy/.According to principle 4 ,this replacement acquires the status of a morpheme because it is the only overt difference between foot and feet. Principle 4 does not mean that there is no zero occurring in the word feet, but only that the replacement constitutes a morpheme. 'Feet' consists of three morphemes:

(1) The stem

(2) Replacement of/u/by/iy/

(3) The zero suffix

Principle 5

Homophonous forms are identifiable as the same or different morphemes on the basis of the following conditions:

1. Homophonous forms with distinctly different meanings constitute different morphemes.

2. Homophonous forms with related meanings constitute a single morpheme if the meaning classes are paralleled by distributional differences, but they constitute multiple morphemes if the meaning classes are not paralleled by distributional differences.

Definition of homophonous forms:

Homophonous forms are phonemically identical. E.g. in English pear, pare and pair are homophonous.

Definition of related forms: It is difficult to define degrees of difference in meaning, and there are no simple means of deciding whether forms are "distinctly different" or "related" in meaning. There are however, some forms which appear to be obviously related, e.g. the word run in the expressions they run and their run. Even in the phrase the run in her stocking the form run appears to be related in meaning to the preceding occurrences of this homophonous form. Similarly, the fish and to fish contain a meaningfully similar item, fish. Another e.g is-in the phrase to pare and the pear appears to be no meaningful relationship between pare and pear. We may explain such similarities and differences by

Saying that fish in the phrases to fish and the fish have same meaning but pare and pear are different.

Types of distributional differences:

There is no limitation on the types of distributional differences, but the most common situations involve occurrence in different major word classes. For e.g. the fish – verb, to fish- noun. To fish and the fish are related but their distribution is different that is they are distributed differently in different constructions and occur with different suffixes. So relation in meaning is paralleled by distributional difference. Eg horn may be either animal horn or instrument. They are related in meaning but not in complimentary distribution.

I bought a horn – from this sentence one cannot understand whether it is an animal horn or instrument, so they are multiple morphemes.

Principle 6

A morpheme is isolatable if it occurs under the following conditions:

1. In isolation.

   Eg. jump, boy, cow in isolation and all are morphemes.

2. In multiple combinations in at least one of which the unit with which it is combined occurs in isolation or in other combinations. Eg. dancer, worker, provider. The morpheme –er never occur in isolation but since the elements with which it occurs may be found in isolation i.e dance, work, provide-in isolation.

   Dancing, danced –with other combinations.

3. In a single combination provided the element with which it is combined occurs in isolation or in other combinations with non unique constituents. Eg. Some morphemes have only single combinations, cran berry or rasp berry.

   Berry-isolation, rasp berry or cran berry-combinations.

Applications of Morphemic Analysis in the Field of Speech-Language Pathology

- Morphemic analysis is required to study the number and kind of morphemes in a given language sample.
- Can be used to analyze an unknown language if glossing is done.
- Morphemic analysis is required to calculate the mean length of utterance.
- Morphemic analysis helps us to develop the norms for morphemic development.
- Based on the presence and absence of morpheme, by comparing it with the developmental norms one can differentially diagnose between the language disorders to certain extent:

E.g. Broca's aphasia: agrammatic speech.
Wernicke's aphasia: pseudo grammatical speech

- Helps us to identify the Allomorphs in a given language

Syntax

Words are organized in principled ways into higher units like phrases and sentences. The rules and principles governing the arrangement of words into such higher units is technically called syntax. Syntax refers to the way in which we arrange words like "building blocks" to construct phrases and sentences that express our ideas. Thus syntax deals with the order of words: the way in which words combine into such units as a phrase, a clause and a sentence.

Word Order

Most modern English grammar is taken up with the rules governing the order in which words and clusters of words can appear. If the word order is changed, it can result in vast or subtle changes in meaning and the sentence becomes unacceptable. There are certain languages in which the word order is not crucial as the endings of the words indicate the relationships between the elements of the sentence. E.g. Latin.

Spoken and written syntax may differ. In spoken language there is no time to plan and polish before uttering the words. Thus they are characterized by false starts, hesitations, interruptions, forgotten words and lost conclusions. But, while writing we have time to think, plan, redraft and proofread the materials.

Phrase

A phrase consists of a group of words within a sentence or clause. It is a small group of words which function as a grammatical unit. The National Literacy Strategy defines phrases as "two or more words, which act as one unit" and gives 5 types of phrase, named after their main word. They are:

(1) Noun phrase: the black dog
(2) Verb phrase: chased the dog
(3) Adverbial phrase – expands the verb
(4) Adjectival phrase – a phrase with adjective and an intensifier
(5) Prepositional phrase – starts with a preposition and explains the relationship between two nouns in a sentence.

Clause

The clause is a component of a sentence. A sentence can be made up of one or more clauses. A clause contains a verb, a subject and a predicate. Modern clause analysis recognizes that the predicate needs to be further analyzed, and so a clause may have 5 elements: subject, verb, object, complement and adverbial.

Sentence

It is the chief syntactic structure, but difficult to define. The sentence is the largest structural unit treated in grammar. In written language the sentence is signalled by punctuation, primarily by a full stop, and contains one or more clauses.

Sentence types:

(1) A *simple* sentence consists of only one main clause. E.g. the drain has been repaired.
(2) A *compound* sentence has two or more main clauses linked by the coordinators *and* or *but*. E.g. The drain has been repaired, *but* the contractors will still be returning tomorrow.
(3) A *complex* sentence consists of one main clause within which there are subordinate clauses. E.g. *The baby,* who cried all afternoon, *was happy and playful at bedtime.*

Complex sentences are sometimes difficult to understand because of their length. If the main clause can be identified, the meaning is easier to ascertain. The skill of understanding longer sentences is dependent not only on the readers' knowledge of the subject, but on his knowledge of sentence structure too.

Functional categories of sentences:

Sentences can also be classified according to their dominant function in discourse, according to the communication they are. That is, whether they state something, ask a question, give a command or exclaim. These are referred to as:

(1) Declarative

(2) Interrogative

(3) Imperative

(4) Exclamatory

Constituent Structure of Sentence

Sentences are constructed from various elements – words, phrases, clauses. These are the constituent structures of a sentence. The syntax of a sentence defines the underlying roles played by the constituent structures in the sentence. A constituent structure might consists of a word serving as a noun (man), which serves a part of a noun phrase (the man) which furthermore might serve as the subject phrase of the overall sentence.

Hierarchical Structures

The relationships between the constituents (words and phrases) of sentences are organized in a hierarchical structure. This means that the words and phrases are each related to structures at higher and lower levels. This hierarchy describes the underlying relationship within the sentence. The hierarchical structure of a sentence can be illustrated through a *sentence tree*. In the following figure, it is possible to say that the two phrases, the man and the door, are similar constituent structures (noun phrase), but they relate to the verb phrase in quite different ways.

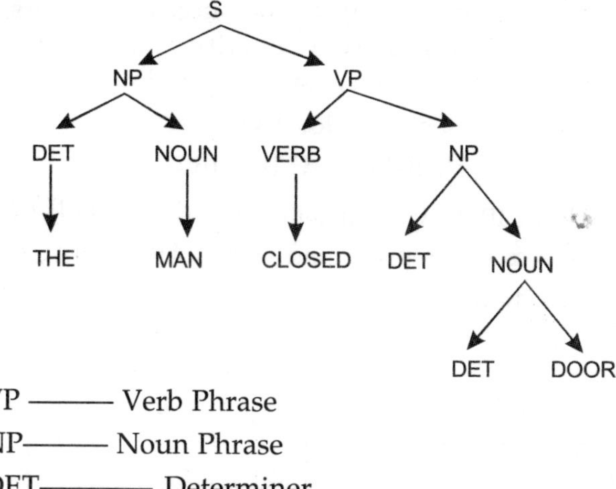

VP ——— Verb Phrase

NP——— Noun Phrase

DET——— Determiner

S ——— Sentence

Syntactic Analysis

Syntactic analysis of a language is a description of the structure of a sentence and of the principles of sentence construction of that language. The various syntactic analysis tools are:

Immediate Constituent Analysis (ICA)

ICA is essentially a structuralist tool for syntactic analysis. It was first introduced and termed by Bloomfield and systemized with theoretical formulations by Roulon Wells and Zellig Harris. This kind of analysis aims at analyzing each utterance into the smallest meaningful units possible. In this model, we begin by cutting the sentence into its natural divisions, and each of these is again cut into two and this process of binary segmentation is continued until we reach the smallest meaningful units namely "morphemes" at the morphological level and "words" at the syntactical level. These units at the last level are called the *ultimate constituents.* ICA helps us to discover how units are hierarchically layered in sentences, each lower level unit or constituent being a part of a higher level construction. Thus a phrase of sentence (called a construction) is broken up in the successive layers, with each layer consisting of two constituents of the closest relationships. For example consider the following:

(1) { The boys} {shouted loudly}

(2) {[The] [boys]} {[shouted] [loudly]}

(3) {[The] [(boy) (-s)]} {[(shout) (-ed)] [(loud) (-ly)]}

The same can be represented with a TREE DIAGRAM

The boys shouted loudly

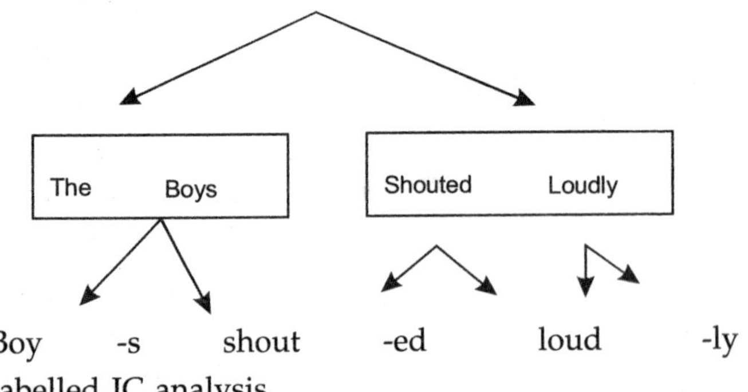

Labelled IC analysis

Once having broken up a sentence into its constituents at different levels, we can label the constituents.

Eg: Little Ram walked slowly (*construction)* can be represented as:

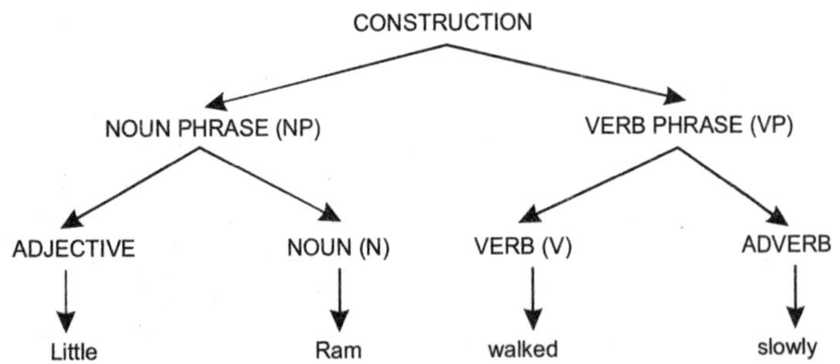

These labels are categorical or formal, indicating the category to which each constituent belongs. Functional labels like subjects, predicates, objects etc can be used to label the constituents. Such labels can show the relationships among the constituents which formal labels cannot. A NP, for instance, can function as subject or object. In terms of the functions of the constituents, constructions can be grouped into 5 types. They are:

(1) The structure of prediction
(2) The structure of modification
(3) The structure of complementation
(4) The structure of subordination
(5) The structure of coordination

Advantages of ICA

(1) Layers of relationships can be graphically displayed by analyzing it into units and showing how they are hierarchically organized to form the sentence

Limitations of ICA

(1) The problem of discontinuity: a construction cannot be cut into two continuous IC's because elements that belong together are separated in the sequences. Eg: She *made* the whole story *up*. Here *made up* belongs to the same category, so it's difficult to do the ICA.
(2) The problem of conjoining: occurs when elements are added or joined to other similar elements. Eg: I will go and meet him.
(3) The problem of embedding: one sentence having another sentence like constructions embedded inside. Eg: the boy who won the prize is my cousin.
(4) The problem of ambiguity/constructional homonymy: these are structures which are outwardly identical, but with different structures and meanings. Eg: hunting dogs.
(5) The problem of structural similarity and different grammatical relations among constituents.
(6) The problem of inter-sentence relationships: ICA fails to reveal the essential relationships between sentence types such as active, passive, affirmative etc.

(7) The problem of group genitive: consider the phrase "The king of Denmark's son". The IC's of this construction are "the king of Denmark's" and "son". The IC's of "the king of Denmark's" are "the king of Denmark" and "son". It's rather strange for one constituent to consist of four words and the other only a single bound morpheme.

(8) The problem of overlapping IC's: consider the sentence "He has no love or kindness to dogs". Here 'no' is applicable to both "love of dogs" and "kindness for dogs". ICA doesn't have any provision to show this.

(9) The problem of understood elements: Eg: in "please pass the salt", *you* is understood, but there is no way for showing this in ICA.

Unlabelled bracketing or tree diagrams do not show the relationships among the constituents. This inadequacy has been removed by introducing the notion of labelling. The labels indicate the functions of ICs. This kind of labelled analysis is the basis of PSG which forms the basic component of TG grammar.

Phrase Structure Grammar (PSG)

A PSG is an alternative way of expressing the information found in a tree diagram by means of rewrite rules. IC analysis, the traditional sentence analysis and phrasing may be referred to as "phrase structure grammar" i.e.: grammar designed to answer the following questions: What share the constituents of a sentence? How are they organized?

It was noted that our ability to distinguish the various constituents of the constructions such as the immediate, mediate and ultimate, depends upon a certain grammatical intuition concerning the relations of elements of sentences.

ICA analyzes each utterance into its basic linguistic units, in order to discover its constituents and how they are organized. A more sophisticated model of grammar called phrase structure grammar has been evolved out of this. This is a method described by Noam Chomsky. PSG contains a set of rules called *Phrase Structure rules or PS rules or rewrite rules.* Rewrite rules are capable not only of generating strings of linguistic elements but also of providing a constituent analysis of the string. They provide a set of directions which if followed mechanically, will generate the abstract frame work of basic English sentences. PS rules are represented by the following general form of rules – schema:

X ⟶ Y

This means that the symbol X is to be rewritten as the symbol Y. The symbol that is used to initiate the rewriting operations is called the initial symbol.

Eg: S ⟶ NP + VP

S - Initial symbol.

The plus sign is used to indicate *concatenation* (chaining together)

Labels such as NP, VP are *nodes* that can be further expanded or rewritten.

NP ⟶ determiner + noun

VP ⟶ Auxillary + Verb + NP + Prepositional Phrase

Prep Ph ⟶ Preposition + NP

A *node* is a point in a tree diagram from which one or more branches emanate.

In PSG the labels are inbuilt in the rewrite rules and the rules themselves can be arranged in the sequence in each rule can be used to rewrite the output of the previous one:

(1) S ⟶ NP + VP

(2) VP ⟶ V + NP + Prep Ph

(3) NP ⟶ D + N

(4) Prep Ph ⟶ Prep + NP

By applying these rules on each other, we get:

S ⟶ D + N + V + D + N + Prep + D + N

A tree may have one or more branches or no branches at all. Every point in a tree where there is a branch is called a branching node and there is a label representing the category at every node. Nodes that can be further expanded or rewritten are called *terminal nodes*. Eg; NP, VP etc.

The final string beyond which the symbols cannot be divided is called *terminal string*. The representation of the structure of a sentence ie: its abstract framework is called its *Phrase marker or P marker*. The usual form of P marker is a tree with labelled nodes.

The PS rules can produce sentences of different structures.

Eg: (1) The girl will sing a song (D + N + AUX + V + D + N)

(2) He can teach grammar (N + AUX + V + N)

But the same rules can generate non – sensical sentences also.

Eg: A song will sing that girl (D + N + AUX + V + D + N)

In order to avoid such constructions there are selection restrictions i.e.: restrictions on the co-occurrence of two or more classes of words in a language and the positions in which they can occur in a sentence.

Limitations:

(1) Cannot account for all types of sentences in a language

(2) They fail to show the relationships between sentence types and the relationships within parts of sentences (they show how sentences are made up of phrases, words etc but do not show the relationships between declarative, interrogative/active, passive sentences etc. they do not show how the simple, compound, complex sentences are interrelated.

(3) Discontinuous constituents cannot be accommodated by PS rules as they treat constituents as continuous units. It is possible to show these through tree diagrams by the crossing of branches but impossible in the form of PS rules.

(4) The close relationships between the verb and the particle in phrases like care off, take off etc cannot be shown with PS rules.

(5) They cannot account for lexical or structural ambiguities.

(6) The property of Recursion cannot be accounted by PSG

(7) Stylistic variations can't be accounted by PSG

Grammatical theory such as ICA and PSG analyse individual sentences to show the functions of their various parts and their relationships. TG grammar shows the essential relationships between sentences like active, passive, affirmatives etc. it shows how different types of sentences are derived from basic types of simple sentences

Transformational Generative Grammar (TGG)

TGG is one of the most influential of modern linguistic theories, introduced through Noam Chomsky's "Syntactic Structures" (1965). Some of its basic concepts were already there in the existing theories. Chomsky's theory about the underlying organizational structure of language became known as TGG. Two concepts fundamental for understanding TGG are *linguistic universals* and the *language acquisition device*.

Linguistic universals: all human language is based on several shared principles called linguistic universals. Eg: all languages include simple active declarative sentences. These features suggest that language is an innate species specific capacity of humans.

Language Acquisition Device (LAD): Chomsky proposed LAD as a concept to represent the special innate organization of the human brain structured for processing language.

In linguistics, a transformational grammar, or transformational-generative grammar (TGG), is a generative grammar. *Generative grammar* refers to a particular approach to the study of syntax. A generative grammar of a language attempts to give a set of rules that will correctly predict which combinations of words will form grammatical sentences. In most approaches to generative grammar, the rules will also predict the morphology of a sentence) that has been developed in a Chomskyan tradition.

Components of TGG

Deep and surface structures: Chomsky's developed the idea that each sentence in a language has two levels of representation—a deep structure and a surface structure. The deep structure represented the core semantic relations of a sentence, and was mapped on to the surface structure (which followed the phonological form of the sentence very closely) via *transformations*. Chomsky believed that there would be considerable similarities between languages' deep structures, and that these structures would reveal properties, common to all languages, which were concealed by their surface structures. The surface structure is the actualized production of a sentence expressing the relationships and meanings.

To comprehend someone else's sentence, the listener must process the surface structures heard to derive the meanings and relationships in the underlying deep structures.

Any grammar that claims to assign to each sentence that it generates both a deep - structure and a surface structure analysis and systematically to relate the two analyses is a transformational grammar.

There are two related components involved in these mental processes and as the term "transformational generative" suggests they are the "transformational component" and "generative component", the two independent aspects which interact.

In the 1957 model, TGG is organized into 3 components:

(1) The Base components, also called the constituent structure or the phrase structure
(2) The Transformational components
(3) The Morphophonemic component

The 1st and 3rd components are obligatory while the 2nd component is optional. In basic types of simple sentences no transformation is involved.

(1) Base/PS component: By means of rewrite rules (PS rules) the PS components generate the structure underlying a kernel sentence, in the form of a string of symbols. For eg: Tom chased the elephant

(1) S ⟶ NP + VP
(2) NP1 ⟶ N
(3) VP ⟶ MV + NP2
(4) NP2 ⟶ DET + N
Therefore, S ⟶ N + MV + DET + N

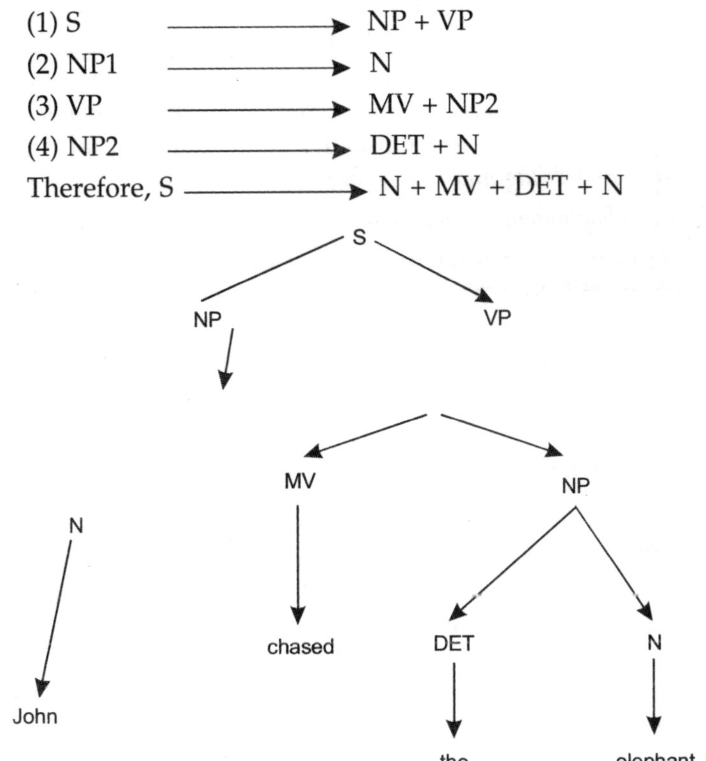

(2) The transformational component:

This component has supplementary rules; the T rules not necessarily constrained to the form of the PS rules. The T rules were to be 'supplementary' in the sense that they were to operate after, and upon the output of the PS rules. The output of the PS rules is a kernel string. A kernel sentence is any sentence which is generated from a single kernel string without the application of any optional transformations. No sentences are generated without the application of at least a limited number of obligatory T rules. Thus this part has the rules known as T rules which can transform the kernel sentences in various ways.T rules operating solely upon one terminal string (and its subsequent transforms) are referred to as *singularly or single base transformations* and are specified as *optional or obligatory* and which operates on the combination of 2 or more strings (by the successive concatenation of pairs of strings) by means of optional *generalized or double base transformations.* All generalized transformations fall into 2 classes: *embedding and conjoining rules.*

(3) Morphophonemic component:

This part converts the output of the transformational component into a phonemic transcription. It consists of the process by which terminal strings are given shapes which can be identified as utterance. Thus the string,

DET + N + V + Adj can be converted into an utterance represented as:

The (DET) girl (N) is (V) clever (ADJ)

(4) *The generative component (added later)*:

TGG is generative since it must be able to generate all and only the grammatical sentences of a language. By following its rules and conventions we could produce all or any of the possible sentences of that language. The TGG has a finite number of rules which enable us to generate the infinite set of sentences in the language that is the actual sentence of the language and also the possible ones. To generate is thus to predict what could be the sentences of the language. Thus a grammar should generate, specify and predict sentences.TGG is a theory of competence.

Performance versus Competence:

As we have studied in the first chapter, Linguistic competence represents speaker's idealized, underlying knowledge of their language. It refers to our hypothetical, unconscious linguistic ability. While, linguistic performance is the actualized production of linguistic units by a speaker and refers to the reality that this idealized knowledge must be applied in actually producing language. Linguistic performance will be influenced by a variety of real limitations, such as memory lapses, fatigue, illness etc.

Chomsky postulated a syntactic base of language (called deep structure), which consists of a series of phrase-structure rewrite rules, i.e., a series of (possibly universal) rules that generates the underlying phrase-structure of a sentence, and a series of rules (called transformations) that act upon the phrase-structure to form more complex sentences. The end result of a transformational-generative grammar is a surface structure that, after the addition of words and pronunciations, is identical to an actual sentence of a language. All languages have the same deep structure, but they differ from each other in surface structure because of the application of different rules for transformations, pronunciation, and word insertion. Another important distinction made in transformational-generative grammar is the difference between language competence (the subconscious control of a linguistic system) and language performance (the speaker's actual use of language).

Although the first work done in transformational-generative grammar was syntactic, later studies have applied the theory to the phonological and semantic components of language. This was marked as the second phase in the history of TGG. The 3 components are interrelated. The central part, the syntactic component, consists of the base and transformational subcomponent. The base contains PS rules which generate the Kernel string, which undergoes certain transformations which are specified and ordered. The transformed kernel sentences then gets phonetic representation from the phonological component and semantic representation from the semantic component and becomes a sentence. (A PSG depends exclusively on a set of PS rules).

Grammaticality, Acceptability, Appropriateness

Grammaticality and acceptability are two distinct but related notations. What is grammatical need not always be acceptable, but what is acceptable will be grammatical also.

For eg: *Colourless green ideas sleep furiously - This is the famous example cited by Noam Chomsky. It is a grammatical sentence, since it is permitted by the rules of sentence construction in English, but obviously such a sentence will not be acceptable to the native speaker of English since it does not convey anything sensible.*

Consider,

(1) Hurry up chaps, to the hall.

(2) Would you please go to the hall?

Both the sentences are grammatical, but (3) is acceptable only in an informal gathering of friends and unacceptable in a formal gathering of guests, where (4) may be more acceptable. Thus, even grammatical sentences can be unacceptable depending upon the ideas it tries to express, as in Eg: (2) or depending upon the context in which it is used as in (3).

Acceptability determined by the context or situation is referred to as *Appropriateness*. Appropriateness is decided by the context. Perfectly grammatical or 'correct' sentences may be appropriate or inappropriate, depending upon the situation or context.

Thus, unacceptability may be due to either ungrammaticality or inappropriateness. Yet another source of unacceptability is *complexity*. Extremely complicated and involved sentences, even though grammatical, will be difficult to understand and hence may not be acceptable. In short, sentences may be acceptable or unacceptable, acceptable sentences will be grammatical, appropriate and semantically sensible. Unacceptability may be due to ungrammaticality, inappropriateness, complexity or semantic oddity.

Grammatical Acquisition/Development

Children start producing true words at the age of

approximately 10-12 months. This stage is often referred as pre syntactic stage.

Soon after their first 50 words, at approximately 18 months of age, toddlers begin to combine words into 2 word phrases. By the time most utterances are two words long, at about 2 years of age; children begin to produce three word utterances. Between 2 and 5 years of age, preschoolers will develop the ability to use grammatical morphemes, produce basic grammatical sentence type, and combine those into even more advanced grammatical constructions.

Bloom and Lahey (1978) described the early word combinations as 'syntactic- semantic'. 'Semantic' in that, their basis for combinations is the meaning relation, 'syntactic' in that, children make use of word-order rules in generating them. Word order is a strategy that controls language production and acquisition.

A landmark study in children's development of grammatical morpheme was conducted by Roger Brown (1973) and his colleagues. He gave 5 stages of language development.

Mean length of Utterance (MLU)

Brown found that the typical length of child's utterances is the indicator of children's grammatical development. As many of the grammatical morphemes are inflectional morphemes, Brown found that counting morphemes, as opposed to words, was the most sensitive measure of the important developments resulting in increased utterance length.

For eg:	words	morphemes
The two boy want two cookie	6	6
The two boys wanted two cookies	6	9

These two examples reflect their level of grammatical development that would not be apparent through counting words.MLU is a moderate predictor of the complexity of the language of young English speaking children. Upto an MLU of 4.0; increase in MLU corresponds to increase in utterance complexity. Above 4.0 increase in utterance length slows considerably and individual variation increases, resulting in MLU becoming a less reliable measure. From age 18 months to 5 years, MLU increases by approximately 1.2 morphemes per year, although there is some indication of decreased rate after 42 months (Davidson etal, 1986)

$$MLU = \frac{\text{Total no of morphemes}}{\text{Total no of utterances}}$$

Brown's Stages of Development

The focus of development changes with increased MLU. Brown (1973) summarized each level of development in 5 stages:

Stages	Characterized by	Features	Examples
1	2	3	4
Stage I MLU: 1.0-2.0 Age:12-26 months	First words semantic roles expressed in simple sentences	Single word utterances combining semantic roles	Naming significant objects, persons,and events in their daily experience (cup, spoon, mommy, etc) Agent + action, action + object, to cation, entity + location, entity + attribute, demonstrative + attribute.
Stage II MLU:2.0-2.5Age : 27-30 months	Modulation of meaning	Emerging of grammatical morphemes	Present progressive (ing), prepositions (in, on), plural (-s) irregular past (eg: ran, ate) etc
Stage III MLU: 2.5-3 Age: 31-34 months	Development of sentence form	Noun phrase elaboration and auxiliary development.	Big boy running fast

1	2	3	4
Stage IV MLU: 3.0-3.75 Age: 35-40 months	Emergence of complex sentences	Embedding sentence elements	Embedded wh questions: *I know who' s hiding*
Stage V MLU: 3.75-4.50 Age: 40 months and above	Emergence of compound sentences	Conjoining sentences	I have a book and you have a toy

According to Brown the five stages represented an overview of development in children's language.

Mastering Grammatical Morphemes

Once preschoolers begin to combine two and three semantic relations they begin to modulate or fine tune their utterances by producing grammatical morphemes which are function words and word endings that modulate the meaning of the more basic terms in their utterances. Although other important aspects of language are also developing in the preschool years, as these grammatical morphemes gradually emerge, the preschooler's language takes on a more mature adult like texture. Several morphological developments begin in stage II but continue well into school age years. The period of greatest acquisition is from 4-7 years.

Variables related to mastery

Brown examined three major variables:

(1) *Semantic complexity*: was gauged by the number of discriminations required to use a morpheme correctly.

Eg: Fewer discrimination related to labelling the spatial relationship 'on'(an item either is on or is not).than are related to use of 'were'(more than one participant serving as agent in an action occurring in a previous time frame.)

(2) *Grammatical complexity*: of each morpheme was gauged by the number of transformations related to its correct use.

(3) *Frequency of occurrence of each morpheme in caregiver's speech*: not related to order of mastery.

Brown determined that the order of mastery correlated best with a rank order of combined semantic and grammatical complexity.

The 14 Grammatical Morphemes

The appearance and mastery of 14 grammatical morphemes in relation to the stages of development became the central focus in Brown's research. Each of the morphemes appeared in stage II (aprox. 2-2.5 years of age).These morphemes generally convey meaning that could only be implied through simple word orders exhibited in stage I. Brown isolated 14 obligatory morphemes that appear early in child language. He reasoned that if use is obligatory, rather than optional, then the absence of morpheme should indicate nonacquisition, rather than choice.

The 14 selected morphemes have the following characteristics:

- They are phonetically minimal forms. In general they include simple phonemic addition or changes.eg addition of-s.
- They receive only light vocal emphasis
- They belong to a limited class of construction, as opposed to the larger number of nouns and verbs.
- They possess multiple phonological forms and can vary with the grammatical and phonetic properties of words to which they are attached.

  Eg: *s* in cats is pronounced/*s*/, whereas the *s* in dogs is pronounced/*z*/

- Their development is very gradual, and considerable individual variation exist

Order of Acquisition of 14 Grammatical Morphemes

Age of mastery	Rank order of grammatical morphemes	Meaning	Example
1	2	3	4
19-28 months	Present progressive verb endinging	Ongoing process	He's sitting down
27-30 months	Preposition 'in' 'on'	containment support	It's in the box It's on the chair
24-33 months	Plural-s	number	The dogs bark
25-46 months	Irregular past Eg:went	Earlier in time	Daddy went out.Jimmy fell down
26-40 months	Possessive noun-'s	possession	The girl's dog ran away
27-39 months	Uncontractible copula (was, were as in question)	Number, earlier in time.	Are they boys?
28-46 months	Articles (a, the)	Non specific/ specific	Jane has a book.
26-48 months	-ed (past regular)	Earlier in time	He jumped the stream.
26-48 months	Third person singular regular	Number; earlier in time	She runs fast

1	2	3	4
28-50 months	3rd person singular irregular	Number earlier in time	He has books.She does work
29-48 months	Uncontractible auxiliary verb (is, were)	Number earlier in time (ongoing process)	Is he coming? That's tom, that is
29-49 months	Contractible copula	Number, earlier in time	I'm good.She's nice.
30-50 months	Contractible auxiliary	Number, earlier in time (ongoing process)	They are running fast. I'm eating.

Other early morphemes

Develop within the preschool years and not studied in detail by Brown.

Auxiliary verb

Auxiliary and helping verbs in English can be classified as primary, such as *be ,have, and do* or as secondary or modal such as *will, shall, can, may* and *must.*

Wide variation exists in the acquisition of auxiliary verbs. Most children use the auxiliaries do, have, and will by 42 mths.

Adjective and noun suffixes

Between 3 and 5 years of age, children understand and begin to use comparative and superlative inflectional suffixes, - 'er', and – 'est'. The comparative – 'er' indicates a comparison between only two items, as in -

"This cookie is bigger than that cookie". Comparative – 'er' is mastered by 5 years of age.

The superlative form- 'est' appears to emerge by 4 years of age. The irregular versions (better, best and more), most go through a period in which over application of suffix results in forms such as *bestest* and *more bigger*.

Use of derivational suffix –'er' appears to be mastered by around 5 years of age.

Advances in Syntax

At the same time that preschoolers' utterances are expanding with additional grammatical morphemes, they are also being modified in other ways. These changes reflect preschoolers' advances in syntactic abilities.

Hierarchical syntactical relationships

The earliest multiword utterances (Eg: Two word utterances in Brown's stage I) were characterized as expressing linear semantic relations. In these, the toddler seemed to produce relatively straight forward "one + one" = two proposition.

Once preschoolers are producing two word utterances at approximately two years of age three and even four word utterances begin to appear. At this level it is possible that the expanded sentence elements represent hierarchical sentence structure. Two patterns in preschool language development that suggest the beginning of hierarchical syntactic structure include recombination and expansions.

Recombination

Recombinations are results of preschoolers combining utterance from the level that occurred previously, resulting in a single, long utterance. For example, two common structures at the two word level would be agent + action and action + object, as in 'mummy eat' and 'eat cookie'. In building up a longer utterance and expressing all the relevant relationships, the preschoolers recombine these without repeating the common element to eliminate the redundancy:

Eg: 'Mommy + *eat*'

$$\frac{\text{'Eat + cookie'}}{\text{'Mommy + eat + cookie'}}$$

Expansions

Expansion includes additional information to elaborate on one of the terms in the utterance.

Eg: 'Want milk' ———— 'want *more* milk'.

The same pattern results in expansion to four word utterances.

Phrase structure

Noun phrase elements: The simple sentences children produce can be divided into two types:

Those with a main verb between two nouns; and those with a copula between two nouns.

Eg: 'The dog ate the candy'.

Versus

'The puppy is a pet'.

It emerges in Brown's stage II. The greatest surge occurs at stage IV, noun phrase elaboration appears in both subject and object position.

Verb phrase elements: Syntactically verbs can be classified according to the role they play in sentence structure. They might be classified as grammatical verbs and lexical verbs:

Grammatical verbs: include such structures as copula and auxiliary forms (eg: is, are, was, were, etc.) that play a grammatical role in sequencing structures.

Lexical verbs: (For example, run, sit, write, etc.) convey specific content in a sentence and are also classified according to what structure may follow them.

Transitive verbs are lexical verbs that are capable of carrying a direct object.

Eg: The boy hit the ball.

Intransitive verbs are lexical verbs might not carry direct objects.

Eg: She is smiling at the baby.

Development in verb phrase:

During stage I when utterance is predominately one and two words, preschoolers produce primarily lexical verbs. The most common lexical verbs (e.g.: eat, put, make, get,) also tend to be transitive in nature.ie they relate to an object affected by the action named.

In stage II the present progressive inflection, '-ing' appears.

The ever present semi-auxiliaries or (catenatives) hafta, gonna, wanna also appear during stage II

In stage III the modal auxiliaries can and will and "be" auxiliary verbs appear.The *be* auxiliary will not be mastered until after stage Vas it require noun verb agreement(I-am/was, He-is/was).

By stage-V preschoolers will have mastered the distinction between regular tense inflections and irregular past tense forms. They will be able to use the third person present tense inflection and the contractible copula.

Most of the grammatical aspects of language have been mastered by age 5 years and after stage V.

Time and reference

In English, time and reference to that time are marked by both tense and aspect. Tense, such as past or future, relates the speech time, which is in the present to the event time or the time when the event occurs. Aspect concerns the dynamics of the event relative to its completion, repetition, or continuing duration.

Children's sense of time and reference to it go through phases of development during preschool years:

(1) Child talks about things that are occurring now. There is no tense or aspect marking. Eg: want juice.

(2) 18 months - 3yrs: children speak about past and present, although reference point is always in present.

(3) 3-3.5 years: child gains a sense of reference other than present. Eg: Kim drove yesterday.

(4) 3.5-4 years: child acquires a flexible reference time that enables him to describe events in past, present or future. Eg: yesterday, grandma asked "would you like to go to the zoo next week"?

Pronouns and their Acquisition:

Pronouns/pronominal are a group of forms (eg. he, she, they) that can replace nouns or entire nounphrase.The substitution process described by linguist is called pronomilization.

Anaphoric reference: pronoun refers to person or thing that has been mentioned previously.

Eg: Jhon ran away because *he* was scared.

Cataphoric reference: pronoun precedes the noun they represent. Eg: when he was finished dad took a nap.

Personal pronouns are used to replace nouns referring to persons. Personal pronoun vary depending on person number and gender.

Reflexive pronouns: are forms that reflect back on the preceding subject of a sentence.

Eg: when I looked in the water I saw myself.

Demonstrative pronoun: include the demonstrative forms, this, that, these, and those, which replace nouns rather than modifying them. Eg: Using *That is mine* for *That book is mine.* In first sentence *that* replaces book and in second sentence *that* modifies book.

Indefinite pronouns: are compound words composed of *any, every, no* and some combined with *one, thing, place, or body.* They are named indefinite as they do not have specific referent, as in bring me something to drink.

Pronouns develop slowly and variably in preschoolers. The earliest forms (this, that, it) occurs in stage I. Most personal pronouns emerge after stage II. Generally subjective pronouns are mastered (I, you, he, she, they) tend to be mastered earlier than objective pronouns (me, he, her, them). Possessive pronouns are acquired later except first person forms (my, mine) which are acquired much earlier. The last pronoun to be mastered, reflexive pronouns (myself, himself, herself, themselves) are acquired after stage IV. With the exception of reflexive pronouns, most pronouns are mastered by approximately 5years of age, although sequence of mastery might be different for each preschooler.

Sentence types and their acquisition:

Declarative sentence forms-

Declarative sentence or statements gradually increases in complexity in preschool years.

Stages:

Agent+action/action+object ⟶ beginning

Subject +verb+object ⟶ 30 months

Subject+aux+verb+object ⟶ stage III

Subject+aux+copula+complement ⟶ stage III/early stage IV

Subject+verb+indirect object+objectform ⟶ stage V

Later development include embedding, conjoining, and internal development of noun phrase

Interrogatives

Interrogative sentences are forms that request, confirmation, denial or information as in are you coming with us? Commonly they are called questions and are of three types: yes/no, wh- and tag questions.

Development of yes/no question and wh question.

Period	Yes/no question formation	egs	Wh question formation	egs
Early	Word+rising intonation	Milk?		
Stage I	NP+rising intonation	That kitty?	What+NP? What+NP	What this? What mommy

			(+doing) Where (+NP+go)	doing?
StageII			What+NP+ verb? Where + NP+ copula?	What mommy make? Where mommy is?
Late stage II			Where+ copula+NP?	Where is mommy?
StageIII	Auxiliary+ NP+Verbcop +NP+ complement	Do kitties swim? Is daddy happy?	What+NP+ auxiliary+ verb? Where+ NP+ aux +verb?	What mommy is making? Where daddy can go?
Final	Inverts all auxiliary and copula to form adult question	Can I go play? Are the boys here? Does he likes me?	Preposes all wh words and inverts all aux and copula to form adult questions.	How did he do that? When are they coming? Why cant he help?

Mastery of grammatical forms for questions occurs over 3 distinct periods. (Klima and Bellugi, 1966):

- Initially a child's rising intonation applied to a nucleus word (ball) is all that is needed to evoke an answer from a responsive listener.
- Klima and Bellugi located the beginning of grammatical questions in period I. When rising intonation applied to basic nucleus statements, as in *That doggie*? - to produce yes or no question.
- Development of *wh* question in period I consist of most frequently including subject and predicate.
- No real growth in yes or no question occurs at period II.

- In period III the copula and auxiliary forms appear in most preschoolers' sentences. The forms are not inverted.
- Beyond Period III preschoolers go to correctly invert copula and auxiliary forms in *wh* questions and produce adult like question forms.

Tag questions

Develops much later. Tag questions are little request for confirmation.

Eg: It is Saturday, isn't it?

Brown and Halon (1970) noticed that to form tag question a series of transformation must be made of declarative sentence.

- Shortening verb phrase - truncation (Tr)

Eg: they are playing ⟶ yes they are

- Negation (N)

Eg: they are playing ⟶ they aren't playing

- Inversion (Q)

Eg: They are playing ⟶ Are they playing

The (SAAD) simple active affirmative declarative should come first, then forms involving one of the transformations.

Finally tag appears as they require all 3 transformations:

Development of imperative forms:

The imperative sentence requests, demands, commands, and insists that the listener performs some action. Eg: Pass the butter (you)

'You' is understood and hence ommited.The imperative sentence forms develop in Brown's stage III where children gain mastery by deleting subject.

Development of negatives

Negatives are those forms that express non appearance, cessation, rejection, prohibition and denial.(Bloom and Lahey, 1978)

Eg: I m not ready to go.

Period	Negative formation	Examples
early	Neg (indicating nonexistence, rejection or denial)	No! allgone! no more!
Stage I	Neg+NP Neg+NP+verb (presentence)	No bath! No daddy play!
Stage II	NP+NEG+VERB (prepredicate) NP+cant/don't+verb	Daddy not sleeps. I can't go. I don't like it.
Stage III	NP+can/do/does/did/will+verb NP+isn't/aren't+verb	That boy will not play. She isn't helping me.
Late	NP+wouldn't/shouldn't/ couldn't+verb	She wouldn't believe it.

Embedding and conjoining

The units within sentences are composed of words, phrases and clauses.

A *phrase* is a group of related words that does not include both a subject and a predicate and is used as a noun substitute or as a noun or verb modifier.

Eg: I love candy.

A *clause* is a collection of related words with both a subject and predicate. A clause that can stand alone as grammatically complete is a simple sentence.

Eg: Sita wept.

When sentence is combined with a main sentence it becomes main clause.

Subordinate clause: some clauses cannot stand alone even though they contain a subject and predicate.

Eg: whom *we met* last week

↓ ↓

Subject predicate

Development of complex and compound sentences: With increased experience and understanding preschoolers between age 2 and 3 years begin to combine several ideas in longer utterances (Bloom and Lahey 1978).

Brown characterized stage IV as the period in which preschoolers learns to embed additional information creating complex sentences. The emergence of embedding is one of the primary characteristics of stage IV. In embedding a phrase or clause becomes the grammatical element of a sentence. And stage V was described as the period in which conjoining ideas into compound sentences is mastered.

Complex sentences:

A sentence made up of a main clause and at least one subordinate clause is called a complex sentence. These have been observed in children between 18 months and 3 years, when MLU is between 3.0nd 4.0.these take the form of I think (X) where X is a clause introduced by that, as in "I think that I like candy".

The second form of complex embedding observed at approximately the same time is the *wh-adverbial clause*. In these, the subordinate clause is introduced with a wh-word serving as a conjunction.(who, what, when, where, which, how, why) these also take the form of *I know* (X) in which X is the subordinate clause. Eg: I know what I like to eat.

The third form to appear as an embedded structure is the *infinitive phrase*. Eg: 'I like to play' in which the verb serve as an object of the verb. These forms are observed during late stage IV, in three year olds with MLUs between 3.0 and 4.0.

*Relative clause*s are subordinate clauses that follow and modify noun. Observed in stage V and later as the preschoolers approaches 4 years of age with an MLU of 4.0-4.5.

Eg: This is the toy *that I want*

Compound sentences:

A compound sentence is one in which two basic sentence structures are linked together by conjunction. A coordinating conjunction is a connecting word that links the two structures into one sentence. This process is called *conjoining or co-ordinating*. Coordination constructions are of 2 types:

Phrasal coordination: simultaneous or near simultaneous events in same location. Eg: *Mary ran and Mary fell.*

Here Mary is redundant and can be deleted

Mary ran and fell.

Sentential coordination: Used for events that occurs at different times and different location. Eg: *Mary ran and John fell* - Cannot be shortened.

Developmentally toddlers express the notion of compound sentence in stage I as soon as they were able to simply string words together. "And" is the first conjunction to emerge in stage II. First "and" is used to express additive meanings, to express collections. Eg : A ball and a block and a.......

Next "and" is used to express temporal relationships to order a series of events, as in 'I fell down and got hurt and ran home.'

In stage III and beyond, the adversative conjunction 'but' and the alternative conjunction 'or' appears.

The grammatical development that occurs during school years include more consistent comprehension and production of wh-questions, compound and complex sentences, passive sentences, and various morphological features related to nouns and verbs.

Later Syntax

School age language development consists of simultaneous expansion of existing forms and acquisition of new ones. Children expand their understanding and use of conjoined sentences with the addition of 'although, unless, and therefore, which are used to join clauses. Correct interpretation of these structures usually does not emerge till 7 years of age.

Passive sentences:

Emerges in preschool years and *acquired beyond age 5.*

Gerund embedding:

Gerunds appear after stage V. The gerunds are one of the first forms of derivational suffixes acquired, using –ing to change a verb to a noun.

Grammatical odds and ends

Count nouns: Some items occur in quantities that can be distinguished as individual countable units (eg: spoon, rocks, trees) the nouns that label such items are called count nouns.

Mass nouns: Items like milk, hair, sand are quantities that are perceived as indivisible. These are labelled as mass nouns. If they are expressed in units they can be counted. E.g.: Grains of sand.

Count nouns accept the plural inflection whereas mass nouns do not. Eg: We can have rocks but we do not have sands.

Mass nouns accept modifying quantifiers like much and little. Count nouns are modified by many and few. Eg: Many rocks but we can't find many sands.

Once children master regular plural form used with count nouns they begin to modify them with many. It may take until adolescence to become consistently accurate in using much with mass nouns.

Reflexive pronouns: The mastering of reflexive pronoun may not come until the later elementary school grades in some children. Most common is confusion in using subjective (he, she, they) and objective pronoun (him, her, them).

Irregular past tense and plurals

Irregular past tense verbs and irregular plural nouns are forms that each vary from their base form that each vary from their base form in ways that do not follow any regular pattern. Eg: run-ran, eat-ate. In both it has been found that common irregular forms appear early in toddlers and young preschoolers only to vanish when regular inflection forms are learned.

Clinical application:

- Many test for language assessment is based on the order of grammatical development in particular language. Eg: Malayalam language test (MLT).
- Language therapy for language impaired children is also given on the basis of age appropriate grammatical development especially for hearing impaired children.
- Studies on syntactical development on language impaired children are not possible without knowing normal grammatical development.

Eg: Study by Mathews (1994) to find grammatical deficit in SLI children shows they lack inflectional morphological rules (with particular reference to past tense deficit)

Grammatical Analysis

Grammatical analysis is a method that leads us to recognize the form or structure of a system, which consists of many categories.

Grammatical analysis necessary because:

1. Analysis gives us an insight into the client's disability.
2. It supplies goals for therapy.
3. Helps to understand normal process of grammatical development and the deviancy the child exhibits from normalcy.
4. Helps in formulation of a diagnosis of a condition.

Grammatical Analysis can be divided into analysis of morphology and analysis of syntax. On the morphological level, we can examine the paradigms into which word enter. In syntactic analysis we deal with colligations or syntagmatic relations between grammatical categories.

Main tasks in syntactic analysis:

- To identify the sentences in the data
- To analyze their structure and function
- To analyze the way they combine into connected speech.

A. Identification of sentences in the data: The analysis begins with the identification of sentences. In writing, there is no problem: sentence begin with capital letters and end with one of the punctuation marks. In speech sometimes, there is a problem, falling intonation tones and presence of pause mark a sentence ending but they do not always.

B. Analysis of sentence structure: Three main sentence structures are recognized. They are:

(*a*) Patterns of sentence and clause structure

(*b*) Patterns of phrase structure

(*c*) Patterns of word structure.

In addition, there is also,

(*d*) Patterns of sentence connection.

(a) Patterns of sentence and clause structure:

It is helpful to begin by making a broad classification of sentences. They can be classified in two main types:

- major sentence
- minor sentences

Major sentences have a subject predicate structure. It can be either simple major sentence or multiple major sentences. Simple major sentence comprise of only one clause. E.g. Simple major sentence: John kicked the ball.

Multiple major sentences: a multiple major sentence contains a sequence of clauses which are linked in various ways. E.g. John kicked the ball and he fell over.

Minor sentences are sentences that usually lack the characteristic SV pattern of major sentences and if they do have a SV structure this tend to be fixed. Minor sentences mainly comprises of stereotypes including proverbs, rhymes etc. and social sentences including greetings.

(b) Patterns of phrase structure:

- Structure of noun phrase: There are three main positions-the centre, the dependent words which precede it, the dependent words which follow it.

- Structure of verb phrase: It involves expressing the following range of contrasts-tense, aspect, mood, voice, negation and number.

(c) Pattern of word structure:

In word structure we have to note the use of the following:

- In the NP: plurals, genitive, comparative, superlative.
- In the VP: third person present singular, present participle form, past participle form, past tense, and contracted forms of auxiliary.
- The adverb marker and the objective case in some pronouns.

(d) Patterns of sentence connection:

There are four main ways of connecting sentence together:

- Using pronunciation by linking them with intonation.
- Using vocabulary, replacing a word in one sentence by a related word.E.g. George Best is still abroad. The handsome footballer has not being seen.
- Using commonsense semantic connection. E.g. He died on Thursday. He was buried on Saturday.
- Using grammatical links of which there are three main kinds:
  - (*a*) Adverbials of time, place, consequence

    e.g., John came in. Then Bill went out.
  - (*b*) Cross reference using articles, pronouns.

    e.g. John came in. He was angry.
  - (*c*) A major sentence may omit elements of clause structure when these are present in previous sentences. It is referred to as ellipses.

    e.g. Where are you going? To town (instead of I am going to Town)

Assessment Tools

Analysis and assessments can be carried out with the help of standardized tests.eg.

- Northwest Syntax Screening Test
- Linguistic Profile Test
- Screening Test for Syntax in Kannada
- Kannada Language tests.
- Malayalam language tests
- Bankson Language Screening Test

Grammatical Analysis in L.A.R.S.P:

Crystal (1982) initiated analysis covering several linguistic levels:

1. LARSP (morpho syntax)
2. PROPH (phonology)
3. PROP (prosody)
4. PRISM (semantics)

LARSP (Language Assessment, Remediation and Screening Procedure) consists of Sampling, Transcription, Segmentation, Grammatical analysis, Profiling, Interpretation and Remediation goals and procedures.

Steps involved in grammatical analysis:

Crystal recommends the following guidelines to work through the data. There are eight scans. In each scan, the data are examined from a specific point of view.

Scan-1

This determines the range of sentences which cannot be analyzed. It includes 3 categories of utterances:-

(*a*) Sentence is unintelligible

(*b*) Symbolic noises are taken separately

(*c*) Deviant sentences which we want to keep separate from expected sentence types.

The first scan tries to ensure that subsequent scans will be as unproblematic as possible so that a rapid and continuous analysis can be made.

Scan-2

It establishes the proportion of spontaneous sentences to responses sentences in the sample and provides an analysis of the type of response.

(*a*) *Responses*. Various response patterns are sub classified in the following way:-

- Normal response type:

(*i*) One may answer with a full major sentence. Eg. Q. Where is the book?

A. It is in the box.

(*ii*) One may answer with an elliptical major sentence. Eg. Q. Where is the book?

A. In the box.

(*iii*) One may answer with a minor sentence usually yes, no, mhm etc.

- Abnormal response type:

(*i*) Zero response: some response is clearly expected but it is not provided.

(*ii*) Structural deviance: a syntactic pattern is used which is not a possible match for the syntax of the stimulus sentence.

e.g.Q. where are you going?

A. yes.

(*b*) *Spontaneous sentences*: The main division made under this heading is to distinguish self repetitions from novel sentences.

(*c*) *Repetitions:* This category subsumes automatic repetition of previous speech i.e. echolalia and elicited imitations.

(*d*) *Problems*: We include any case where allocation to one of the above category is uncertain.

Scan-3

Data is analyzed sentence by sentence at the level of sentence connectivity. Each type of sentence is tabulated and a count is made.

Scan-4

Sentences are analyzed for coordination and subordination.

Scan-5

Clause structure is analyzed, in terms of subject, verb, clause etc. and the range of constructional types are established

Scan-6

Phrase structure is analyzed, in terms of noun phrase, verb phrase etc.and the range of construction established.

Scan-7

Word structure patterns are analyzed.

Scan-8

Problem cases are scrutinized, to see if, in the light of other analyses difficulties can be eliminated.

Grammatical Disorder/Disability

Grammatical disability can be located in four main levels:

- Connectivity difficulties
- Clause difficulties
- Phrase difficulties
- Word difficulties

This example will make us understand each types of difficulty in a better way:

The sentence in question is: *The man broke his arm because the ladder slipped and he fell off.*

Connectivity difficulty: *The man broke his arm and the ladder slipped because he fell off.*

Clause difficulty: *The man his arm and because the ladder and he off* (verb omission).

The man his arm broke because slipped the ladder and fell off (element order).

Broke his arm because slipped and fell off (subject omission).

Phrase difficulties: *Man broke arm because ladder slipped and he fell off* (no phrase development).

Man the broke arm his because ladder slipped and he off fell. (word order in phrase).

Word difficulties: *The man break he arm because the ladder slip and he fall off.* (no inflections).

Interaction of Grammatical Levels and other Disorders

The problem may involve clause or phrase integration or phrase or word integration and in the more advanced patient, connectivity may be affected by residual difficulties from earlier stages of phrasal or clausal development:

Agrammatism: Agrammatism is characterized by reduction in the use of free and bound inflectional morphology. It is regarded as characteristic of Broca's aphasia. Syntactic deficits in language comprehension are also found in these patients (Kolk and Weijits 1996). Omission of functional elements and inflectional errors are seen. In agrammatic patients the functional categories in their syntactic representations have lost their internal feature specification.

Para grammatism: It is usually seen in Wernick's apashia cases. Patient speaks at fluent rate but syntax is often erratic (word order is affected). Although the sentences the patients produce are quite long and complex, they are not syntactically well formed and contain various kinds of errors.e.g. word exchanges and exchanges of whole constituents. This cluster of properties is called paragrammatism in clinical literature. No difficulty with phonological production. Morphological markers are not absent but are not used appropriately. Frequent neologism is seen. Paragrammatism is not a genuine syntactic disorder but rather a secondary effect of the client's lexical disorder.

Grammatical disability in children with Specific Language Impairment (S.L.I.): Grammatical problems of SLI subjects lie mainly with inflection and word order is intact. Within the area of inflection, subject- verb agreement, case marking, gender and auxiliaries are strongly affected than noun plurals. The only difference with a SLI subject and normal is that a SLI child does not produce as many as verb forms as required by the language.

CHAPTER

4

Semantics

Concepts, Acquisition/Development, Disorders and its Clinical relevance

Semantics

Semantics refer to the study of meaning system of a language. It involves translation of one's cognitive representation of life into language. Semantics can be defined as the study of the meaning system of a language (Berko Gleason, 1993).

Semantics involves the translation of one's cognitive representation of life experiences into language (Bloom and Lahey, 1978). This means that as an individual interacts with the world, these events are cognitively processed and stored as mental images, which then must be translated into language for the purpose of communication, problem solving and social relations.Thus receptively; semantics involves comprehension and requires accurate delineation of meaning from our linguistic symbol system. And expressively, semantics is the appropriate choice of vocabulary and language structure to transfer meaning and is dependent on the content and purpose.

Semantic study explores the process of encoding meaning into language and decoding meaning from language which includes the lexicon i.e. words/vocabulary, the relationship of these words to the concepts they represent, and the organization of these words (Cromer, 1988). In this context, before entering into various types of Semantics, we must know about the below mentioned concepts which are based upon the *truth relationship*:

Entailment

Entailment means *something which is inferred*. Entailment is the relationship between two sentences where the truth of one (A) requires the truth of the other (B).

For example, the sentence (A) *the president was assassinated.* Entails (B) *The president is dead*. Notice also that if (B) is false, then (A) must necessarily be false. To show entailment, we must show that (A) true forces (B) to be true and (B) false forces (A) to be false.

First, consider two sentences

E.g.: I (*a*) *Tom managed to finish his dinner*

(*b*) *Tom finished his dinner*

Suppose that if sentences I (a) is true, then sentence in I (b) is also true. There is no possible way that if (a) is true while I (b) is false. In these circumstances we say that I (a) entails I (b).

A general definition of entailment is:

A sentence (S_1) entails a sentence (S_2) if and only if whenever s1 is true, s2 is also true.

This relationship of entailment doesn't obtain between the sentences which is happened to be true in the current or any other state of affairs.

E.g.: II (*a*) The dodo is extinct

(*b*) Mumbai is the capital city of Maharashtra.

In this case II (a) does not entails II b, because there is no meaningful relationship between the sentences, knowing that II b is true does not help at all in understanding II (a). This is called material implication or semantic implication. But this is not the case in first example where I (a) helps in understanding the meaning of the I (b).

Presupposition

A presupposition is background belief, relating to an utterance that:

- must be mutually known or assumed by the speaker and addressee for the utterance to be considered appropriate in context.
- generally will remain a necessary assumption whether the utterance is placed in the form of an assertion, denial, or question, and can generally be associated with a specific lexical item or grammatical feature (presupposition trigger) in the utterance.

  The utterance *Sunil regrets that he stopped doing linguistics before he left Delhi* has the following presuppositions:

  - There is someone uniquely identifiable to speaker and addressee as *Sunil.*
  - John stopped doing linguistics before he left Delhi.
  - John was doing linguistics before he left Delhi.
  - John left Delhi.
  - Sunil had been at Delhi.

Structural Semantics

It is a branch of structural linguistics that considers language as a set of interrelated elements which are not valid i.e. are meaningless except in relation to each other. Meaning in a language has been found to be hierarchically organized and rule governed in a similar way to syntax and phonology. Structural semantics defines the structure of the lexicon, the relation between lexemes, which can be analyzed in terms of the complementary dimensions of Syntagmatic and paradigmatic.

Syntagmatic Relationship

It is the linear arrangements of units; sounds, letters, words etc. Each string is dependent on the other. The choices which can be substituted are constrained by the other elements in the sentence. So, if any choices are made outside a certain range will result in semantic incoherence.

E.g. a)

P I N

T I N

B I N

S I N

E.g. (b) John drank a glass of water

In the above example (a) four words have been represented in a table. The four words are pin, tin, bin and sin. In the word pin, the phonemes/p/,/i/and/n/occurs one after the other in a sequence and these phonemes are said to be in Syntagmatic relation with each other.

In the above example (b) John–drank-a-glass-of-water all the elements are placed in relation to each other. Here each string is dependent on each other. Hence they share Syntagmatic relation with each other. If the word "water" has to be substituted by any other word then it is constrained by the presence of other elements in the string.

Paradigmatic Relationship

Paradigmatic relationship is the vertical arrangement of units, sounds, letters, words etc. This reflects the semantic choices available at a particular structure point in a sentence.

E.g. a)

P I N

T I N

B I N

S I N

E.g. b) this tea is very hot.

In the first example the word pin, the phoneme/p/can be replaced by/t/,/b/and/s/. By replacing these phonemes we can get different meaningful words. These are the available number of phonemic choices. If we replace it with the phoneme/a/then it does not make any sensible word. So, we can say that the phonemes/p/,/t/,/b/and/s/are in paradigmatic relationship with each other.

In the second example, the word hot can be replaced with cold, tepid and scorching etc. Making any of these changes would alter the meaning of the sentence but it would still make sense. These connections which exist between the elements are called paradigmatic relations.

Paradigmatic relationship is not only seen in nouns but, also in verbs, adjectives, and adverbs. These are called paradigms. The way these classes are put together to form a sentence shows its Syntagmatic aspect.

To explain conveniently, we shall divide paradigmatic sense relations into two categories. They are:-

(*a*) Paradigmatic relationship of identity and inclusion between word meanings

(*b*) Paradigmatic relationship of opposition and exclusion.

Paradigmatic Relationship of Identity and Inclusion

Synonymy: It is a type of sense relation where the selection of one lexeme rather than another has no effect on the meaning of the sentence.

E.g. (pointing to a women picture) who is that?

The answer could be a female, women, lady or girl. In this context these words could be said as synonymous with each other. In a different context one lexeme can be preferred to the others.

E.g. A girl is going to the school. In this example the lexeme is preferred over other women, lady or female.

There are different types of synonymy based on their degree. They are:

(*a*) Cognitive synonymy

(*b*) Absolute synonymy

(*c*) Propositional synonymy

(*d*) Near synonymy

1. Cognitive synonymy: This is defined in terms of entailment, where S (L) means that L occurs in sentential contexts.

Lexemes L1 and L2 are cognitive synonyms if and only if S (L_1) entails S (L_2) and S (L_2) entails S (L_1).

To illustrate, consider the pair of lexemes HORSE and STEED. These are cognitive synonyms because if we consider a sentential context such as Ramu rode a white ———Both the entailments is obtained.

(*a*) Ramu rode a white horse entails Ramu rode a white steed

(*b*) Ramu rode a white steed entails Ramu rode a white Horse.

Why can we not simply drop the modifier 'cognitive' and say that these two lexemes are synonyms? Because there are sentential contexts where their appearance, while not affecting the truth value of the containing sentence, certainly affects its acceptability.

For e.g.

(*a*) Horses eat hay

(*b*) Steeds eat hay.

Here in the above example "steeds eat hay" is not acceptable and seems to sounds odd with "Horses eat hay".

2. *Absolute synonymy:* It means the greatest resemblance between two lexemes. This is based on contextual approach where it says the absolute synonym's as items which are equally normal in all contexts. That is to say , for two lexical items X and Y, if they are to be recognized as absolute synonyms, in any context in which X is fully normal, Y is, too; in any context in which X is slightly odd, Y is also slightly odd, and in any context in which X is totally anomalous, the same is true of Y. This is a very severe requirement, and few pairs, if any, qualify.

E.g.

(*a*) Brave: courageous

Little Billy fought bravely in the war

Little Billy fought courageously in the war.

(*b*) Big: Large

He's a big baby, isn't he?

He's a large baby, isn't he?

(*c*) Almost: nearly

She looks almost Chinese

She looks nearly Chinese.

3. ***Propositional synonymy:*** Two words are propositionally synonymous if they can be used in any truth functional expression and not change the value of the sentence.

Sally took the can from the box.

Sally took the tin from the box.

Alex plays the violin

Alex plays the fiddle.

In a sentence like "Alex plays the fiddle in the orchestra" the use of 'fiddle' (a word which in this context typically is only used by professionals) preserves the truth value for the sentence and so is appropriate for propositional synonymy.

In any language there will be very few absolute and propositional synonyms, so majority of what lexicographers call synonyms are near synonyms.

4. Near synonyms: Plesionyms, or near synonyms, are words, that are almost synonyms but they differ in relatively minor aspects. Eg.

It was *misty* last Friday or, more exactly, it was *foggy*.

It was *foggy* last Friday or, more exactly, it was *misty*.

He was killed but not murdered.

In this example it is shown, that it is nearly impossible to distinguish between the two truth conditions. Both sentences are referring to the same thing, but they seem to exclude each other, though it is impossible to tell what the difference in the truth condition may be. This hints to the assumption that plesionyms rely much more on personal impressions than on actual states of reality. Though there is a difference between the lexemes *foggy* and *misty*, this difference exists only in connotation and the speakers expressed attitude. Other examples point to that observation.

Other examples: Handsome; pretty
Laugh; chuckle

Hyponymy: Hyponymy is a sense relation in semantics that serves to relate word-concepts in a hierarchical fashion. Examples are:

Apple: fruit

Car: Vehicle

Stool: furniture

Cow: Animal

The more specific concept is known as the hyponymy and the more general concept is known as the hypernym or super ordinate. *Apple* is the hyponym of *fruit* and *fruit* is the superordinate of *Apple*.

E.g.: Cow (x) and animal (y)

Here if x is a Cow, it follows that y must be an animal and it doest not follow that if y is an animal, x is therefore a Cow. This represents one-way relationship. To put in this another way, being an animal is a *necessary condition* for being a lion; it is not, however a *sufficient* condition

Thus "one-way" relation is an important property of hyponyms. In dictionaries, hyponymy is represented by a *definitional formula*, as-

An x is a kind/type of y.

E.g.: cow is a hyponym of animal, similarly lion is a type of animal, and snake is a type of reptile.

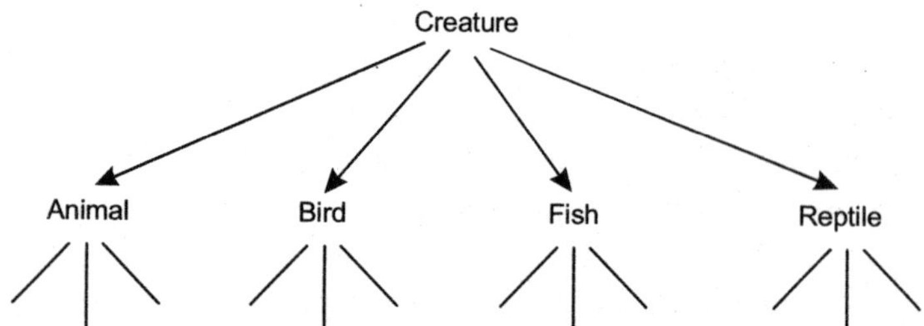

Lion Dog Cow Sparrow Eagle Ostrich trout eel shark Snake Lizard newt

First we must recognize that animal being a *super ordinate* of Lion, it is also itself a hyponym *of Creature.* From this example super ordinate is animal, the lion, dog, cow are the co-hyponyms of the super ordinate animal, which is a co-hyponyms of creature along with bird, fish and reptile.

Thus this example illustrates the relation between the super ordinate with that of its hyponyms. In English lexicon, taxonomy means the structure in which we meet more general terms as we ascend to higher levels are defined by the semantic relation of hyponymy, which is multilayered.

It is readily apparent that this taxonomy can be further extended at certain points to include another level. For instance, dog has spaniel, corgi, Rottweiler etc. and snake has cobra, riper, anaconda etc as co-hyponyms. However this is not the case for all the items at the lowest level e.g. Ostrich and for other cases, extension of the taxonomy involves a resort to morphologically complex form. (White shark, blue shark, basking shark).

All the words appearing in the taxonomy are nouns. There can be a question like do other word classes words enter into hyponymy relation?

For verbs there are some clear instances.

E.g.: 1. (a) X borrowed/stole/found/bought Y
(b) X got Y
2. (a) X walked/ran/staggered/crawled to Z
(b) X moved to Z

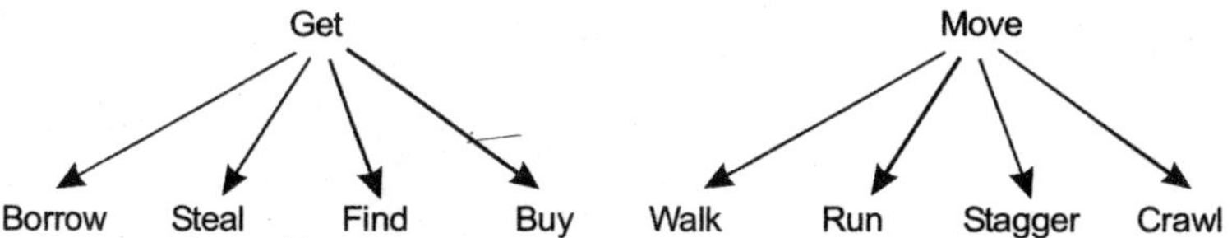

In both of these sentences cases, the various sentence in (a) entail the sentence in (b). There is no possible, state of affairs in which someone can borrow something and not get it. So we can justify the partial taxonomies as follows.

We cannot straight forwardly extent x is a kind/type of y in this example. However if we manipulate the syntax appropriately, it is easy enough to come up with a formula, which produces a simple test for whether, a verb x is a hyponym of another verb y.

i.e. x-ing is a sort of/type of y- ing

Meronymy: Meronymy, derived from the root *mer-* meaning "part" is a relation in semantics that expresses the part-whole relationship that lexical items may have. Examples of this are:

Finger: hand

Wall: house

Sleeve: shirt

Arm, elbow

House, roof

In this relation, the part is known as the meronym and the whole is called thc holonym.In theory, the meronymic relation is transitive meaning that if an item is a part of a part, then that first item is part of the larger whole.

For example *if John has a scar on his elbow, we know that John has a scar on his arm.*

It is easy to see that the one-way entailment that we have seen, to be the characteristics of hyponymy does not obtain for cases such as these.

E.g.: X is a body entails x is an arm

X is an arm entails x is a body

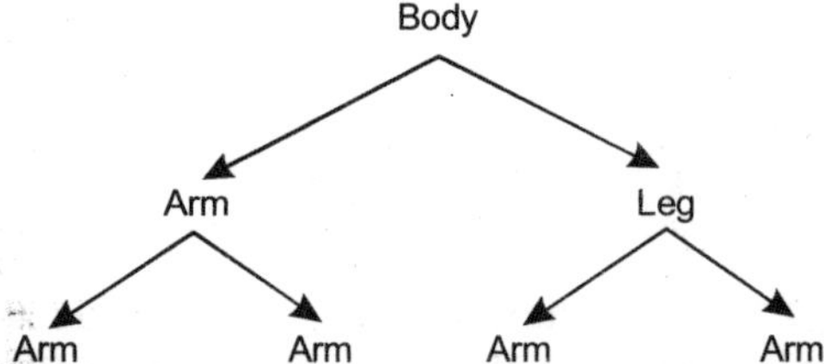

The relationship between arm and body is one whereby the objects to which they refer are in a part-whole relation and the term used for this relation is meronymy. We say arm is a Meronymy of body and that arm, leg, etc are co-meronyms. The structures such as these are not to be confused with taxonomies.

While large sections of the vocabulary of a language can be analyzed in terms of relation such as hyponymy and meronymy, such analysis is not always straightforward. For instance consider the set of verbs, think, believe, hope, wish, know, realize. For these verbs in English which qualifies as a super ordinate for members of this class. In these circumstances, there is a lexical gap.

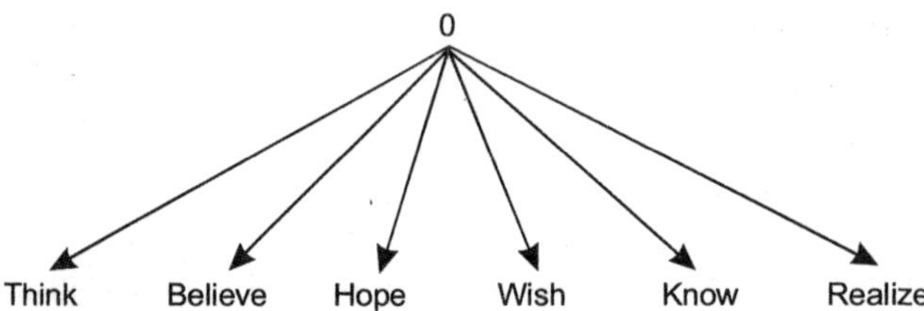

These verbs are known as propositional attitude verbs, i.e. they are all used to express something about the nature of the attitude of someone.

Paradigmatic relation of opposition and exclusion: It is a kind of sense relation, where one lexeme involved in the substitution must be in some way opposite in meaning to the other. Oppositeness is perhaps the only sense relation to receive direct lexical recognition in everyday language. It is presumably, therefore, in some way cognitively primitive. E.g.: If X is male, X cannot be female and vice versa.

There are many kinds and degree of oppositeness. According to Lyons (1977) all oppositions, in their technical sense, are binary, that is involving lexemes, which are seen as being at particular extremes.

Complementaries: These constitute the very basic form of opposites and display inherent binarity in perhaps its purest form. Some definite conceptual area is partitioned by the term of the opposition into two mutually exclusive compartments. Hence if any thing falls into one of the compartments, it cannot fall into the other compartment.

E.g.: Single/Married
Alive/Dead
Male/Female
True/False
Stationary/Moving
Obey/Disobey
Inside/Outside

It is important to emphasize that the relation of complementarity holds only within some specific domain which is frequently implicit. E.g. the relation between dead and alive presupposes the domain of animate things and implicitly excludes anomalous entities such vampires and zombies.

Antonymy: It is derived from the Greek word anti (opposition) and onoma (Name). Lyons reserves these terms for those binary contrasts which are gradable i.e., it is possible to identify degree of contrast between the extremes. It is frequently used as synonym for opposite. It falls into several relatively well defined groups. E.g.: Happy and Sad

Polar Antonyms:

E.g.: *Long: Short*
Fast: Slow
Wide: Narrow
Deep: Shallow

High: Low

Heavy: Light

Thick: Thin

Diagnostic features of polar antonyms.

1. Both terms are fully gradable, that is to say they occur normally with a wide of degree modifiers.
2. They indicate degree of some objective, uni-dimensional physical property, prototypically one which can be measured in conventional units such as centimeters, kilograms, and miles/hour.
3. They occur normally in the comparative and superlative degrees: long, longer, longest; light, lighter, lightest.
4. They are incompatibles, but not complimentaries. It's neither long nor short is not a contradiction.

Equipollent antonyms:

In this neither term is impartial (i.e., both are committed).

For instance, Hotter presupposes "hot" and "colder" presupposes "cold"—this antonym pair typically denote sensation or emotions.

E.g.: Hot: Cold
Bitter: Sweet
Painful: Pleasurable } typically denotes Sensations

Happy: Sad
Proud of: Ashamed of } typically denotes Emotions

Overlapping antonyms:

In this pair one member yields as impartial comparative and the other a committed comparative. E.g.: Good: Bad

'John is an excellent tennis player, but he is worse than Tom'.

'John's a pretty useless tennis player, but he is better than Tom'.

Reversives: This belongs to broader category of directional opposites which include straight forward directions such as *Up: Down; Forwards: Backwards; Into: out of; north: south.*

Reversives has the peculiarity of denoting movement in opposite direction between two terminal states. They are all verbs. The most elementary exemplars denote literal or relative movement in opposite directions. E.g.: Rise: Fall, Advanced: Retreat, Enter: Leave.

Converses: This term is reserved for binary contrast which display and interdependence of meaning such that one member of the pair presupposes the other member. This sense relation is especially found in the definition of reciprocal social roles or special relationships. Converses are often considered to be a subtype of directional opposite.

E.g.: Above: Below
Buy: Sell
Employer: employee

One cannot be an employer without having employee and vice versa. This is the one essential difference with complimentarity, where there is no such symmetry of dependence, these terms of in gradable; hence, there is a difference with antonymy.

Markedness: This notion is often applied to two pairs of opposites: one term is designated as the marked term and the other as the unmarked of the opposition. Lyons (1977) distinguishes three major conceptions of Markedness which may or may not coincide in a particular instance or type of instances.

Morphological Markedness:

The constructions, where one member of opposition carries a morphological mark. This mark, in the case of opposites, is invariably a negative prefix.

E.g.: Possible: Impossible
Happy: Unhappy
Kind: Unkind

True: Untrue

Distributional Markedness:

The unmarked term according to this conception is the one which occurs in the widest variety of context.

E.g.: long is marked with respect to short, because it occurs in a variety of expression from which short is excluded.

This one is 10 meter long.

What is its length?

How long is it? (Neutral Question)

Semantic Markedness:

Unmarked form is one which is used in the context where the normal opposition between the terms is neutralized. In such contexts, the meaning of the term is what is common to the two terms of the opposition. E.g.: Lion and Lioness, in the sentence- *The lion and the lioness were lying together*; there is a gender contrast between the terms. But if we see a group of lions in the distance, the sex contrast is neutralized. The group may well contain both males and females.

Componential Analysis

It is also called *feature analysis* or *contrast analysis* or *lexical decomposition.*

One of the earliest and still most persistent and widespread ways of approaching word meaning is to think of the meaning of a word as being constructed out of smaller, more elementary, invariant units of meaning, somewhat on the analogy of the atomic structure of matter (although the immediate inspiration for the 1st proposals on these lines were not physics but phonology). These 'semantic atoms' or 'the alphabet of thought' are variously known as semes, semantic feature, semantic components, semantic markers, semantic primes, *semanteme or* sense component (few of the terms).

All lexeme in all languages are complexes of universal atomic concepts, comparable with the allegedly universal feature of phonology. Semantic atoms of a natural language are the meanings of its lexical items. On this view complex meanings are certainly built up out of combinations of simpler ones. E.g.–

Word	**Semantemes**
Father	male + parent
Mother	female + parent
Son	male + offspring
Daughter	Female + offspring
Brother	male + sibling
Sister	female + sibling

M. Bierwisch, writing in 1970, said that semantic features do not differ from language to language, but are rather part of the general human capacity for language, forming a universal inventory used in particular ways in individual languages. The process of breaking words down into semantemes is known as *componential analysis, w*hich is given as "present", "absent" or "indifferent with reference to feature".

Componential analysis is a method typical of structural semantics which analyzes the structure of a words meaning. Thus, it reveals the culturally important features by which speakers of the language distinguish different words in the domain (Ottenheimer, 2006, p. 20). This is a highly valuable approach to learning another language and understanding a specific semantic domain of Ethnography.

Componential analysis is usually conceived as binary opposites: one of the members is then used as a base form; contrast being signalled through the use of plus and minus.

e.g.

	Man	Woman	Boy	girl
[adult]	+	+	-	-
[male]	+	-	+	-

Or,

- *man* = [+ male], [+ mature]
- *woman* = [– male], [+ mature]
- *boy* = [+ male], [– mature]
- *girl* [– male] [– mature]
- *child* [+/– male] [– mature]

Hjelmslev 1961, Lyons1968 and Lehrer 1974

Bovine	bull	Cow	Calf
Equine	stallion	Mare	Foal
Ovine	ram	Ewe	Lamb
	male	female	Young
	Adult		

Words can be analyzed and described in terms of their semantic components, which usually come in pairs called semantic oppositions: "Up" and "Down," for example, are related in that they both describe vertical directions, one in one direction (call it "plus") and the other in the other (call it "minus").

To summarize, one word can have basic underlying meanings that are well established depending on the cultural context. It is crucial to understand these underlying meanings in order to fully understand any language and culture.

It has been most often used to analyze kinship terms across languages. The components are often given in more detail. Kroeber 1969 postulated the following components of a kinship system:

- Generation
- Relative age with in a generation
- Consanguinal v/s collateral
- Sex of ego, kin and linking kin
- Condition living or decreased of kin

For instance, kinship terms like those shown below might have three components: sex, generation, and lineage. Sex would be male or female; generation would be a number, with 0 = reference point's generation, -1 = previous generation, +1 = next generation; lineage would be either direct, co lineal (as in siblings) or ablineal (as in uncles and aunts).

Word	Generation	Lineage	Sex
Mother	-1	Direct	Female
Father	-1	Direct	Male
Aunt	-1	Ablineal	Female
Uncle	-1	Ablineal	Male
Sister	0	Colineal	Female
Brother	0	Colineal	Male
Daughter	1	Direct	Female
Son	1	Direct	Male
Niece	1	Ablineal	Female
Nephew	1	Ablineal	Male

This can be the starting point of a more detailed analysis of English terms.

Structural semantics and the componential analysis were patterned on the phonological methods of the Prague School, which described sounds by determining the absence and presence of features. On one hand, componential analysis gave birth to various models in generative semantics, lexical field theory and transformational grammar. It was first proposed by anthropologists as a technique for describing and comparing the vocabulary of kinship in various languages.

Only some years later it was taken up and generalized by such scholars as Lamd (1964), Nida (1964.1975) and Weinreich (1963,1966), as well as by Katz and Fodor (1963), which led to the integration of semantics and syntax within the framework of transformational grammar. The earliest and most influential proponents of componential analysis in the post Saussurean structuralist tradition were Hjelmslev and Jakobson.

Within modern linguistics, the componential analysis of meaning was adapted from distinctive feature analysis of morpho-syntax which in turn had its roots in the methodology of Prague school of phonology.

Procedure for SemanticFeature Analysis

Very often one will find her/himself in a situation in which he/she needs to sort out the similarities and differences among a group of events, people, objects or ideas. A technique that can help you do that is called Semantic Feature Analysis.

Semantic Feature Analysis uses a grid to explore how a set of things are related to one another. By analyzing the grid a person is able to see connections, make predictions and master important concepts.

Steps (Things to do):

1. Identify the general topic to be analyzed.
2. Make a list of typical examples or ideas related to the topic.
3. Make a list in the leftmost column of the grid some features or characteristics that some of the elements might have.
4. Put a "+" sign in the grid if element have this feature. If the answer is no, put a "-". If you don't know, leave it blank.
5. When the grid is completed, it's time to take a look at it and see what patterns emerge. Ask yourself...
   - Which columns are similar to each other?
   - What features do the elements in these columns have in common?
   - Is there a name for the grouping of these elements?
   - Could you make one up?
   - Which rows are similar to each other?
   - What elements are tagged in the same way in those rows?

- What does this similarity tell you about these features?
- Which cells are still blank?
- Where can I go to find the information I'll need to complete those cells?

6. When you've completed this first look at your grid, write up a summary of what you've learned. Your summary should answer the questions listed above.

Example:

	DSL	Aphasia	Autism	Alzheimer's	Dysarthria
Speech disorder	+	-	-	-	+
Language disorder	+	+	+	+	-
Degenerative	-	-	-	+	-
Acquired	-	+	-	+	+
Congenital	+	-	+/-	-	-

Add more columns and rows as ideas for additional features and elements occur to you. After completing the grid; summarize what you've found and what you still don't know.

Advantages of componential analysis:

Lexical decomposition, as a method for characterizing the sense of words has several advantages. There are few reasons that have been put forward for lexical decomposition:

(1) Componential analysis is very popular in linguistics; it shows heterogeneity, complexity of lexical meaning.

(2) Componential analysis helps to differentiate between words (especially between synonyms) the difference between small and little lies in the presence of an additional seme (pleasant, nice) in the word "little" '! not absolute synonyms.

(3) Componential analysis helps to explain semantic derivation (metaphor, metonymy, etc.)

(4) Componential analysis to create the so called language of semantic primitives – minimal units of sense.

(5) It can explain or give evidence regarding partial similarities and correlations between different words.

E.g. horse and mare have some similarity

[Male] and [female] are correlated with widely distributed words in language such as mother, daughter, wife, girl, woman, aunt and many others.

(6) Reduction: an important aim of many componentialists has been to achieve a genuinely reductive analysis of the realm of meaning.

(7) Lexical relations and entailments.

E.g. hyponymy: reptile and snake; meaning of reptile is actually included in snake

antonymy: tall-[+ avg]

Short [-avg]

Wide [+ avg]

Narrow [-avg]

(8) This method allows us to characterize the sense of a potentially infinite set of words with a finite no. of semantic features.

(9) To identify "holes" in a language's vocabulary, areas for which it lacks a direct term.

For instance, English lacks a genderless word for an aunt or uncle; you can't fill in the blank for the statement:

"Parent is to mother and father,

as *** is to aunt and uncle".

One can still express this concept in English but s/he will likely express it less often than you would if there was a word for it

Another gap is the lack of words for either "male cousin" or "female cousin". The paradigm parent/mother/father, sibling/sister/brother is just not carried out for cousin.

This is unlike other Germanic languages, including Danish (Faetter and Kusine for male and female cousins respectively), Dutch (neef and nicht) and German (der Vetter and die Kusine).

Problematical aspects of Lexical Decomposition (Disadvantages)

- The discovery procedures for semantic features are not clearly objectifiable.
- Only part of the vocabulary can be described through more or less structured sets of features. Nouns especially concrete nouns seem to land them to lexical decomposition more readily than do other parts of speech. E.g. mind
- Features used may not have clear definitions.
- Limited in focus and mechanical in style.
- While componential analysis is useful for some exercises, it is not a representation of how language works; no one has ever been able to develop a complete list of semantic primitives. Invariably, some of the primitives identified are actually molecules that can be broken down into new atoms. For instance, parent, offspring and sibling are all interrelated terms; the word parent can be defined as "a person who has offspring" and sibling can be defined as "a person with a parent who has other offspring". If semantic primitives were to exist, they would number in the thousands and would resemble a mathematical logic system more than the mind's loom of language.
- One of the main problems with lexical decomposition is that many times our decomposition leads us to bogus analyses. Let's take the example:

  Kill = Cause + Die

This decomposition worked very well in explaining the ambiguousness of "almost killed", but we are left with the problem that in many cases, 'kill' does not actually equal the sum of the senses of 'cause' and 'die'.

1. John caused Bill to die on Saturday by poisoning his soup on Friday.
2. John killed Bill on Saturday by poisoning his soup on Friday.

The first sentence is correct, while the second seems a bit odd. There are senses where 'cause' and 'die' seem to make sense, but differ from the meaning of 'kill'. The response to this is that these meanings are very abstract and should not be equated completely the meanings of the real words. When we say that Kill = Cause + Die, we don't mean that it has the concrete meanings of 'cause' and 'die', merely that it means generally what they mean abstractly. The linguist Anna Wierzbicka has argued against this interpretation, arguing that these meanings should in fact be very concrete and intuitable.

In sum lexical decomposition provide a useful tool using semantic features with some what limited account of the meaning of word.

Lexical Semantics and Non-lexical Semantics

Lexical semantics studies the meaning of words; the focus here is on 'content words' where meaning is most obviously located to lexicon. On the contrary it can be argued that all levels of linguistic organization contribute in some way to the meaning of an utterance which includes phonetic, phonological and grammatical meaning. This forms the part of non-lexical semantics.

Non-lexical Semantics

J.R.Firth was one who advanced the view that meaning could be seen as a "spectrum" of modes involving all linguistic levels. The insight of this approach can be given immediate clinical interpretation.

Firth's ideas are fundamental to his conception of language, as he considered the analysis of the meaning of utterances to be the main goal of linguistics; Firth proposes to use the term 'semantics' to describe his whole approach to language, which is to link all levels of linguistic analysis (from phonetics to lexicography) with their contexts and situations. He extends the meaning of 'meaning' in remarkable ways by writing about the 'phonological meaning' of phones and the 'grammatical meaning' of constituents.. These usages of 'meaning' allowed Firth to perceive a fundamental unity among linguistic levels, linked through the search for statements of 'meaning' at each level. It has frequently been pointed out, not least by Lyons (1966), that this stretches the meaning of 'meaning' until it snaps, and that while situations must be understood for the interpretation of utterances, considerably more is required to give a full description of meaning.

Phonetic meaning and its clinical relevance: Here a meaning is attached to the sounds of a language, i.e. sound symbolism- a phenomenon which is normally limited to a few cases of onomatopoeia and to literary and rhetorical expression:

Onomatopoeia: means the "name" given to a sound. It's a word imitation of noise. e.g.: "Bong, a bell sound.

Rhetoric: It essentially means the art of speaking persuasively; using the phonetic, semantic and syntactical resources of language in a formalized way in order to convince or have an effect on an audience. E.g. - metaphor, simile.

Phonetic meaning is clinically relevant

- In order to make rapport with patient, therapist adopts a particular voice quality as norm like speaking in loud resonant voice with widened pitch range.
- With children therapist adopts lively exaggerated melodic style aim being to generate enthusiasm, interest and involvement in therapy situation.
- Another example can be of an aphasia patient who can maintain a reasonably fluent level of expression only if she uses what she called "her television voice".

Phonological meaning: In certain linguistic genres(such as poetry), pattern of phoneme in an utterance can be interpreted as conveying a meaning of sorts, for e.g. the way in which alliteration, assonance and rhyme act to interrelate words that are spatially apart—the similarity of sound promoting a connection of sense.

According to J.R.Firth phonological entities have meaning because they can contrast and have relations with other entities in particular phonological environments. At a lexical level, this embraces the notion of the' collocation', that is, which other words a particular word consistently co-occurs with(part of the 'meaning' of words in collocations, such as 'an egregious ass' is that they co-occur together).

Alliteration: The repetition of the same letter at the beginning of two or more words immediately succeeding each other, or at short intervals. Many expressions and tongue twisters rely on alliteration. It can be used in poetry as well as music.

For example:

She sells sea shells by the sea shore

or Peter Piper picked a peck of pickled peppers.

The first letter, s or p, is a consonant which is repeated many times. (If you use a syllable rather than a consonant, it is assonance.)

Alliteration can take the form of assonance, the repetition of a vowel, or consonance, the repetition of a consonant

Assonance:

The repetition of similar vowels in the stressed syllables of successive words. Assonance is repetition of vowel sounds to create internal rhyming within phrases or sentences, and together with alliteration and consonance it serves as one of the building blocks of verse.

Rhyme:

Correspondence of sound in the terminating words or syllables of two or more verses, one succeeding another immediately or at no great distance can be termed as rhyme. The words or syllables so used must not begin with the same consonant, or if one begins with a vowel the other must begin with a consonant. The vowel sounds and accents must be the same, as also the sounds of the final consonants if there be any. E.g. "hat and cat rhyme".

The word "rhyme" can be used in a specific and a general sense. In the specific sense, two words rhyme if their final stressed vowel and all following sounds are identical; two lines of poetry rhyme if their final strong positions are filled with rhyming words. A rhyme in the strict sense is also called a "perfect rhyme". Examples are sight and flight, deign and gain, madness and sadness.

Grammatical meaning: The meaning of the sentence is the product of both lexical and grammatical meaning i.e. of the meaning of the constituent lexeme and of the grammatical construction that relate one lexeme, syntagmatically to anther. Although there is a distinction between these two kinds of meaning in clear case the boundary between them is not always as easy to identify as we might like it to be.

Grammatical meaning becomes clear if we compare pairs of sentences such as following:

1. The dog bit the postman.
2. The postman bit the dog.

These 2 sentences differ in meaning but this difference can not be attributed to any of the constituent lexeme. The semantic difference between 1 and 2 is additionally explained by saying that in 1 "the dog" is the subject and "the postman" is the object, whereas in 2 grammatical roles are reversed.

The difference between lexical and grammatical meaning depends, in principle, upon the difference between the vocabulary (or lexeme) and the grammar.

A category such as tense, or number, can be identified in terms of the formal features of syntax and morphology which mark the contrast involved, or in terms of the meaning conveyed by these formal contrasts.

It is evident that the main element of sentence structure (subject, verb, complement, object and adverbial) can be studied, not only in terms of their syntactic form and distribution in the clause (SVO,VOA etc), but also in terms of the type of information that such grammatical patterns convey.

The various categories and constructions of grammar can be discussed from both formal and semantic points of view:

Formal: a category such as tense, or number, can be identified in terms of formal features of syntax and morphology, which marks the contrast involved. E.g. no. in English is formally a two-term system involving an unmarked singular form and a marker of plurality (by form of s).

Semantic: semantically it will be meaning conveyed by these formal contrasts like for above e.g. the number conveys the difference between "one and more than one".

A construction such as a grammatical statement can be identified formally (e.g. NP + VP or subject-verb) and also semantically (e.g. actor-action, or topic-comment)

It is evident that the main elements of sentence structure(subject, verb, object, adverb) can be studied, not only in terms of their syntactic form and distribution in the clause (SVO, VOA), but also in terms of the type of information that such grammatical patterns convey. In the given example:

1. The key opened the door.
2. He used the key to open the door.
3. The door was opened with the key.

The key is subject in (1), object in (2) and adverb in (3).

Certain semantic features do however seem to be widely recognized and these will form basis of the clinical analyses below. The usual procedure is to recognize the centrality of the category of verbs, identifying the two main functions of ACTION (or DYNAMIC), e.g. kick, run, go, and STATIVE, e.g. know, see, want, be. The remaining semantic functions are then specified with reference to the verb, as follows:

ACTOR: the animate being that causes an action or change of state, e.g. John kicked the ball, the ball was kicked by John.

EXPERIENCER: the animate being that experiences an action or change of state, e.g. John is happy, John saw a car.

GOAL: the object or being which undergoes the result of

an action or change of state, e.g. John kicked the ball, John saw Jim.

INSTRUMENTAL: the inanimate cause of an action or change of state, e.g. The rock broke the window; He broke the window with a rock.

LOCATIVE: the location of the action or state specified by the verb, or of the goal, e.g. Mysore is in Karnataka; Greenland is cold.

TEMPORAL: the time of the action or state specified by the verb as expressed outside of the tense forms, e.g. Later, he came in; We went at 7'o clock.

During the acquisition of language, all the components; namely phonology, morphology and syntax, are interrelated in both typical and atypical development. But this is particularly relevant to the area of semantics because semantic development and semantic problems are intertwined with the other component areas. (Camarata and Schwartz, 1985; Norris and Damico, 1990).

This can be explained as follows:

Language is used to transfer a message and to translate meaning and meaning is derived from individual words and word combinations, language form (syntax and morphology), and context (pragmatics). Thus *language form* and *language use* are dependent on the meaning one intends to express.

Semantic Development

This process of learning to encode and decode meaning i.e. semantic acquisition can be studied at the word level, sentence level and at discourse level.

Semantic Development at Word Level

The process of attaching meaning to words is just a part of the cognitive process of organizing and categorizing information learned about the world. The categories and classes that a child generates to understand the world help him to become more efficient at assimilating and accommodating new information about the world (Owens, 1996). This interrelationship that between cognition and language demonstrates the internal overlap that occurs in learning across developmental domains. Before, getting into the semantic development at word level, some concepts and facts should be made clear.

(a) Referential Meaning: Referential meaning is the ability to use a word as a sign or symbol to represent a referent, which may be an object or an event, or a concept. The assignment of a word or symbol is arbitrary. There is no particular reason why a certain word represents a certain object. The referent itself is not the meaning of the word but the cognitive representation of that object is the meaning. Example: In *bird*, the actual bird is the referent but not the meaning of the word *bird* but the cognitive representation of the word i.e. the meaning. If the bird flies away, the word *bird* still has meaning.

Concept formation occurs through the environment and is never identical for any two individuals. Example: The word *cat* has different meaning for different individuals depending upon the experiences with cats. Though the representation for the word is the same but there may be variations in meaning. Like- *Cat* can also be associated with pain and fear if somebody has an experience of being scratched by a *cat*.

Variation in meaning will be greater with young children because of their lack of experience. Preschoolers' semantic development is coupled with the motor, social and cognitive abilities. The motor abilities of preschoolers are more fully developed and thus they are better able to explore their environment and examine the things they find around them. The growing language abilities allow them to inquire about the objects and expanding cognitive abilities permit them to organize and store all the new-found information.

Preschoolers are not aware that words have lexical meanings i.e. they may not recognize that a word may stand apart from its meaning or that several words can share similar meaning. Example: If a three year old child is asked say all the words that mean *yummy,* the response would likely be to name the favourite snack or to simply say the word *yummy.*

The first words appear to be responses that simply occur in association with the gestures, items, or actions they have accompanied in the past. Some words have early connections as words serving as signs for their referent. Later, those words occur in new situations and also in the absence of the items they refer.

During the school age years, children become more conscious of word meanings in the lexical use. At a metalinguistic level, they recognize that words share similar meanings and that same word can have several different meanings. Example: a fifth grader will typically know that the word *block* may refer to a section of land containing houses, or a unit of concrete used to build those houses, or an act of preventing someone from walking.

Three primary hypotheses provide explanations for the attachment of referential meaning (Owens, 1996; Valletutti, McKnight- Taylor, and Hoffnung, 1989).

(b) Semantic feature hypothesis (Clark, 1973): Semantic feature hypothesis suggests that the attachment of meaning to words (vocabulary development) occurs through the process of abstracting or recognizing attributes or features. Clark suggests that children initially identify perceptual features, or some combination of perceptual features, to generate a word meaning. The child attaches one or two features to a word and then adds other features over time.

As the child's interaction with the environment continues, s/he gradually adds more features until adult meaning is eventually reached. It is during this process that the child learns that an addition of features may mandate a new name or linguistic level. Example: it is highly likely that a child will first categorize a zebra as horse. Upon additional experience, the child will come to realize, with addition of additional features such as black and white and striped that the more appropriate label is *zebra.* Generally, the perceptual features of shape, size and movement are the first to be attached.

Example:	*horse*	*zebra*
	+living	+living
	+animal	+animal
	+four legged	+four legged
	+mane	+mane
		+black and white
		+wild
		+striped

Words that have identical or very similar features are known as *Synonyms*.

Example: happy and glad

Beautiful and lovely

Words with similar features except for one opposite or polar feature are known as *Antonyms*.

Example: heavy and light

Night and day

The features attached to a word impose certain restrictions on word combinations. These are known as *Selection Restrictions*.

These restrictions prohibit feature conflicts that result in confusion, conflict, or redundancy.

Example 1: A bachelor's wife

This word combination is not acceptable as one of the features of bachelor is +unwed, therefore this combination is contradictory in meaning and unacceptable.

Example 2: An unwed bachelor

This word combination is unacceptable because it is redundant as one of the features of bachelor is +unwed.

(c) Functional core hypothesis (K. Nelson, 1974): Functional core hypothesis is another explanation for the attachment of word meaning and is based on the Piaget theory of development. This theory suggests a process by which a child

organizes experiences with the world through structures Piaget referred to as *schemes* (Berk, 1994). It is through these that a concept develops. According to Piaget, the earliest stage of development is sensorimotor stage, it is hypothesized that early schemes are built on motor actions. Concepts will be built upon how something acts or can be acted upon.

Example provided by K. Nelson related to the concept of *ball*.

Ball (1) In living room, porch
Mother throws, picks up, hold
I throw, pick up, hold
Rolls, bounces
On floor, under couch

These schemes form the functional relations experienced by the child and the ball. These functional relations then form the core of the understanding of the concept. Additional concepts will cause addition, deletion, and modification of the concept.

Ball (2) On playground
Boy throws, catches
rolls, bounces
Over ground, under fence

The mature scheme will eventually form:

Ball (1, 2) Location of activity: living room, porch, playground
Actor: mother, I, boy
Action: throw, pick up, hold, catch
Movement of ball: roll, bounce
Location of object: on floor, under the couch, under fence.

For the child to identify the object in pictures and in static situations, the child must recognize the characteristics of the object which includes the functional and perceptual information. Later on, the child recognizes that there is a relationship between a word and a concept. The word or object are embedded in the experience or schema and not identified in isolation (K.Nelson, 1974). Therefore, the concepts that the child develops may not be the same as the adult and therefore are unnamed.

The child develops the concepts and the pre-concepts that organize objects and are acted on in the similar ways (K.Nelson, 1974). The child attempts to translate dynamic experiences into relationships between objects, animals, people and activities and into cognitive and linguistic meaning. Linguistic representation (i.e. the word) is dependent on the experiences and the different relationships that the child observes with the object.

(d) Prototypic complex hypothesis (Bowerman, 1978): Prototypic complex hypothesis suggests that the child develops a prototype or a best example of a concept or a category (Rosch, 1973). This prototype is normally learned by the first experience with a referent from a category (Rosch and Mervis, 1975) or from the frequency of use from an adult caregiver (Valletutti et al., 1989). Additional examples within that category are introduced and added upon the child's experiences. Referents that resemble the prototype will be included in the category and those most similar to the prototype will be central, leaving those with less similarity on the periphery.

Development of Early Expressive Vocabulary

- Children begin to use their first words at about 12 months of age.
- Vocabulary development will then slowly progress to about 50 words or more by about 18 months.
- From 18 to 24 months, toddlers' expressive vocabulary develops from 50 words to 200-300 words.
- 3 year old preschoolers' vocabulary is of 900-1000 words i.e. it almost triples.

- At 5 years of age i.e. the kindergarten stage, their vocabulary will be more than double i.e. almost 2100-2200 words (Owens, 1996).
- It is estimated that children add words to their vocabulary at the rate of 2-5 words per day during their preschool years (Owens, 1996; Pease and Berko Gleason, 1985).
- It is also estimated that children learn nine new words per day, accumulating a receptive vocabulary of about 14000 words by 6 years age (Carey, 1978).
- Initial vocabulary is predominantly made up of nouns i.e. substantive words. (Gentner, 1982; Nelson et al., 1993). According to nelson et al., it could be because there are more nouns than verbs in language. Whereas Gentner suggested that action words are more semantically complex and therefore nouns are easier to learn. However in terms of usage, relational words are used more frequently. Although there may be more nouns in their vocabulary, the frequency of use may be higher for relational words (Bloom, 1973).
- While examining children's early lexicon (the first 50-75 words), two different types of vocabulary have emerged (nelson, 1973) possibly indicating two language learning strategies. They are:
  (i) Referential or Analytical: The vocabulary of referential children is dominated by common nouns and is primarily used for labeling the environment. They connect a string of phonemes i.e. a word to an object or concept in the environment by labeling it (bates et al., 1994).

  (ii) Expressive or Gestalt: An expressive child focuses more on interaction and has a vocabulary that consists of more proper names, action-type words and social communication words such as *go bye-bye, thank you* and *stop it* (Nelson,1973; Hampson, 1989). They use language primarily for social interaction or instrumental functions.

Studies of language development reveal that early vocabulary development consists of *substantive words* and *relational words* (Bloom and Lahey, 1978).

(a) Substantive words are objects or class of objects. It can be single word like *mommy* or *daddy*, or a class of objects that share perceptual and/or functional feature such as *car* or *dog*. First words tend to be objects or concepts that are important and familiar to the child such as family, pets, food, animals, or animal noises (Nelson, 1974).

(b) Relational words describe the relationships that a referent has with him- or her or other referents, including movement (Reed, 1986). *Reflexive relational words* are words that refer to a relationship with itself. These relationships are represented in four general meanings: existence, nonexistence, disappearance, and recurrence (Bloom and Lahey, 1978). These are very useful words; they enable the child to express what he wants.

The learning process: A small set of words is learned early. These words tend to be dominated by categories such as people, animals and food (Nelson, 1974). Although children follow a general pattern of development, there is a great deal of variation in the rate of learning (Bates, 1994).

Nelson also noted that children will make up words if they don't have a word to describe something. They create new words to fill in the gaps in their vocabulary. They may also interchange classes of words such as using nouns for creating verbs. Example: A two year old child saying *body boo- boo* to let her mother know that she has stomach ache; or a child saying pumpkin house for a pumpkin shaped house.

Also it was noted that acquired words are often generalized by children. In the early productive language of the children, two processes occur, *overextension* and *underextension*. They occur most frequently in the age 1-2.5 years. If these processes continue beyond this age, they may be an indicative of language delay.

Overextension: Overextension is overgeneralization of the meaning and occurs when the range of meaning for a particular word is much greater than it is for the adult's referent for that word. Example: a young child may call the babysitter mama where is only attempting to communicate with his limited knowledge about the world with even more limited lexicon.

Young preschoolers tend to use certain features to produce certain overextensions. The features are often used to categorize or determine sameness are perceptual features and occasionally functional features. The most common perceptual features may include shape, movement, size, sound, texture and taste.

Overextension may be a result of a comprehension error which occurs if the child does not have adequate semantic representation. But this is not the case every time. It may also due to the performance error which is due to limited vocabulary or a retrieval problem.

Underextension: Underextension occurs when a range of meaning for a particular word is more limited than the adult's meaning of that word. Example: the child learns the word kitty for his pet cat and then uses that word only for his cat and not other cats. It has been hypothesized that the child's word learning process occurs in two stages. These are:

Fast mapping: This is a hypothetical process in which children apparently associate a word and its referent after the initial exposure (Carey and Bartlett, 1978). Upon hearing the new word, the child may store some initial information or associations, as to what the word might mean.

Extended mapping: During this stage, the information will be gradually expanded and modified as an additional experience with that word clarifies its full meaning (Carey, 1978). This stage might be a prolonged process extending for several months or even years. And the child will be dealing with many words in the similar way. There are a number of factors that appear to influence how rapidly preschoolers map meaning onto a new word. These factors include each child's learning style, phonetic composition, syllabic structure, situational factors and linguistic context.

Situational factors:

- Like object words are learnt more quickly than action words. Of object words, those that refer to objects that are acted on in specific ways are learned more quickly (example- only frying pans are used for frying).
- It is also seen that simultaneous pairing of a new word with its referent leads to more efficient learning.
- Children learn a new word more readily when it occurs in an unambiguous context, being the only new word with its referent more apparent as opposed to being embedded among several new words and various references.

Linguistic context:

- Familiar words (e.g. colours that are already known) make it easier to learn new words for an instance of that same property (e.g. new colour word). For example, if the child knows *red* and *blue* then it will easier for him to learn *yellow.*

Children exhibiting referential learning style are more likely to imitate new words.

- Phonetically, new words composed of phonemes already used by the child are more easily learned than the words with phonemes which are not there in their phonetic inventory.
- In terms of syllable structure, words that consist of reduplicated syllables (e.g./*toto*/) are generally learned more quickly than words consisting of non-reduplicated syllables (e.g./*fumo*/).

Lexical Learning Principles

These are the speculated principles that guide the children as they learn new words (Cairns, 1996).

- *Principle of reference*: this principle states that children assume that words refer to objects, events and attributes around them.
- *Whole object principle*: This principle states that there is a tendency in children to assume that a novel word applies to the entire object and not just a part of it.
- *Principle of extendibility*: This principle states that children generalize a new word to other similar objects quickly.
- *Taxonomic principle*: This principle states that children have tendency to extend a new word to another similar object as opposed to an item merely associated with the original object.
- *Mutual exclusivity assumption*: this principle refers to the fact that a new name applies to for which they do not yet know a name.

Semantic development at the two-word to sentence level: It has been noted by Prather (1984) that the vocabulary test scores are higher for 12th grader than for a 5th grader. In contrast tests focusing on syntax and morphology showed less noticeable increases. This implies that the size and scope of a typical student's vocabulary will continue to grow at a noticeable level throughout development.

According to Wiig, Freedman and Secord (1992), the *'principle of translating into world knowledge'* does not hold good for middle and secondary school level children. Instead vocabulary understanding will aid in the understanding of the world and in the development of efficient strategies for problem solving.

Some vocabulary proves difficult for children especially for children with disabilities. These vocabulary terms include *shifters, relational* and *kinship terms*.

Shifter is a word that changes its referent depending on who the speaker is and where and when he is speaking (Reich, 1986).

- These words lack a one-to-one word correspondence with the referent. For example pronouns like *I, me, mine, you, yours* etc shift referents depending on who the speaker is. Example: I refer to the speaker and then I become you when you are talking about me.
- This concept is very difficult for the children until after the age 5 years. Thus, when the caregivers speak to young children, they tend to use child directed speech (CDS) and tend to avoid pronouns because possibly, they understand the level of difficulty and thus attempt to make language easier to understand.
- In learning pronouns, it is common to first witness some redundancy. It is developmental to initially use *me* as in first person pronoun and later replace it with *I*.
- The use of shifters like this/that and here/there depends on the location of the referent to the speaker. Example: *This* book is the same book when it is moved across the room and it becomes *that* book.

Come/go will indicate motion from one location to another but the usage is dependent upon the direction.

Relationals are vocabulary terms that express a relationship between two or more objects or events and depend on context.

- Children find temporals like *before, after, until, since, while* etc difficult and will use word order if they do not yet understand the time concept. Time is the most abstract relationship to contemplate. Words indicating duration like since, until are mastered later. And words like while, until; which indicate simultaneously occurring events are understood by 5 years of age.
- Locational terms such as *inside/outside, in, on, under, at, above, below, top, in front of, behind* etc. these terms are commonly found in the directions that are given to children.

- Physical attributes like *more/less, hard/soft, big/little, thick/ thin* etc.

Dimensional words refer to words that are adjective pairs used to indicate the various dimensions of objects. The positive terms are learnt before negative terms. The reason might be that the positive member reflects the presence of the dimension, which makes it more conspicuous; and perhaps big things are more notable than the little items. Moreover, the positive member refers to the entire continuum, thus the positive marker tends to occur more frequently. Complexity depends on the specificity of the attributes that must be analyzed. Example: wide/narrow is more difficult than big/ small.

Kinship terms like *father, mother, sister brother* precede *son, daughter, grandfather, grandmother* and *aunt, uncle, niece, nephew* are learnt even later.

- And it's only by 10 years of age that the most major kinship terms are understood.

Colour words: Younger preschoolers are able to sort and categorize items according to their colour. But it somewhat later that they begin to comprehend and express color names accurately.

- Younger preschoolers 1st demonstrate that they recognize color as a perceptible part of objects i.e. they can be identified apart from the object. By 4-5 years age, preschoolers can name basic colours.

Spatial words indicate the location of a referent, typically in relation to some item. Children generally begin to comprehend spatial words before they use them expressively and continue to rely on their caregivers for additional cues. The nature of items involved in the situation are may influence the younger child's interpretation.

- By 4 years of age, most children master in meanings of *in, inside, on* and *under* (Clark, 1980). By 5 years of age, all spatial relations are generally mastered.

According to a study by Backsheider and Gelman, children as young as 3 years know some homonyms. This means that children realize that labels can be misleading and that a single label can represent different categories. The fact that homonyms exist complicates the encoding of meaning and this is referred to as *semantic mapping*.

Each time a new word is learned, the child must map that word into the previous knowledge. But there are numerous mappings of the same sort which contribute to the possibility of error.

Semantic restrictions: beyond one word stage, words rarely occur in isolation and occur together and relate to each other in several ways. As lexical items certain words may not occur together because the semantic features of each word introduce selection restrictions. Example: mature speakers are unlikely to use the word *angry* in relation to the word *rock*.

Semantic relations: At around 18 months of age, children begin to combine words into multiword utterances. These utterances and define the relationship between semantic categories. Bloom and Lahey (1978) discussed the importance of the interrelationship of syntactic and semantic roles once the child moves beyond the one-word utterances stage. The same word may play a different semantic role depending on the word order (syntax). This reflects the preschoolers' new understanding of other roles that can be played by the objects and people they talk about.

Brown (1973) suggested that most early utterances are based on combining two or three basic semantic relations. The following are the most basic combinations used by preschoolers.

Construction	Example
Agent+action+object	Mommy bake cake
Agent+action+locative	Mommy bake kitchen
Agent+object+locative	Mommy cake kitchen
Agent+action+object+locative	Mommy bake cake kitchen

The utterances appear to lengthen as they elaborate on one of the major terms in the basic relationship. Example: an early *agent+action* relationship utterance may take the form *boy eat*. Later, this might be lengthened on *agent* term with an *attributive* relation as in *big boy eat*.

However beyond these basic relationships, preschoolers are soon compelled to express their ideas more clearly. Thus they elaborate the meaning with the production of grammatical morphemes.

Semantic Organization at Multiword, Sentence and Conversation Level

Now the individual has reached a level of semantic sophistication that allows the comprehension of language by processing pragmatic, syntactic, morphological and lexical information simultaneously. This allows the understanding of multiple and complex ideas, events and theories. This level of semantic sophistication allows the individual to competently translate complicated events and abstract ideas into language through accurate structure and appropriate use. In addition, these language abilities will affect the encoding of experience to memory and retrievability of that experience at a later date (Lindfors, 1987)

Figurative language: school age children develop figurative language which allow for creativity. According to Hakes (1982), children invent many creative because of a lack of vocabulary. Example: Gardner and Weiner (1979) related the description of a *bald man* by a preschooler as having a *barefoot head*.

Early use of figurative language is based on physical resemblance and similarities of use or function. Metaphors become less frequent after the age 6 as the child's basic vocabulary increases, requiring less of a need to create new words (Owens, 1992). The decline in the spontaneous production may also be evidence of the elementary school child's focus on the real and the literal. Usually the quantity of metaphors increases in creative writing in later elementary school. But the comprehension of figurative language increases. The 8 to 9 year old begins to appreciate psychological states like *feeling blue, being a cold person,* although misinterpretation may still be there.

However, proverbs such as *don't put the cart before the horse* are very difficult for young school age children and may be interpreted literally. The ability to understand proverbs and idioms develops slowly throughout childhood, adolescence and adulthood (Nippold, 1985). Figurative expressions are easier for adolescents to comprehend in context than in isolation, and the interpretation may depend on how transparent they are. Thus, *hold your tongue* would be easier than *kick the bucket.*

Semantic Developmental Patterns

Semantic development can be divided into following age levels:

(*a*) 0-2 years

(*b*) 3-6 years

(*c*) 6-8 years

Zero to two years:

1st year:

- During first year, meaning is mostly used in context of certain activities rather than referring to any object.
- Then relational meaning is formed since it is contextualized.

  Example: *spoon* with *eating* and *car* with *travel.* I.e. symbolism is developed.
- Mental representation is created. It is crucial for language i.e. relating arbitrary symbols to meaning (Piaget, 1951).

1.5 years:

- Overextension i.e. words refer to, but do not match with the denoted concept. This is called as naming explosion.

- Concepts are formed based on holistic event analysis.

Some common word categories which can be observed are:

- Specific objects (mama, dada)
- General objects (dog, cat, toy)
- Manipulating objects (cup, juice, shoe)
- Action words (give, up, on)
- Attributes (dirty, nice)

End of 2 years:

Semantic development is based on concepts like:

- synonyms, antonym, hyponym etc and not on event analysis.
- In building initial vocabulary, children accomplish 3 linguistic tasks:
  (*a*) Labeling: matching object/image with word.
  (*b*) Packing: underextension (vehicle means only papa's bike)
  (*c*) Network building: It includes semantic relations like
- Hyponymy: example-*cat, dog* etc belong to category called *animals*. Hyponyms have collocational relations.
- Synonymy: words having same meaning. Example: *cry, weep* etc.
- Antonymy: words having opposite meaning. Example: *hot-cold, thick-thin.*

Three to six years

- Vocabulary grows dramatically
- Active word stock nearly 2500 words
- Passive lexicon up to 14000 words.
- About 500 words are added to active vocabulary every year.
- Meaning of 'that' and 'this' are grasped first, presumably because 'this' and 'here' are semantically

more complex since they express the extra component of nearness. This develops by 6 years.

- Polar denotational meaning (antonyms) develops by 3-6 years age. Example: more-less, big-little, short-long.
- Semantics continues to grow in terms of
- Extension of vocabulary
- Refinement of meaning representation
- Extension of non-literal meanings
- Words are not added as isolated terms, but as number of already existing fields. So extension of vocabulary proved through enlargement of semantic network selection (hyponyms, synonyms, antonyms etc.). So this learned information is encyclopedical than lexical.
- Verbs like *give-take, buy-sell* etc are learnt through environmental demonstration/action.
- Semantic meaning of concrete activity is known.
- Meaning of nouns (*dogs, chair* etc) are easier to learn as they are perceptually available than meaning encoded by verbs (*go, give* etc).

Six to eight years

- Familial words with single meaning take additional meaning. Example: 'paper' can mean a piece of paper, written essay, examination paper etc.
- Metaphorical expression arises by this age.

Semantic Disorders/Disabilities

There are two types of semantic disabilities namely *lexical and sentential*. Within each category there are two subdivisions namely *delay and deviance.*

Lexical Delay

In the present state of knowledge, only gross patterns of delay can be isolated.

(*i*) Patients whose vocabulary is largely or wholly composed of social/relational/stereotyped lexemes or who lack specific lexemes.

(*ii*) Patients who are within the area of specific lexemes show the inability to use the later semantic field.

(*iii*) Patients who continue to underextend or overextend vocabulary beyond the developmental peak period.

(*iv*) Patients who are unable to use the more advanced semantic features contrast to develop and extend their vocabulary.

(*v*) Patients who fail to develop the expected range of collocational relations.

The clearest cases of semantic delay would be children whose lexicon, in terms of number of lexemes, lexeme meaning and interrelationship is the replica of their juniors. There will also be unbalanced delays in which these variables are in different levels of maturity and this is where deviant patterns intervene.

Lexical Deviance

It is very difficult to be sure whether an abnormal lexical use in a patient is an instance of lexical delay or something which would be outside the path of normal lexical development. Example: Taking lexemes as synonyms when they are not. On first encounter they may strike one as deviant usage; but if we observe closely, it shows that it has features of normal development. Or the path of normal lexical development like any of the paradigmatic sense relation could go wrong in that pairs of lexeme or could be interrelated in unacceptable ways.

On first encounter with such problems, they inevitably strike as one as deviant usage but it may be that the syntagmatic observations show that they are feature of normal development. They may be common features but it not clear whether the phenomenon is widespread or not and by no means invalidate to delay/deviance distinction. Example: an aphasic my respond saying 'as big as big' which might strike as abnormal but is quite expected from a preschooler.

Same implies to paradigmatic relation as well. Example: *fat* as opposite to *pretty* or child producing *baby* as opposite of *big*.

The term word finding can also be called as lexeme finding. This is the problem of retrieving a lexeme in a specific grammatical form. The main problem that arises is whether there is evidence of pattern underlying the lexeme finding behavior of the patient, and whether this pattern is governed by linguistic (specifically semantic) factors. There are logical possibilities for taking decision about lexeme finding behavior:

(*i*) The lexeme seems totally unavailable in some modes like auditory, speech, reading, writing, comprehension, production and imitation.

(*ii*) The lexeme is sometimes available i.e. in some modes in some tasks. It is available only in one subset of semantic fields but have difficulty with those from the other field. If the target lexeme and produced lexeme does not demonstrate synonymy, oppositeness, hyponymy; then it does not belong to the same semantic field.

When a lexeme is comprehended incorrectly then 3 kinds of responses can be observed.

- Zero response
- Treats it as related lexeme
- Treats it as unrelated lexeme

  Example: when asked to open the door, the child may,

- Look uncertain and do nothing
- Might point at the window
- May point to the tree.

(*iii*) The lexeme is available but not compatible with therapists use i.e. patient has different semantic system, at least for the field to which the lexeme belongs.

Sentential Delay

This involves:

- Patients whose sentences are restricted to a single, early emerging semantic function example reflexive meaning only.
- Patients are unable to connect sentences semantically as well and are restricted with 2 or 3 semantic function sentences.
- Patients whose sentential semantic expression is incomplete being dependent on context to make the meaning clear. It includes non-verbal behavior like gestures as well.

Sentential Deviance

This is referred to the inability to express a specific semantic set of functions which are unrelated to any development order of emergence.

It involves:

- Inability to use only single semantic function unrelated to developmental order, or to development semantic functions in an unexpected development order.
- Inability to use semantic formations whether developmentally early or not, but in an abnormal way. Example: restricting locative expression to the semantic field of vehicles.
- Unnecessary use of a semantic function either because it is repeated or because it is redundant or irrelevant to the context.
- Mismatch between the order of grammatical elements and semantic values attributed to them. Example: subject-verb-object being interpreted as goal-action-actor.

Semantic Disorders in Children

The following features may be found in presence of other language problems in children:

Word retrieval versus word learning:

Word finding problems may be found in language impaired children and adults. A distinction needs to be made between word retrieval and word learning. If the language impaired child has restricted lexical knowledge, cueing to help find a word will be of no use because the child will search for a word which is not available. The use of such overt behaviors may indicate that a child is attempting to find a word which is known. There are a number of such behaviors:

1. The use of initial speech sounds or silent articulatory gestures preceding the target word
2. Giving semantic information. Example: 'I see one of them, Mrs. Walker got.'
3. Using a filler or empty word. Example: 'serve thingies and cook.'
4. Self-correcting, starting, stopping and restarting. Example: 'A woman is going in...a woman is going in...in the station.'
5. Gesturing, signing, miming or using symbolic noise
6. Extra verbalizations and starters
7. Frustration gestures

It may be helpful to consider whether a particular search behavior predominates and assists the child iaccessing the word. Of so, the child could be encouraged to use the effective search behavior when difficulty occurs. Alternatively, it may be that the child does not attempt a search and may need to be taught to do so. Test of word finding (TWF) (German, 1986) is a standardized assessment which aims to assess accuracy and speed of naming in children in five different ways:

Picture naming of both nouns and verbs, sentence completion, naming of an object from a given description and naming the category a group of objects belong to (pliers, axes, screwdriver: tools). Also, analysis of naming behavior involves looking for substitutions the individual produced. These categories would be useful for monitoring the child's naming behavior in informal testing and spontaneous language.

Word finding and word learning studies concentrate on the relationship between lexical and phonological knowledge. For children to acquire a new item of vocabulary, they have to understand its conceptual attributes. They must also be able to perceive and produce its phonological form and store this in memory in order to access it later. Normal children are able to do this readily. They are able to gain basic conceptual knowledge necessary to fit the new item into their new lexicon. This is termed as fast mapping (Carey, 1978).

Gathercole (1993) discusses the role of short term and long term memory in the learning of new words. She concludes that language impaired children have exceptional difficulty in short term retention of new words. Thus research should further investigate the short term retention of new words and effective remediation of this problem.

Overextensions:

Here the lexical item is used to refer to a larger category of objects in adult usage are often present in the speech of children with developmental language delay and are generally recognized as characterizing an immature semantic system. In normal developing children, overextensions generally disappear by age 3 years.

Clark's (1973) hypothesis of semantic feature acquisition suggests that the child has identified an object by one particular perceptual feature. Example: *apple* by the fact that it is round. The term *apple* becomes overextended when the names another round object (namely *plate*) as *apple*. It thus becomes necessary to for the child to perceive another feature which distinguishes *apple* from *plate* which could be the fact that apples are edible whereas plates are not. According to Clark, shape is the first attribute to control word meaning followed by size, sound, movement, and then taste.

Confusion of polar opposites:

This is the second common feature of delayed language development i.e. confusion in polar terms as *more/less, high/ low, before/after*. Example: Immature child will choose a tree containing *more* apples in response to a request for *more* and also choose more apples in response to *less.*

Clark (1973) considers it to be another form of overextension because both the terms have large number of semantic features in common and differ in respect of one feature only. At the stage of confusion, the child has realized that *more* and *less* are both measurements of quantity but not that *more* refers to positive quantity and *less* refers to negative quantity.

Semantic-Pragmatic Disorder/difficulties (now Considered as Pragmatic Disorder broadly)

This term was coined by Rapin and Allen (1983) in their classification of developmental disorders. Semantic-pragmatic disorder without autism is used to describe a group of children who present with very fluent expressive language and yet are not affective communicators. The utterances will be syntactically and phonologically well formed but the children demonstrate severe difficulties with language processing and use. Problems of discourse comprehension, irrelevant responses to questions, echolalia, disruption of syntax and prosody are all noted.

Examination of child's lexical system may reveal one or more of the following features:

1. **Slow development and difficulty in acquiring semantic field boundaries**

Example: child aged 13 is asked to list lexemes from semantic field fruit:

Child	apple
	Banana
	Pineapple
	Cabbage

Therapist	Is cabbage a fruit?
Child	No-carrots
Therapist	Are carrots fruit?
Child	Yes
Therapist	No. cabbage and carrots are _____?
Child	Vegetables

Here although child appears to know both the superordinate terms fruit and vegetable, she is unsure which lexemes belong in each of these semantic fields.

2. Rigid concept boundaries

A rigid concept boundary is observed as preposition and particle error in children with semantic-pragmatic difficulties.

Example: children when told that a butcher sells meat lists beef, pork and chicken as types of meat but would not accept the suggestion of sausages as he considers it to be food and not meat.

3. Incorrect semantic ordering in part-whole relationships

This may be caused due to poor knowledge of the associations between words and alternatively the error may be a failure to comprehend the syntax of the question.

Example: In response to a question such as 'what's got a roof on?'. The child answers 'chimney'. This happens because of his knowledge that a chimney is a part of the roof which in turn is a part of the house.

4. Overuse of deictic items

Deixis is the term for lexemes whose meaning is dependent on shifting referents. Crystal suggests four deictic terms:

Animate: *him, she, I* etc.

Inanimate: *it, that* etc.

Scope: *then, there, now, down* etc.

Overuse of deictic terms can result in ambiguities. Analysis of this overuse suggests semantically based problem i.e. Poor lexical knowledge or that the speaker may fail to appreciate the listener's state of knowledge or the listener's perspective.

5. Lexical access difficulty

Problems with lexical access can result in:

- Literal paraphasias (words which contain at least 50% of the same sounds as the target items).
- Semantic paraphasias (words which belong to the same semantic category as the target item).
- Neologisms (made up words)

It is recommended that the child's reasoning ability be investigated. It is difficult to determine the word boundaries between semantic, pragmatic, syntactic and world knowledge. Our understanding of a particular word meaning in a given utterance is affected by our individual experiences, the possible contexts both in terms of syntax and situation as well as the particular context given. Child with semantic-pragmatic difficulties fails to integrate this information successfully and therefore his or her reasoning through language is affected.

The following features may be observed:

(*a*) *Failure to make inferences:* the child finds it difficult to interpret information which may be given in visual and verbal form.

Example: child is given a picture of an accident victim being put in an ambulance but is unable to answer the question 'where will the ambulance go next?'.

This implies that the child is in some way unable to use the information provided in the picture to assess the situation, integrate this with knowledge of the world i.e. where ambulances normally take accident victims and reach the conclusion of hospital.

(*b*) *Literal interpretations:* Literal interpretation of idiomatic expressions is often noted as a feature of the language behavior of children with semantic-pragmatic difficulties.

(*c*) *Reasoning may be logical but idiosyncratic:* Mctear (1985) reports on a conversation with a child where the child seemingly failed to understand the interviewer's questions. When the child's half of the conversation was analyzed, it is shown to progress logically but not in the way the adult expects.

Careful assessment and data collection is essential and should not be restricted solely to the areas of semantics and pragmatics because the problem involves the breakdown of conversational interaction, it is important that conversational analysis is undertaken.

Semantic Disorders in Adults

Semantic disorder in adults is prominently seen in aphasic individuals wherein problems in language expression persist.

Problems in Language Expression

Word retrieval errors are present in aphasics i.e. impairments in the ability to produce lexical items like naming, spontaneous speech or reading. Meaningful and non-meaningful word substitutions in fluent speech indicate lack of awareness of errors. Whereas different types of blocking and searching behaviors such as pauses, hesitations and re-attempts at initial sounds and syllables or at whole words; are displays of awareness of difficulty.

The following are some of the language features reflecting problems in lexical retrieval:

I. *Circumlocution:* In an attempt to retrieve a word or convey its meaning, the subject talks around the target word. Intentional strategies are sometimes adopted like descriptions and definitions. When a person has extreme difficulty in accessing content words, empty runs of speech may be heard such as 'it is over there, like the other one, the one he has'.

II. *Semantic paraphasia:* A real word which has the same grammatical function as the target and also has semantic association with its substitute. Example: walking for running, glass for window. These examples show that the phonological structure of the substitute word will generally be dissimilar to the target.

III. *Verbal paraphasia:* A real word which has the same grammatical function but there is no recognizable semantic association with the target. The error may show a degree of intactness of the structural features of the target word such as number of syllables and some similarity with phonemes like walking for wishing; chair for chalk.

IV. *Perseverative paraphasia:* A word which has been expressed in the previous context is inappropriately expressed in later utterance. It can be both linguistic and non-linguistic and usually implies to the failure in processing of new response which is more difficult than reproducing the former one.

V. *Anomia:* This refers to the disorder of naming rather than word retrieval in running speech and may be due to a failure to recall words from a variety of concept groupings, or may be restricted to specific word categories, notably body parts, colors and objects. The problem may be in:

(*i*) Visual perceptual analysis causing visual agnosia

(*ii*) Linking sensory and perceptual information with conceptual and semantic information

(*iii*) Accessing the semantic representation of an appropriate lexical item

(*iv*) Eliciting the phonological structure of an appropriate lexical item

Depending on the underlying difficulty, the anomic response may present as failure to evoke a word attempt, a semantic paraphasia, circumlocution, neologism, or feature phonemic paraphasia.

In an aphasic connected speech, lexical retrieval problems will be realized by searching behavior or any types of error described. Additionally, there may be difficulty in placing the semantic representations or themes that convey sentence meaning into sentence framework.

Problems in Receptive Language

- If a spoken word heard by an individual with aphasia fails to evoke appropriate and sufficient sense relations, its meaning or referent cannot be accessed, or is only partially accessed by semantic memory. The word will be perceived as meaningless nonsense word or may be interpreted as another concept from a related semantic field. Example: *turnip* for *potato.*
- A person with lexical comprehension deficit generally has more difficulty correctly associating a heard word with one of two closely related pictures or items or rather than with one of two unrelated pictures or items. Example: knife is more likely to be recalled from pictures of a *knife* and a *boat* rather than pictures of *knife* and *fork*.
- The treatment at a single word level depends on a variety of influences including degree of abstractness and familiarity that affect the ability to understand and use lexical items.

  Often, difficulty arises in understanding single words because there is an absence of information to support semantic processing. Linguistic and extralinguistic context is used to comprehend specific semantic and syntactic information as natural communication provides a great deal of contextual information (Pierce, 1991).
- Sentence meaning can also be affected by semantic comprehension problems. This occurs where there is impairment in the ability to interpret the thematic relations of a particular verb. Example: *The mouse chased the cat;* here the thematic roles of *mouse* as agent-subject and *cat* as theme-object can only be appreciated if the lexical entry *chase* is understood. A person with a sentence meaning deficit might fall back on knowledge,

experience and expectancy and so interpret the sentence as *The cat chased the mouse.*

- The effects on information load and memory span also affect semantic comprehension. In most of the people with aphasia, memory deficit is the influence of memory span, information load, semantics, and syntax that affects the ability to comprehend.

Semantic disorder is seen in aphasic impairment and has been divided into 2 broad categories: *selection* and *combination* (Jakobson, 1956). Semantic disorders may be observed in both these categories.

Word finding/access difficulties may be seen as a problem of selection, along the paradigmatic axis. At the syntagmatic level, problems in linking linguistic elements to form larger units i.e. sentences are classed as combination difficulties.

The complexity of aphasic disturbances is reflected in the diversity of typological classification of aphasic impairment. When working with an adult who has acquired a semantic deficit following brain injury, it is assumed that pre-trauma, the individual was working with a mature semantic system. Linguistic description of the communicative ability of the person with aphasia is required before a therapy is planned. However, developments through cognitive neuropsychology and processing theory have highlighted the necessity of psycholinguistic assessment. Cognitive neuropsychology studies patterns of behavior in brain injured individuals i.e. which aspects of behavior have become abnormal and which remain intact. It is based on the assumption of an internal processing system and that system is modular. Separate cognitive activities are carried out by separate modules. Each modules works independently of other modules unless in direct communications. This was initially used to investigate lexic disturbances and later applied to brain injured individuals with aphasia and now being applied to developmental disorders of speech and language.

CHAPTER

5

Pragmatics

Concept, Acquisition/Development, Disorder and its Clinical relevance

Pragmatics

Pragmatics is a subfield of linguistics concerned with speech acts, and how communication is achieved in a given instance of language use; it studies how the transmission of meaning depends not only on the linguistic knowledge (e.g. grammar, lexicon etc.) of the speaker and listener, but also on the context of the utterance, knowledge about the status of those involved, the inferred intent of the speaker, and so on. In this respect, pragmatics is the study of how the meaning of a sentence (or other linguistic unit) changes depending on how and where it is expressed, or on the *structural ambiguity* in language.

'Pragmatism' was first clearly defined by Pierce and developed by Prof. James of Harvard and Prof. Dewey, Columbia. Pragmatism confines itself wholly to those truths, which are definitely correlated to actual facts of existence. Pragmatic language ability involves the appropriate use and interpretation of language in relation to the context in which it occurs (Bishop, 1997) and requires skill in turn taking, topic maintenance, attention control, interpreting subtle non-literal aspects of meaning, conversation repair and listener empathy (Mc Tear and Conti-Ramsden, 1992; Ripley, Barrett and Fleming, 2001). Pragmatics is a set of sociolinguistics rules related to language use in the communication context.

Definition of pragmatics:

Pragmatics is the systematic study of meaning by virtue of, or dependent on, the use of language. Linguistic pragmatics studies the meaning that sentences have when they are uttered (as text sentences, in particular classes of contexts).

Hulit and Howard (1997) define pragmatics as the study of functions, purposes or intents of communication.

Pragmatics was introduced into the child language literature by Bates (1976). He defined pragmatics as the 'rules governing the use of language in context'

The Domains of Pragmatics:

It will be necessary to distinguish pragmatics from other branches of linguistics that are also concerned with the study of language usage. For example, the study of psychological aspects of language usage, such as linguistic perception and processing, overlaps with the field of psycholinguistics, while the study of social aspects of language usage overlaps with sociolinguistics.

More positively we can identify several areas within the study of language usage that may be seen as relatively independent of the study of structure. These are:

- *Language as social action:*

  This is concerned with the study of linguistic acts in social contexts. We need to study the nature of intention, beliefs, wishes and plans. Social actions such as these which involve the use of language have been referred to as speech acts.

- *Language as appropriate behavior:*

  Speakers can achieve their goals in different ways, choosing from alternative ways of expressing the same intention. While there are many different ways to ask someone to close the door, it is usually the case that not all of the theoretically possible forms are appropriate in a particular context.The terms 'context' and 'appropriacy' are two concepts in pragmatics that are the central to the study of language usage.

- *Language as a means of function/intentional communication:* Language has been described as the primary means that human use to communicate.

Framework of Pragmatic Abilities

There are many aspects of pragmatics. An organizational framework for these aspects has been described by Roth and Speckman (1984).

They included:

- Communicative intention
- Presupposition and Entailment.
- Discourse and its Organization.

Communicative Intention

Communicative intention is one's purpose or reason for speaking that is the act or force of illocution. Communication is such an effective tool for humans, and it serves so many purposes, it is for this reason we learn language in the first place. Depending on our intention or illocutionary act, different language form and content will be used. The contexts in conjunction with those intentions will affect language production or locutionary act.

There are numerous reasons for using language, including soliciting information, providing information, responding to request and gaining attention. These are statements, assertion, denials, request, commands, promises, apologies, thanks, condolences, warning and much other speech acts.

Presupposition (in continuation to the last chapter):

Presupposition is an implicit assumption about the world or background belief relating to an utterance whose truth is taken for granted in discourse. Examples of presuppositions include:

Question: Do you want to do it again?

Presupposition: that you have done it already, at least once.

Statement: Jane no longer writes fiction.

Presupposition: that Jane once wrote fiction.

A presupposition must be mutually known or assumed by the speaker and addressee for the utterance to be considered appropriate in context. It will generally remain a necessary assumption whether the utterance is placed in the form of an assertion, denial, or question, and can be associated with a specific lexical item or grammatical feature (presupposition trigger) in the utterance.

Crucially, negation of an expression does not change its presuppositions: I want to do it again and I don't want to do it again both presuppose that the subject has done it already one or more times - *My wife is pregnant*; and *My wife is not pregnant* - both presuppose that the subject has a wife. In this respect, presupposition is distinguished from entailment and implication. For example, *The president was assassinated* entails that *The president is dead*, but if the expression is negated, the entailment is not necessarily true.

Entailment (in continuation to the last chapter):

Entailment is the relationship between two sentences where the truth of one (A) requires the truth of the other (B). For example, the sentence (A) The president was assassinated; entails (B) The president is dead. Notice also that if (B) is false, then (A) must necessarily be false. To show entailment, we must show that (A) true forces (B) to be true and (B) false forces (A) to be false.

Entailment differs from implicature (in their definitions for pragmatics), where the truth of one (A) suggests the truth of the other (B), but does not require it. For example, the sentence (A) Mary had a baby and (B) got married implicates that (A) she had a baby before (B) the wedding, but this is cancellable by adding — not necessarily in that order. Entailments are not cancellable.

Entailment also differs from presupposition in that in presupposition, the truth of what one is presupposing is taken for granted. A simple test to differentiate presupposition from entailment is negation. For example, both The king of France is ill and The king of France is not ill presuppose that there is a king of France. However The president was not assassinated no longer entails The president is dead. Presupposition remains under negation, but entailment does not.

Discourse and its Organisation

Discourse means either "written or spoken communication or debate" or "a formal discussion or debate." The term is often used in semantics and discourse analysis.

Discourses are linguistic units composed of several sentences; in other words, conversations, arguments, or speeches. In discourse analysis, which came to prominence in the late 1960s, the word "discourse" is often used as shorthand for "discursive formation" meaning large heterogeneous discursive entities.

According to Michel Foucault, discourse has a special meaning. It is "an entity of sequences of signs in that they are enouncements (enouncés)" (Foucault 1969: 141). An enouncement (often translated as "statement") is not a unity of signs, but an abstract matter that enables signs to assign specific repeatable relations to objects, subjects and other enouncements (Ibid: 140). Thus, a discourse constitutes sequences of such relations to objects, subjects and other enouncements. A discursive formation is defined as the regularities that produce such discourses. Foucault used the concept discursive formation in relation to his analysis of large bodies of knowledge, such as political economy and natural history. (Foucault: 1970).

Studies of discourse have been carried out within a variety of traditions that investigate the relations between language, structure and agency, including feminist studies, anthropology, ethnography, cultural studies, literary theory and the history of ideas. Within these fields, the notion of "discourse" is itself subject to discourse that is, debated on the basis of specialized knowledge. Discourse can be observed in the use of spoken, written and signed language and multimodal/multimedia forms of communication, and is not found only in "non-fictional" or verbal materials.

There is no agreement among linguists as to the use of the term discourse in that some use it in reference to texts, while others claim it denotes speech which is for instance illustrated by the following definition: "Discourse: a continuous stretch of (especially spoken) language larger than a sentence, often constituting a coherent unit such as a sermon, argument, joke, or narrative" (Crystal 1992:25). On the other hand Dakowska, being aware of differences between kinds of discourses indicates the unity of communicative intentions as a vital element of each of them. Consequently she suggests using terms 'text' and 'discourse' almost interchangeably betokening the former refers to the linguistic product, while the latter implies the entire dynamics of the processes (Dakowska 2001:81). According to Cook (1990:7) novels, as well as short conversations or groans might be equally rightfully named discourses.

Seven criteria which have to be fulfilled to qualify either a written or a spoken text as a discourse have been suggested by Beaugrande (1981). These include:

(*i*) Cohesion - grammatical relationship between parts of a sentence essential for its interpretation;

(*ii*) Coherence - the order of statements relates one another by sense.

(*iii*) Intentionality - the message has to be conveyed deliberately and consciously;

(*iv*) Acceptability - indicates that the communicative product needs to be satisfactory in that the audience approves it;

(*v*) Informativeness - some new information has to be included in the discourse;

(*vi*) Situationality - circumstances in which the remark is made are important;

(*vii*) Intertextuality - reference to the world outside the text or the interpreters' schemata.

Nowadays, however, not all of the above mentioned criteria are perceived as equally important in discourse studies, therefore some of them are valid only in certain methods of the research (Beaugrande 1981, cited in Renkema 2004:49).

Discourse Analysis

The term discourse analysis (DA) first came into general use following the publication of a series of papers by Zellig Harris beginning in 1952 and reporting on work from which he developed transformational grammar in the late 1930s. Formal equivalence relations among the sentences of a coherent discourse are made explicit by using sentence transformations to put the text in a canonical form. Words and sentences with equivalent information then appear in the same column of an array. This work progressed over the next four decades (see references) into a science of sublanguage analysis (Kittredge and Lehrberger 1982), culminating in a demonstration of the informational structures in texts of a sublanguage of science, that of immunology, (Harris et al. 1989) and a fully articulated theory of linguistic informational content (Harris 1991). During this time, however, most linguists pursued a succession of elaborate theories of sentence-level syntax and semantics.

Although Harris had mentioned the analysis of whole discourses, he had not worked out a comprehensive model, as of January, 1952. A linguist working for the American Bible Society, James A. Lauriault/Loriot, needed to find answers to some fundamental errors in translating Quechua, in the

Cuzco area of Peru. He took Harris's idea, recorded all of the legends and, after going over the meaning and placement of each word with a native speaker of Quechua, was able to form logical, mathematical rules that transcended the simple sentence structure. He then applied the process to another language of Eastern Peru, Shipibo. He taught the theory in Norman, Oklahoma, in the summers of 1956 and 1957 and entered the University of Pennsylvania in the interim year. He tried to publish a paper Shipibo Paragraph Structure, but it was delayed until 1970 (Loriot and Hollenbach 1970). In the meantime, Dr. Kenneth L. Pike, a professor at University of Michigan, Ann Arbor, taught the theory, and one of his students, Robert E. Longacre, was able to disseminate it in a dissertation.

Harris's methodology was developed into a system for the computer-aided analysis of natural language by a team led by Naomi Sager at NYU, which has been applied to a number of sublanguage domains, most notably to medical informatics. The software for the Medical Language Processor is publicly available on Source Forge. In the late 1960s and 1970s, and without reference to this prior work, a variety of other approaches to a new cross-discipline of DA began to develop in most of the humanities and social sciences concurrently with, and related to, other disciplines, such as semiotics, psycholinguistics, sociolinguistics, and pragmatics. Many of these approaches, especially those influenced by the social sciences, favor a more dynamic study of oral talk-in-interaction. In Europe, Michael Foucault became one of the key theorists of the subject, especially of discourse, and wrote The Archaeology of Knowledge.

Organization of discourse refers to the rules that must be mastered to effectively communication or discourse. This includes skills related to topic management, such as turn taking, topic maintenance as well as productive repair strategies. The skills included in this area are:

Selection of topic is important because it will influence the level of interest on the part of listener, and as result, influences the quantity and quality of social interaction that occurs

Introduction or initiation of a topic begins the social communicative and must be presented in a manner acceptable to the listener and in way that encourage participation. This is extremely important for positive peer interaction

Topic maintenance refers to the ability to respond appropriately during a conversation in order to keep the conversation going. There should be some level of responsiveness on the part of the listener or the conversation will not be maintained. The listener must demonstrate skills that acknowledge attention to the speaker and include making meaningful comments about the topic in an order that makes sense and increases understanding.

Change in topic during a conversation, there will be times when the conversant changes topic. It requires a smooth transition, closure to the previous topic, and then the introduction and maintenances of the new topic must be practiced.

Turn taking involves the ability to take the role of the both listener and speaker and the knowledge of when to appropriately switch roles. A conversation partner listens to comments and then makes a statement regarding the topic, asks a question or uses verbal and non verbal modes to indicate listening and interest, such as nod or verbal acknowledgements, such as 'okay,'uh-huh'.

For all speakers, there are times when the intended message is not understood. The speaker must recognize this misunderstanding and then repair the communication breakdown. This can be accomplished through a variety of strategies, including revisions to the language form and content.

Discourse analysts carefully scrutinize universal circumstances of the occurrence of communicative products, particularly within state institutions. Numerous attempts to minimize misunderstandings between bureaucrats and citizens were made, resulting in user-friendly design of documents. The world of politics and features of its peculiar communicative products are also of concern to discourse analysts. Having carefully investigated that area of human activity scholars depicted it as characterized by frequent occurrence of face saving acts and euphemisms. One other sphere of life of particular interest to applied linguists is the judicature and its language which is incomprehensible to most common citizens, especially due to pages-long sentences, as well as peculiar terminology. Moreover, educational institutions, classroom language and the language that ought to be taught to enable learners to successfully comprehend both oral and written texts, as well as participate in real life conversations and produce native-like communicative products is the domain of discourse analysis. Last but not least, influence of gender on language production and perception is also examined (Renkema 2004, Trappes-Lomax 2004).

Spoken Language Analysis

The examination of oral discourse is mainly the domain of linguists, who at first concentrated on the language used during teacher - learner communication, afterwards altering their sphere of interest to more general issues. It was said that certain characteristics are common to all societies in relation to communication, for instance, indicating the end of thought or end of utterance. The words that are to point the beginning or the closing stages of a phrase are called 'frames'. McCarthy (1991:13) claims people know when they can take their turn to speak in a conversation. However, in spite of the fact that frames can be noticed in every society, their use might differ, which is why knowledge of patterns of their usage may be essential for conducting a fluent and natural dialogue with a native speaker. Moreover, these differences are not only characteristic of cultures, but also of circumstances in which the conversation occurs, and are also dependent on the rights (or 'rank') of the participants (McCarthy 1991:13).

Apart from that, it was pointed out that some utterances are invariably interrelated, which can enable teachers of foreign languages to prepare learners adequately to react as a native speaker would. Among the phrases whose successors are easy to anticipate there are for instance: greeting, where the response is also greeting; apology with the response in the form of acceptance or informing - and acknowledging as a response. Such pairs of statements are known as adjacency pairs. While the function of the reply is frequently determined by the former expression its very form is not, as it depends on circumstances in which the conversation occurs. Thus, in a dialogue between two friends refusal to provide help might look like that: no way! I ain't gonna do that! But when mother asks her son to do something the refusing reply is more likely to take different form: I'm afraid I can't do that right now, can you wait for five minutes? Frequently used phrases, such as "I'm afraid", known as softeners, are engaged when people want to sound more respectful.

Written Texts Analysis

One of the major concerns of written discourse analysts is the relation of neighbouring sentences and, in particular, factors attesting to the fact that a given text is more than only the sum of its components. It is only with written language analysis that certain features of communicative products started to be satisfactorily described, despite the fact that they were present also in speech, like for instance the use of 'that' to refer to a previous phrase, or clause (McCarthy 1991:37). As mentioned before written language is more integrated than the spoken one which is achieved by more frequent use of some cohesive devices which apart from linking clauses or sentences are also used to emphasize notions that are of particular importance to the author and enable the reader to process the chosen information at the same time omitting needless sections (Salkie 1995:XI).

Links in discourse studies are divided into two groups: formal - which refer to facts that are present in the analyzed text, and contextual - referring to the outside world, the knowledge (or schemata) which is not included in the communicative product itself (Cook 1990:14). Since it is difficult to describe the processing of contextual links without referring to particular psychological inquiries, therefore, this section is devoted to representation of formal links.

By and large five types of *cohesive devices* are distinguished, some of which might be subdivided:

(*i*) *Substitution*: in order to avoid repeating the same word several times in one paragraph it is replaced, most often by one, do or so. So and do in its all forms might also substitute whole phrases or clauses (e.g. "Tom has created the best web directory. I told you so long time ago".)

(ii) *Ellipsis*: it is very similar to substitution; however, it replaces a phrase by a gap. In other words, it is omission of noun, verb, or a clause on the assumption that it is understood from the linguistic context.

(*iii*) *Reference*: the use of words which do not have meanings of their own, such as pronouns and articles. To infer their meaning the reader has to refer them to something else that appears in the text (Ram: "How do you like my new Honda Activa?" - Mohan: "It is a nice scooter, which I'm also thinking of buying".).

(*iv*) *Conjunction*: specifies the relationship between clauses, or sentences. Most frequent relations of sentences are: addition (and, moreover, etc.), temporality (afterwards, next e.g. "He bought her perfume at a local perfume shop and afterwards moved toward a jewellery store.") and causality (because, since).

(*v*) *Lexical cohesion*: denotes links between words which carry meaning: verbs, nouns, adjectives. Two types of lexical cohesion are differentiated, namely: reiteration and collocation. Reiteration adopts various forms, particularly synonymy, repetition, hyponymy or antonymy (Collocation is the way in which certain words occur together, which is why it is easy to make out what will follow the first item).

It is clear from the analysis of written language that when people produce discourse they focus not only on the correctness of a single sentence, but also on the general outcome of their production. That is why the approach to teaching a foreign language which concentrates on creating grammatically correct sentences, yet does not pay sufficient attention to regularities on more global level of discourse, might not be the best one (Cook 1990, McCarthy 1991, Salkie 1995).

Narratives

Narratives include self generated stories, telling of familiar tales, re telling of movies or television shows etc.:

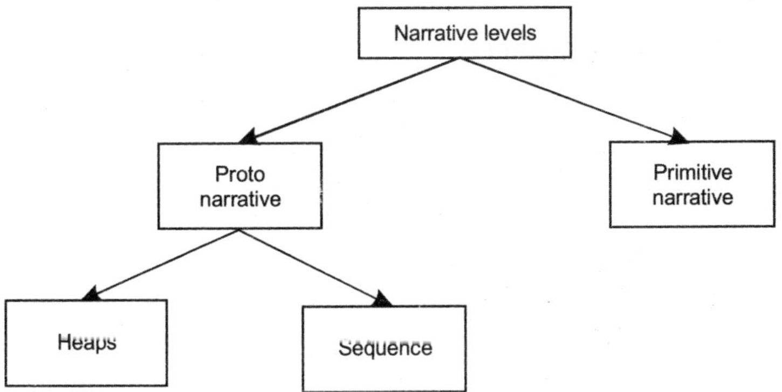

The earliest stories have been called as proto narratives.

Heaps- collections of unrelated elements. E.g. There is a truck. The man has a red hat. This is smoke. I see a dog.

Sequence- produces a collection of story elements similar to heaps but related to a central topic. E.g. The lion lives in a cave. The seal has a cave where he swims. And the monkey has trees in his cage, produced by a preschooler following a visit to zoo.

Primitive narrative- the elements are connected to core topic in a conceptual manner.

Non-referential use of Language

Language can be used non- referentially as well. Roman Jakobson identified six functions of language, only one of which is the traditional system of reference. Others are non-referential.

Referential: conveys information about some real phenomenon

Expressive: describes feelings of the speaker

Conative: attempts to elicit some behavior from the addressee

Phatic: builds a relationship between both parties in a conversation

Metalingual: self-references

Poetic: focuses on the text independent of reference

Structural Ambiguity

The sentence "You have a green light" is ambiguous. Without knowing the context, the identity of the speaker, and their intent, it is not possible to infer the meaning with confidence. For example:

It could mean you are holding a green light bulb.

Or that you have a green light to drive your car.

Or it could be indicating that you can go ahead with the project.

Similarly, the sentence "Sherlock saw the man holding binoculars" could mean that Sherlock observed the man by using binoculars; or it could mean that Sherlock observed a man who was holding binoculars. The meaning of the sentence depends on an understanding of the context and the speaker's intent. As defined in linguistics, a sentence is an abstract entity — a string of words divorced from non-linguistic context — as opposed to an utterance, which is a concrete example of a speech act in a specific context. The cat sat on the mat is a sentence of English; if you say to your sister on Tuesday afternoon: "The cat sat on the mat", this is an example of an utterance. Thus, there is no such thing as a sentence with a single true meaning; it is underspecified (which cat sat on which mat?) and potentially ambiguous. The meaning of an utterance, on the other hand, is inferred based on linguistic knowledge and knowledge of the non-linguistic context of the utterance (which may or may not be sufficient to resolve ambiguity).

Implicature

Implicature is a technical term in pragmatics coined by Paul Grice. It refers to what is suggested in an utterance, even though not expressed or strictly implied (that is, entailed) by the utterance. For example, the sentence "Mary had a baby and got married" strongly suggests that Mary had the baby before the wedding, but the sentence would still be strictly true if Mary had her baby after she got married. Further, if we add the qualification "— not necessarily in that order" to the original sentence, then the implicature is cancelled even though the meaning of the original sentence is not altered.

This can be contrasted with cases of entailment. For example, the statement "The president was assassinated" not only suggests that "The president is dead" is true, but requires that it be true. The first sentence could not be true if the second were not true; if the president were not dead, then whatever it is that happened to him would not have counted as a (successful) assassination. Similarly, unlike implicatures, entailments cannot be cancelled; there is no qualification that one could add to "The president was assassinated" which would cause it to cease entailing "The president is dead" while also preserving the meaning of the first sentence.

Grice's Maxims

1. Maxim of Quality:

Be Truthful: Do not say what you believe to be false. Do not say that for which you lack adequate evidence.

2. Maxim of Quantity:

Quantity of Information: Make your contribution as informative as is required for the current purposes of the exchange. ?Do not make your contribution more informative than is required.

3. Maxim of Relevance:

Relevance: Be relevant: The speakers are assumed to be saying something that is relevant to what has been said before.

4. Maxim of Manner:

Be Clear: Avoid obscurity of expression. ("Eschew obfuscation"). Avoid ambiguity. ("Espouse elucidation"). Be brief. ("Avoid unnecessary prolixity"). Be orderly.

Explanation of Maxims

These maxims may be better understood as describing the assumptions listeners normally make about the way speakers will talk, rather than prescriptions for how one ought to talk. Philosopher Kent Bach writes:

We need first to get clear on the character of Grice's maxims. They are not the sociological generalizations about speech, nor are they moral prescriptions or proscriptions on what to say or communicate. Although Grice presented them in the form of guidelines for how to communicate successfully, I think they are better construed as presumptions about utterances, presumptions that we as listeners rely on and as speakers exploit. (Bach, 2005).

If the overt, surface meaning of a sentence does not seem to be consistent with the Gricean maxims, and yet the circumstances lead us to think that the speaker is nonetheless obeying the cooperative principle, we tend to look for other meanings that could be implicated by the sentence.

Grice did not, however, assume that all people should constantly follow these maxims. Instead, he found it interesting when these were "flouted" or "violated" (either purposefully or unintentionally breaking the maxims) by speakers, which would imply some other, hidden meaning. The importance was in what was not said. For example: "It's raining" is in violation of quality and quantity of spoken language; however, in context (e.g. when someone has suggested a game of tennis) the reasoning behind this 'fragment' sentence becomes clear.

The cooperative principle describes how people interact with one another. As phrased by Paul Grice, who introduced it, it states, "Make your contribution such as it is required, at the stage at which it occurs, by the accepted purpose or direction of the talk exchange in which you are engaged." Though phrased as a prescriptive command, the principle is intended as a description of how people normally behave in conversation.

Put more simply, people who obey the cooperative principle in their language use will make sure that what they say in a conversation furthers the purpose of that conversation. Obviously, the requirements of different types of conversations will be different.

The cooperative principle can be divided into four maxims, called the Gricean maxims, describing specific rational principles observed by people who obey the cooperative principle; these principles enable effective communication.

The cooperative principle goes both ways: speakers (generally) observe the cooperative principle, and listeners (generally) assume that speakers are observing it. This allows for the possibility of implicatures, which are meanings that are not explicitly conveyed in what is said, but that can nonetheless be inferred. For example, if Alice points out that Bill is not present, and Carol replies that Bill has a cold, then there is an implicature that the cold is the reason, or at least a possible reason, for Bill's absence; this is because Carol's comment is not cooperative — does not contribute to the conversation — unless her point is that Bill's cold is or might be the reason for his absence.

Speech Acts

For much of the history of linguistics and the philosophy of language, language was viewed primarily as a way of making factual assertions, and the other uses of language tended to be ignored. The work of J. L. Austin, particularly his *'How to Do Things with Words'* (published posthumously in 1962), led philosophers to pay more attention to the non-declarative uses of language. The terminology he introduced, especially the notions *"locutionary act"*, *"illocutionary act"*, and *"perlocutionary act"*, occupied an important role in what was then to become the "study of speech acts". All of these three acts are nowadays commonly classified as "speech acts".

Austin defined speech acts as the actions performed in saying something. Speech act theory said that the action performed when an utterance is produced can be analyzed on three different levels.

Speech act is the acts that may be performed by a speaker in making an utterance, as stating, asking, requesting, advising, warning, or persuading, considered in terms of the content of the message

Austin's primary assertion was the speakers produces utterances, they are doing more than saying words organized by conversational language rules. John R Searle suggested that every speech act consist of three separate acts:

(*i*) The perlocutionary act

(*ii*) The illocutionary act

(*iii*) The locutionary act

These pragmatic elements are present in an individual instance of a mature speech act. The speaker first has an intention (illocution) that is expressed in an utterance (locution) and subsequently interpreted by a listener (perlocution).

Austin was by no means the first one to deal with what one could call "speech acts" in a wider sense. Earlier treatments may be found in the works of some church fathers and scholastic philosophers in the context of sacramental theology as well as Thomas Reid and C. S. Peirce. Austin's primary assertion was that when speakers produce utterances, they are doing more than saying words organized by conventional language rules.

Austin distinguishes between illocutionary and perlocutionary speech acts. An interesting type of illocutionary speech act is that performed in the utterance of what Austin calls performatives, typical instances of which are "I nominate John to be President", "I sentence you to ten years' imprisonment", or "I promise to pay you back." In these typical, rather explicit cases of performative sentences, the action that the sentence describes (nominating, sentencing, promising) is performed by the utterance of the sentence itself.

The basics of the theory centre on the idea that words, when placed together, do not always have a fixed meaning. Austin's work has had many critics; Gorman (1999, p.109) explains that many people have used his work without fully understanding its criticisms, and Austin's main arguments have had only one notable follow up work, that by Searle in 1969. Speech-act theory is a continuing discourse, still written about and criticised in hundreds of articles and books. MacKinnon (1973, p.235) states that 'the various conceptual systems we have indicated are only intelligible as extensions of an ordinary language framework', meaning that, as its basis, the theory must first have an already working or 'ordinary' set of rules that are indisputable and reliable.

Searle's typology of speech acts (1975):

- Representatives/Assertatives: are those kinds of speech act that commit the speaker to the truth of the expressed preposition and thus carry a truth value. They express the speaker believes such as "describing", "claiming", "hypothesizing", "insisting", and "predicting".

  E. g. I came; I saw; I conquered. (Julius Caesar)

- *Directives*: are those kinds of speech that represent attempt by the speaker to get the addressee to do something. They express the speaker's desire for the addressee to do something (advice, commands, orders, questions and requests).

  E. g. turns the TV down
- *Commissives*: are those that commit the speaker to some future course of action. They express the speaker's intention to do something (offers, pledges, promises, refusals and threats).

  E.g. I'll never buy you another computer game
- *Expressives*: are those that express a psychological attitude or state in the speaker [apologizing, blaming, congratulating, praising, and thanking]

  E .g. well done, Elizabeth!
- Declaration/declaratives: are those that effect immediate changes in some current state of affairs [bidding in bridge, declaring war, excommunicating, nominate a candidate].

  E .g. I hereby pronounce you man and wife

Speech act may be direct or indirect:

1. *Direct speech act:* perform their function in a direct and literal manner. In direct speech act there is a direct relationship between their linguistic structure and the work they are doing.

   Examples: I was going to get another one.
2. *Indirect speech act:* In indirect speech act, the speaker wants to communicate a different meaning from the apparent surface meaning; the form and function are not directly related.

   Example: "Peter, can you open the window?"

   In this example the speaker is asking Peter whether he will be able to open the window, but also requesting that he do so. Since the request is performed indirectly, by means of (directly) performing a question, it counts as an indirect speech act.

Indirect speech acts are commonly used to reject proposals and to make requests. For example, a speaker asks, "Would you like to meet me for coffee?" and another replies, "I have class." The second speaker used an indirect speech act to reject the proposal.

Deixis

Deixis is collectively the orientational features of human languages to have reference to points in time, space, and the speaking event between interlocutors. A word that depends on deictic clues is called a deictic or a deictic word. Deictic words are bound to a context — either a linguistic or extra linguistic context — for their interpretation.

Some English deictic words include, for example, the following:

now vs. then

here vs. there

this vs. that

me vs. you

he/she vs. him/her

go vs. come

It is the context from which the reference is made—in other words, the viewpoint that must be understood in order to interpret the utterance. (If Tom is speaking and he says "I", he refers to himself, but if he is listening to Betty and she says "I", then the origo is with Betty and the reference is to her.)

Types of Deixis

Spatial deixis: A spatial location relative to the spatial location of the speaker. It can be proximal or distal, or sometimes medial. It can also be either bounded (indicating a spatial region with a clearly defined boundary, e.g. in the box) or unbounded (indicating a spatial region without a clearly defined boundary, e.g. over there)

It is common for languages to show at least a two-way referential distinction in their deictic system: proximal, i.e. near or closer to the speaker, and distal, i.e. far from the speaker and/or closer to the addressee. English exemplifies this with such pairs as this and that, here and there, etc. In other languages, the distinction is three-way: proximal, i.e. near the speaker, medial, i.e. near the addressee, and distal, i.e. far from both. This is the case in a few Romance languages and in Korean, Japanese, Thai, Filipino and Turkish.

Spatial deictics are often reused as anaphoric pro-forms that stand for phrases or propositions (that is, items of discourse, not items of the outside reality). Consider the following statement:

'There may be ice hidden in unexplored places of the Moon. This ice could be useful for future lunar expeditions'.

In the above example, this ice is not near the speaker in the physical sense, but the deictic does not refer to real ice. This ice refers to the phrase ice hidden in unexplored places, which is conceptually near the speaker in the discourse flow.

Temporal deixis: Time deixis is reference made to particular times relative to some other time, most currently the time of utterance. For example, the use of the words *now* or *soon*.

Discourse deixis: Where reference is being made to the current discourse or part thereof. Examples: "see section 8.4", "that was a really mean thing to say", "This sentence is false". The last is an example of token-reflexive discourse deixis, in which a word in the utterance refers to the utterance itself.

Switch reference is a type of discourse deixis, and a grammatical feature found in some languages, which indicates whether the argument of one clause is the same as the argument of the previous clause. In some languages, this is done through same subject markers and different subject markers. In the translated example "John punched Tom, and left-[same subject marker]," it is John who left, and in "John punched Tom, and left-[different subject marker]," it is Tom who left.

Person deixis: Pronouns are generally considered to be deictics, but a finer distinction is often made between personal pronouns such as I, you, and it (commonly referred to as personal pronouns) and pronouns that refer to places and times such as now, then, here, there. In most texts, the word deictic implies the latter but not necessarily the former. (In philosophical logic, the former and latter are collectively called indexicals.)

Social deixis: Social deixis is the use of different deictics to express social distinctions. An example is the difference between formal and polite pro-forms. Relational social deixis is where the form of the word used indicates the relative social status of the addressor and the addressee. For example, one pro-form might be used to address those of higher social rank, another to address those of lesser social rank, another to address those of the same social rank. By contrast, absolute social deixis indicates a social standing irrespective of the social standing of the speaker. Thus, village chiefs might always be addressed by a special pro-form, regardless of whether it is someone below them, above them or at the same level of the social hierarchy who is doing the addressing.

Pragmatic Development

In terms of pragmatic skill the child's communication expands as they learn to adopt a role to express own opinion and personality. The development of pragmatic language ability is thought to be dependent on interactions between linguistic, social, cognitive and emotional aspects of development. Thus pragmatic development involves not only the development of social communication rules, but also the flexibility to modify the rules situationally.

In the process of development of the child, even before the production of the first word, communication between infants and caregivers is occurring at some level. Although infants have not yet produced their first words, the evolution of communication throughout infants first 12 months has been correlated with the pragmatic elements of speech acts outlined by Searle and Austin (Bates, 1976).

These pragmatic elements are present in an individual instance of a mature speech act. The speaker first has an intention (illocution) that is expressed in an utterance (locution) and subsequently interpreted by a listener (perlocution). However, the sequence of these elements is somewhat altered in the phases of communication development during infancy.

Perlocutionary Stage

The first half of an infant's first year is considered the *perlocutionary stage***,** a phase in which communication is based primarily on caregivers' interpretation of infants' behaviours. Through this stage, the infant fails to signal specific intensions beyond those behaviours they will sustain an interaction such as cries, coos, and use of face and body nonspecifically, that is infants lack conscious, goal- directed intentions in these earliest interactions.

Initially, the infant's behaviour is characterized by attention *interaction* in which he or she attends to and discriminates stimuli (Wetherby and Prizant, 1989).The child responds to stimulus with diffuse undifferentiated behaviours such as crying, as it is assumed that infants do not exhibit "intentions," as they are incapable of conceiving of cause-effect or means-end relationships.

Crying indicates general pain, discomfort or need but does not identify the cause of the problem. The caregiver interprets the infant's behaviours and responds differentially. The communication system becomes effective as the caregiver learns to interpret the child's behaviour. Communication at this point is a one-sided affair, based primarily on caregivers' willingness and ability to interpret their infant's behavior as signals. Caregivers use baby talk, which makes their speech more noticeable to their infant.

Later the infant recognize the mean end potentials of his or her communication. Gradually, the infant's greater cognitive ability will enable him or her to understand the outcome of the behaviours. Soon the infant will begin to make deliberate attempts to share specific experience with the caregiver's, fully expecting them to respond.

Towards the end of the perlocutionary period, the infant becomes more interested in manipulating objects and begin to use gestures (Bates, Bertherton, Shore and Mc New, 1983)

These gestures demonstrate an understanding of object purpose or functional use, and include such behaviours as bringing a cup to the lips or a telephone receiver to the ear. At this stage, the infant begins reaching for desired objects. For objects that are beyond its grasp, the infant's reach will become a pointing gesture.

Illocutionary Stage

The *illocutionary* stage, in which intentions are signaled, emerges during the second half of the first year. It represents the emergence of intentionality on the part of infants. This stage begins at 8-9 month of age. Within this stage the child uses conversational gestures or vocalizations to communicate intensions i.e infants begin to indicate identifiable intentions with apparent awareness of achieving their goals through the caregivers' behaviour. The child's behaviour becomes differentiated to signal different intentions. Several behaviours mark the emergence of intentional communication (Scoville, 1983):

- Gestures are accompanied by eye contact with the child's communication partners
- The child uses consistent sounds or intonation patterns of his or her own invention as signals for specific intensions.

  Eg: child might say "eh-eh" to express a want.
- The child persists in attempting to communicate. If not understood , he/she may repeat the behaviour or modify it for the communication partner

- There are 3 sequential substages the development of gestures (Bates etal. , 1975)

In first stage, which begins prior to the illocutionary period, the infant exhibit or shows to self? The infant hides its face, raises arms to pick up, or plays peek-a-boo

In second stage infant shows object by extending them towards the care giver but does not release them.

Finally, in the last sub stage, the child exhibit full range gestures such as showing, pointing, giving and requesting

Eg: touching the mouth repeatedly to signal *eat*

Pointing may include the whole hand or only the finger with arm extended. It is the movement of upper trunk in the direction of object.

Requesting is a whole –hand grasping reach towards a desired object or giving gesture accomplished by a call for assistance.

Initial gestures are used to signal two general functions (Bates et al., 1975):

(*i*) Protoimperatives such as request, signal an adult to attain an object.

(*ii*) Protodeclerative such as giving, showing and pointing signal an adult to attain adult attention

Locutionary Stage

The final stage is the *locutionary* stage, which begins with the first meaningful word. In this symbolic interaction, the child's intend become encoded in a language symbol. Words and gestures are combined to express the same basic meanings or intensions that were previously conveyed by gestures or vocalizations

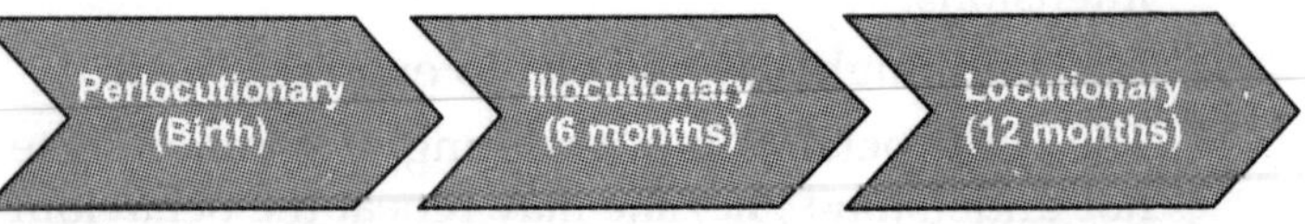

Fig: Development of Pragmatic elements of speech acts.

When the child is of *5 or 6 years*, he/she is able to make judgments about whether enough information is contained in a message, or not. As early as *3 years*, the child understands that the inclusion of the word 'please' make requests more polite; and by the time he/she is *5 years* old, he/she understands the indirect requests are more polite than direct commands. If there is a communicative failure that requires a repair, the preschool child usually faults the listener for the failure, not the speaker. By the time he/she is *8 years* of age, the child understands that the speaker is sometimes responsible for the failure (Robinson, 1981). By the time child reaches adolescence, her/his pragmatic skills are fairly well developed, at least as they are applied in the most common social experiences, the child is likely to face (Berko-Gleason, Hay, and Cain, 1988). In adolescent, the child will sometimes purposely violate the pragmatic skills we could categorize as common rules of courtesy.

Pragmatic Development in Preschool Children

In terms of pragmatics or social language skills, babies between birth and six months of age use perlocutionary behavior- signals issued by the child that have an effect on the word to fill communicative listener but lacks communicative intent. For example, if a mother puts her baby in to the bath and he begins to cry, she might say, *"uh-oh, that water is too cold and you don't like it. I would better warm it up."* But the baby would be crying for many other reasons; his mother has interpreted his cry as indicating that he does not like the temperature of the bath water, and she is now adding warm water in hopes that he will like the bath better.

At *8 months* of age, child uses gestures.

At *9-10 months* of age, the baby uses illocutionary behaviour-a signal to carry out some socially organized action. This is intentional communication (e.g. pointing to desired object), for example, a baby points to balloon; his intent is to obtain the balloon.

At *11 months* of age, child starts giving response to about half of maternal verbal and non-verbal request.

At approximately *12 months* of age, the baby enters the locutionary stage as he/she begins to use true word to fill communicative functions established by gestures. Babies also learn to establish joint reference, or reference by establishing eye contact with the baby in the early months.

Dore (1975) focused on the *12-24 month* period where children used early words to signal communicative intent. Rather focusing on listener's reaction, Dore focused more upon children's intentions. These are:

— Requesting an answer (child: 'sheep?' Adult: Yes it's a sheep)

— Labelling (child is playing with a doll and labels 'mouth, nose,' etc.).

— Protesting ('no' and resisting).

— Greeting ('hi' 'bye').

— Practicing (language) answering (adult: 'what's this?' child: 'elephant').

— Calling/addressing ("daddy!").

— Requesting action (want milk).

— Repeating/imitating (child overhears and repeats the word "car').

Children can assume various roles, especially in their play. Roles require different styles of speaking called registers.

At *one year* of age, child is skilled at initiating a topic by a combination of glance, gestures, vocalization, and verbalization, but is limited to topics about the item that are physically present. Topics are maintained for only one or two turns.

At around *two years* of age, simultaneous talking during infancy between mother and child decrease significantly (Alias 1996) and develop alternative conversational pattern. Conversational turn taking between mother and child is smooth. Less than 5% of turns of either participant are interrupted by other partner. They are capable of using *"please"* at a softer tone. Contingent queries are nonverbal, such as showing a confused expression (Gale, 1981). They respond to request for clarification. The most common clarification strategy used is simple repetition. Two – five year old children use more commands with other preschoolers and more permission requests with older children. The child now, is capable of maintaining a topic which follows a pattern, such as question/answer.eg *"Do you like candy or ice-cream best"?* (Foster, 1981). The child is now able to use some attention getting words with gestures and rising intonation. The child tends to rely on less specific attention-getting forms such as *"hey"*. Request words such as *"more, want, and mine,"* problem statement such as "I'm tired and I'm hungry" and verbal routines are common in children of this age.

Two and half year old child can comprehend and produce I, you and he (Tanz,1980) Deictic words seem to be used indiscriminately, with a gesture to indicate meaning as there are no definitive boundaries between terms such as here, there, so that it's difficult to determine child concept.

The most basic form of stories develops after *two years* of age and occurs more frequently by *three and half, years* of age. The first level of *protonarrative, heaps* emerge by *30 months* of age.

Two to three year old child can make politeness distinctions based on the age or size, familiarity, role, territory, and rights of the listener. Young children use please in a request, especially if the listener is older or bigger, less familiar, in a dominant role, or possessor of an object or privilege desired (Ervin-Tripp and Gordon, 1986). Action request addressed to the child are likely to be answered with the action even when information is sought.

At the age of *three years*, the child begins to use some modal auxiliary verbs in indirect requests (could you give me a.............?), permissive directives (can/may I have a......?), and question directives (do you have a ......?). The level of proto narrative, sequence emerges around this age.

At *three and half, years* of age, three-fourth of child's utterance is on the established topic. Repetition is one tactic used to remain in the topic. By *three years* of age, children are able to determine the amount of information the listener needs (Bretherton and Beeghly, 1982).

At the age of *four years* 20 to 30% of child utterances consist of monologues. They are instances of private speech in which children simply talk to themselves. Pre-sleep monologue of many children consist of songs, sounds, bits of chitchat. Gradually child's monologue becomes more social. The child gets engaged in them when others are nearby; he or she will share a topic with the listener. Throughout preschool years, audible monologue behaviours declines with age, presupposition tools like "know, think, forget and remember are used correctly.

Child understands the use of presupposition verbs such as wish, guess and pretend. Is more skilled with indirect forms although still unsuccessful more than half of the time at getting someone else's attention (Ervin-Tripp et al, 1984).

The child become more aware of partner's point of view and role, and of the appropriate form of request and politeness required (D.Gordon, 1984).the child is able to respond correctly to forms such as "you should........,", "I'll be happy if you......"(Carrel,1981).

Mastery of deictic term *here/there* precedes mastery of *this/that*. Terms such as *in front of* and *in back of* are mastered by 4 years (Tanz, 1980).The level primitive narratives or centring, emerge around *four years* of age. He/she seems to gain a better awareness of the social aspect of conversation. Utterances addressed to conversational partners are clear, well formed, well adopted for listeners. The child demonstrates a form of motherese when addressing very young children. This indicates growing awareness of conversational roles. Children assume various roles in their play. Symbolic play in which child allow one thing to represent another, has been thought to be of particular importance. This reflects:

— Aware of pre-supposition,
— Use of elliptical responses,
— Uses of many affective utterances, discussing feelings and emotions.

Five year children recognize those indirect requests which are more polite. (McCloskey, 1986)

— Young children use questions and contingent queries, or request for clarification (What, Huh).
— Continue to use frequent repetition but change the topic frequently.
— The preschool child becomes increasingly adept at knowing what information to include, how to arrange it, and which particular lexical items and linguistic form to use.
— Increase use of explanation, and justification and their justification are self-contained statements such as "I need it", stop it, because I don't like it."

School Age and Adult Pragmatic Development

Six year old child can convey a simple story or recount a movie or television show, often in the form of long, rambling sequential accounts. According to S. Kemper, children's narratives become causality coherent. Causality involves description of intentions, emotions and thoughts and the use of connectives, such as because, as a result of, and since, to name a few. Children's stories describe motives for actions. The child uses the adverbial conjuncts *"now, then, so", and, though, although* disjuncts are rare. Generally respond to literal meaning. The *six* years old who is asked can you pass the cup?, may respond 'yes' but may not follow through.

Narratives of the *seven* year old typically involve a beginning, a problem, a plan to overcome the problem, and a resolution. Fiction narratives are increasingly clear after age *eight* (Peterson andMcCabe, 1983). Language function increases greatly with the demands of the classroom. Children are required to explain, express, describe, direct, imagine and predict outcomes. Social-perspective taking, the ability to understand and adopt varying points of view, is necessary for unsuccessful communication and is used to persuade, comfort and to be polite(bliss,1992) this occur between 7 to 9 years of age. By age 7, he or she acquires greater facility with indirect forms. Eg.*That's a beautiful shirtt, and it would go so well with my tan.* The school age child is more creative and more aware of social roles than the preschooler. He/she is also aware over politeness; he/she can be more polite to adults than to his/her peers (Parsons, 1980) they are more aware of others and he/she increasingly take their intentions into considerations (Ervin- Tripp 1986).

Eight year olds and adults recognize most non literal request for. The high schoolers now, can use language creatively in sarcasm, jokes, and double meaning. They also make deliberate use of metaphor and can explain natural phenomena (Ackerman, 1978).

The proportion of introduced topics maintained in subsequent turns increase with age, with most of the changes occurring from late elementary school to adulthood (Brinton and Fujiki, 1984). There will be a decrease in the number of different topics introduced or reintroduced, modifying the focus of the topic, as a means of gradually moving from one topic to another while maintaining some continuity in the conversation.

Conjuncts express a logical inessential relationship and are more common in conversation.eg. 'We were up whole night'. As a result of our effort, our group won the competition. Eight year old can be more polite to adults than to his peers (Parsons, 1980) they are more aware of others and he/she increasingly take their intentions into considerations (Ervin- Tripp 1986). Eight year olds and adults recognize most non literal request for actions (Ackerman, 1978). Development of conjuncts occurs gradually from school age to adulthood.

Nine years: Until age 9, the predominant repair strategy is repetition. The 9 year old clearly provide additional input for the listener, are capable of addressing the perceived source of a breakdown in communication by defining their terms providing more background contexts, and talking about the process of conversational repair (Brinton et al, 1986).

By age *eleven*, children are able to use utterance and context to infer the speaker's intent accurately.

By age *twelve* the youth has added *otherwise, anyway, therefore, and however* along with the disjuncts *really and probably...* The school age child is more creative and more aware of social roles than the preschooler. He/she is also aware that over politeness is inappropriate. Eight year old can be more polite to adults than to his peers (Parsons, 1980) they are more aware of others and he/she increasingly take their intentions into considerations (Ervin- Tripp 1986). Eight year olds and adults recognize most non literal request for actions (Ackerman, 1978)...

Beyond 12 yrs

- Learn to recognize and control supra-segmental aspects (e.g., intonation, stress), sty in appropriate physical distance from others (proxemics), and regulate discourse style.
- Situationally, non-verbal language, such as facial expression and body language is adjusted as well, depending on social and language contexts
- The adolescent is able to synthesize information rather than parrot what he or she has heard or read
- Skills in negotiation and persuasion develop further
- Can respond appropriately to idiomatic language
- Learn to make more subtle distinctions between communicative functions, example: promise and prediction
- Can assess the adequacy of communication and comment on where it has gone wrong
- Can read and extract information from books
- Topic of conversation extends into a abstract ideas

- Adapts style of speech to age, status and other variables related to listener develops appreciation and use of social conventions relating to facial expressions
- Gesture, posture, distance and eye contact.
- More proficient at using politeness as a strategy in communicating

The *later school years* and beyond: (*15 years and beyond*):

- Uses sarcasm and irony
- Develops use of non literal language, example; idiom, simile, metaphor
- Skills in negotiation and persuasion develop further
- Can respond appropriately to idiomatic language
- Learn to make more subtle distinctions between communicative functions, example: promise and prediction
- Can assess the adequacy of communication and comment on where it has gone wrong
- Can read and extract information from books
- Topic of conversation extends into a abstract ideas
- Adapts style of speech to age, status and other variables related to listener develops appreciation and use of social conventions relating to facial expressions
- Gesture, posture, distance and eye contact.
- More proficient at using politeness as a strategy in communicating.

Peer acceptance in a group and use of language that fosters peer solidarity is important for teenagers. However the social circles of high school broaden as they develop more independence and explore their interests. They adjust to part time work situations, begins to date other students under take on responsibilities in the home, school and other settings. These expanded opportunities afford teenagers experience assuming social rules and shaping new beliefs and attitudes.

The pragmatic development that categorizes the late school years reflects the broadening of experiences in new social realms and gradual shift from being a part of the peer group to becoming an independent individual older student adopt adult like styles, which becomes more refined with continued education.

Summary of School-age Children's Pragmatic Development

Age in years	Pragmatic Development
5	• Uses mostly direct requests • Repeats for repair • Begins to use gender topics
6	• Repeats with elaboration for repair • Uses adverbial conjuncts now, then, so, though; disjuncts rare
7	• Uses and understands most deictic terms • Narrative plots have beginning, end, problem, and resolution
8	• Sustains concrete topics • Recognizes non- literal meanings in indirect requests • Begins considering others' intentions
9	• Sustains topics through several turns • Addresses perceived source of breakdown in repair • Produces all elements of story grammar
11 12	• Sustains abstract topics 20% of narrative sentences still begin with *and* • Uses adverbial conjuncts (4/100 utterances) otherwise, anyway, therefore, and however, disjuncts really and probably
16-18	• Uses sarcasm and double meanings • Makes deliberate use of metaphors • Knows partner's perspective and knowledge differ from own

Pragmatics is a domain more like the lexicon, in which continued development can occur throughout the life span. Rash, Kemper and Sprott (1989) found that elderly speakers' narratives were more memorable and effective than those of younger, middle aged comparison groups. Continued growth in areas like politeness and communicative effectiveness is probably within the realm of possibility for most adults.

Pragmatic Development at a Glance

Birth to First Year

- *From the first week* - "Self-imitation", reflexive actions (cries) which are treated as meaningful by caregiver.
- *Second week*-Distinguishing of caregiver's voice and face.
- *By one month*- Short visual exchange with caregiver; prefers human face to all else.
- *Second month* -cooing.
- *By around 3 months,* the child begins to -
    - Briefly look at people
    - Follow moving persons with eyes
    - Quiets in response to sounds(responds more readily to speech than non speech sounds)
    - Smiles/coos in responds to another smile/voice(1-4 months)
    - Excites when caregivers approaches(1-4months)
    - Aware of strangers and unfamiliar situation(1-4months)
    - Cries differently when tired ,hungry, in pain(1-4months)
    - Quiets when picked up
- *By around 3-6 months* the child -
    - Fixes gaze on face
    - Responds to name by looking for voice source(4-8 months)

  - Regularly localizes sound source/speaker
  - Occasionally vocalizes in responds to speech
  - Child begin to uses gestures and the caregiver interprets the messages
- *By 9-12 months* the baby uses illocutionary behaviours - a signal to carry out some socially organized action.

  Eg: pointing to desired objects: If the child points to toy, he intended to obtain the toy. In addition to this, child develops:
  - Shouts and cough to attract attentions
  - Shakes head for "no"
  - Wave "bye"
  - Begins directing other's behaviors physically(pat, pulls, tugs on others)
- *By 11 months* response to about half of material verbal and non verbal request.
- *At approximately 12 months of age*, the baby enters locutionary stage as he/she begins to use true words to fill communicative functions established by gestures. Babies learn to established joint reference (involves shared attention and caregiver's utterances are focused on an object) in early months.
  - By 12 months (or so) most children have one or two words that they say with meaning and can comply with simple requests (e.g., 'Can I have your cup?') or commands (e.g., "Don't touch!") and understand little questions (e.g., 'Where's your tummy?').
  - Between the first and second birthday preschooler's conversation will mature in several ways.

Two-three Years

- During second year, three areas developed further in toddlers' conversations: Topic initiation, presupposition and turn taking.

- Child initiates topics by a combination of glance, gestures, vocalizations, and verbalizations but the topics are maintained only for one or two turns.
- Are capable of using "please" at a softer tone.
- Contingent queries are non verbal ,such as showing a confused expression(Gala, 1981).
- They respond to request for clarification .The most common clarification used is simple repetition.
- Child is capable of maintaining a topic which follows a pattern such as question and answer. Eg: Do you like candy or ice cream?
- Child uses some attention seeking words along with gestures and rising intonation Eg: "hey".
- Expresses emotions.
- The most basic form of stories develops after 2 years of age and occurs more. frequently by two and half years of age.

Three–Four Years

- Child now engages in longer dialogues.
- By age four, children assume various roles. Roles requiring different styles of speaking called registers.
- Competence of different registers varies with age and experience.

  Eg: family registers – exhibited in the ability to play various roles such as mother or baby. Roles outside family members - such as playing as nurse, teacher etc appears.
- Uses more filler to acknowledge partner's message, Eg: um-, huh, yeah, ok.
- Request permissions, eg: "Can I open this?"
- Begins uses language for fantasies, jokes and teasing.
- Child makes conversational repairs when listener has not understood.
- Primitive narratives emerge.

Four-five Years

- Uses indirect request.
- At the age of 4 years 20 to 30% of child's utterance consists of monologues. Monologues are instances of private speech in which children simply talk to themselves, eg: child who is playing with a toy aeroplane will verbalize.
- I want to fly, yeah, it'll be fun!
- Presupposition tools like "know, think, forget and remember are used correctly.
- Masterly of deictic term such as this, that, here, their.
- Demonstrate the form of mothers when addressing young children.
- Symbolic play (child allows one thing to represent another), eg: use a 'block' to represent 'car'.
- Child uses many effective utterances, discussing feeling and emotions.

Five to Six Years

- Now children can convey a simple story or recount a movie or television show, often in the form of long, rambling sequential accounts.
- Causality involves description of intensions, emotions and thoughts and use of connectives such as because, as a result of, and since.
- Gives threats and insults.
- Issues promises.
- May give praises.
- Child is more creative and aware of social roles.

Six to Seven Years

- True narratives developed narrative plots and character with sequences events.

Eight years

- Sustains concrete topics.
- Recognize non-literal meanings in indirect request.
- Begins considering others intentions.

Nine Years

- Sustain topics through several turns.
- Addresses perceived source of breakdown in repair.
- The 9 year old clearly provide additional input for the listener, are capable of addressing the perceived source of a breakdown in communication by defining their terms providing more background context , and talking about the process of conversational repair (Brinton etal,1986).

Eleven Years

- Sustains abstract topics 20% of narrative sentences still begin with *and*.
- By the age of eleven, children are able to use the utterance and context to interfere the speaker's intent accurately.

Beyond Twelve Years

- Uses adverbial conjuncts (otherwise, anyway, therefore, and however) and disjuncts.
- As they enter teenage years, students adopt several verbal and nonverbal strategies to communicate effectively in different social situations.
- Learn to recognize and control supra-segments aspects (eg: intonation, stress), stay in appropriate physical distance from others (proxemics) and regulate discourse style.
- Situationally, non verbal language, such as facial expression and body language is adjusted well, depending on social and language context.

- Students learn to recite, tell about, explain, answer, discuss, listen, write, read and apply information in individual, small group and apply information in individual, small group and large group situations.
- They also learn to employ self –regulatory techniques such as inner speech and self-appreciation strategies.
- Can read and extract information from books.
- More proficient at using politeness as a strategy in communicating.
- As the social circles of the high school broaden as they develop more independence and explore their interest.

Pragmatic development is a domain more like the domain more like the lexicon, in which continued development can occur throughout the life span. Rash, Kemper and Sprott (1989) found that elderly speakers' narratives were more memorable and more effective than those of younger, middle and comparison group. Continued growth in areas like politeness and effectiveness is probably within the realm of possibility for most adult.

Clinical Implication

- Various tests are developed by considering the normal pragmatic development (Test of pragmatic skill).
- Only by knowing the normal pragmatic development, an SLP can go in pace with the treatment of children who exhibit difficulties in pragmatic skills.

Pragmatic Disability

Pragmatic disability is used to refer to the problems that a person experiences in using language to communicate. The affected person has little difficulty with language form, but have difficulty using and understanding language in communicative situations.

Types of Pragmatic Disability/Impairment

Classification scheme based on Perkins (2002):

Types of pragmatic impairment	Underlying cause
Primary pragmatic impairment	Cognitive dysfunction • Inference • Executive function • Memory • Emotion and attitude
Secondary pragmatic impairment	(a) Linguistic dysfunction • Phonology • Morphology • Syntax • Semantics • Prosody • Discourse (b) Sensorimotor dysfunction • Auditory perception • Visual perception • Motor/Articulatory ability
Complex pragmatic impairment	Multiple sources

Before discussing these types in detail, we must be aware of the concept of *Theory of Mind*.

Concept of Theory of Mind (TOM)

Alsc :eferred to as mind reading, is a term used to describe the ability to attribute mental states such as beliefs, intentions and feelings to others, and to explain and predict the actions that derive from them (Baron and Cohen, 1995). Eg: If A sees B hide a ball under a cup, but doesn't see B subsequently remove the ball and put it in his pocket , we assume that A still thinks the ball is under the cup. However children under the age of 4 and many people with autism will often intimate that A thinks the ball is in B's pocket, and are thus judged not to have developed a ToM.

Impairment and its consequences: the condition most commonly associated with theory of mind is autism and then RHD (Champagne et al 2003).

An inability to appreciate and engage in communicative activities such as pretending, joking and humour generally has been linked to ToM difficulties.

Inference

Key cognitive process involved in pragmatics by linguist, psycholinguist and neurologists. Inference means how we draw conclusions.

Impairment: Breakdown in the ability to draw inference is most commonly seen in autism, right hemisphere damage (RHD), traumatic brain injury (TBI), specific language impairment (SLI). The manifestation of poor inferential reasoning in communicative problems include difficulties in understanding sarcasm, irony, indirect request, punch lines of jokes, ambiguous utterances, etc

Executive Function

It is a term used to collectively describe a range of higher cognitive processes such as planning, goal setting, monitoring, evaluating, sequencing organizing, reasoning, problem solving, decision making, etc.

Impairment: Associated with damage to the frontal lobes of the brain. It is seen as a major contributory factor in ADHD (Attention deficit hyperactive disorder), autism etc.

Memory

Memory plays a vital role in executive function and on inferential reasoning.

Impairment: Poor communicative interaction resulting from memory impairment has been reported in Alzheimer's disease, amnesia, aphasia, autism etc.

Emotion and Attitude

Our ability to entertain, display and recognize emotions and attitude is a crucial part in pragmatics. Eg: Autism-difficulty to read the emotions and attitude in others facial expression.

Characteristics of Persons Described as Having Pragmatic Disability

Main characteristics of persons described as having pragmatic disability [Rapin and Allen (1983), Bishop and Rosenbloom (1989)] are:

- Early history may include echolalia, jargon, poor symbolic skills, poor social relationships and hyperactivity.
- Delayed speech and language development, but once language develops it appears clean and fluent with syntax and phonology developing fairly normally but with problems with semantics and pragmatics. Eg:
    1. Odd associations and reasoning.
    2. Tangential or inappropriate remarks.
    3. Undue attention to literal rather underlying meaning.
    4. Problems in understanding normal conversation. Eg: descriptions of sequences of everyday events that are related temporally or causally.
    5. Lack of awareness of what knowledge is shared between speaker and hearer.
- Poor social skills- either withdrawn or eccentric or over friendly.

Identification of Pragmatic Disability

Pragmatic disability can be identified on the basis of following disordered skills:

1. Difficulties in communication intentions or speech acts
2. Difficulties in presupposition
3. Difficulties in organization of discourse. Problem in-
    - Topic initiation
    - Topic maintenance and topic changing

- Topic closure
- Off target responding
- Tangentiality
- Topic identification problems
- Turn taking
- Repairs and revisions

Difficulties in Communication Intentions or Speech Acts

Speech acts are often cited as a prime example of pragmatic ability. Speech acts are concerned with the functions rather than the forms of language. The ability to use and understand speech acts depends on both linguistic and pragmatic skills. While analyzing a speech act two aspects are particularly important.

1. Whether the child can interpret the intention expressed by an utterance, especially when the literal meaning is not the intended one (involves comprehension of direct and indirect speech acts). Checking the *Linguistic Competence.*
2. Whether the child is aware of the appropriate use of speech acts in different conversational contexts. (Ability to produce a particular linguistic form that is appropriate to the situation- the task at hand, social characteristics of the addressee, make judgements about the appropriacy of speech act made by another person). Checking the *Pragmatic Competence.*

Eg: *"Would you mind shutting the door?"* (Question or Request)

It has been frequently reported that language impaired children may use a restricted range of speech acts. They fail to use language to describe and inform spontaneously instead they use language mainly to direct the listener's attention. That is, most of the time they are non assertive in conversation and their contributions are limited to back channel responses like verbal and nonverbal responses such as 'umm', nodding, which indicate attention without taking the conversational initiative.

The reason for this non assertiveness may be that the child has linguistic deficiencies that make responding in conversation and maintaining an ongoing topic or introducing a new topic problematic. The adoption of passive role in conversation could be a consequence of poor comprehension skills. An inability to understand the messages of their partners would make conversational participation difficult for these children.

Difficulties in Presupposition

One problem that exists in the area of presupposition is not providing sufficient information (lack of specificity or accuracy) for a message to be understood. There are following types of difficulties observed:

- A person with disability often doesn't supply enough information. The listener must then ask additional question in order to understand the message.

  Eg: A 9 year old boy who calls the office where his mom works and asks *"is my mom there?"*

  They assume that listener has the same knowledge as that of the speaker does.

- If too much of information is given for the listener/ speaker relationship, redundancy can occur. In a case where a great deal of information is shared, less specificity is required.

  Eg: If Tom and Harry had been going out to dinner on every Saturday at 8.00 pm from past 2 months to the same restaurant, Tom may simply say *"We're on for Saturday"* or *"let's meet on Saturday"* instead of *"we need to meet at 8.00 pm at The Hotel Green so we can have our dinner"*.

- They may have a very difficult time taking another's point of view. So they will have problems with quality or quantity of information they give.

Eg: An 8 year old boy having learning disability, telling someone who has not seen the movie, - *"What the movie 'Look who's talking' was about"*.

- They will not be able to make the language adjustments according to the age and social status.

  Eg: *"Get out of here"* may not be perceived as friendly if it is said to a peer, but the same child making the statement to a teacher may lead to a serious consequence.

The amount of information that is explicitly given will depend on the listener and the relationship of that listener to the speaker. If a person is not understood, it may be for reasons related to presupposition.

Difficulty in Organization of Discourse

Topic Related Problems:

Topic management skills encompass topic choice, initiation, maintenance and change. These skills will be dependent on semantic and syntactic proficiency. Problems in one component area may be the result of or compounded by deficiencies in other component areas.

There are appropriate and inappropriate times to discuss a topic. Certain topics should not be spoken about with certain people. Some students with disabilities appear to have difficulty learning these skills. They may select topics that have nothing to do with what else is going on. Hence, topic choice will influence both peer and adult interaction.

1. Topic initiation: Children with disabilities may not initiate topics and social activities appropriately because of poor verbal skills. It may be difficult for them to form a sentence and find vocabulary. Many students have sufficient language, but seem to not know how to use it. Several studies have shown that children with disabilities initiate conversations much less frequently than their peers.

Eg: when a child wants to join a group of children playing outside, the appropriate language or approach would be "Hi, what are you doing? Can I play too?" instead if the child takes the ball and hits one of the children on their head it would hurt and inevitably end up with a lot of negative feedback from the group.

2. *Topic Maintenance and Topic Change:* Mentis (1994) discussed topic maintenance in terms of local cohesion and global cohesion.

- Local cohesion involves a relationship of 1 sentence to the previous one.
- Global cohesion is the relationship of the sentences to the topic.

Example 1: Yesterday we looked at a house we wanted to buy. It had a wonderful garden with lots of fruit trees. I love fruit. I go to Farmer's market every Saturday morning to get the best fruit available. Sally also goes to Farmer's market. She's an old friend. We went to college together. Our reunion was last month. It was in California. The weather there is really lovely at this time of year.

Example 2: Yesterday we looked at a house we wanted to buy. The renovations will cost a lot. The estate agent will let us know on Monday. It had a very modern kitchen. We'll never go to that bank again for a mortgage. Our son will love the garden.

The first example is locally coherent but not globally coherent, that is, all of the sentences are linked to each other but not to topic.

In contrast, in the second example, all of the sentences are linked to the topic but the speaker does not link one sentence to another.

Example 3: Students are in cafeteria queue, making comments:

S1: What are you having?

S2: Noodles.

S3: (a student with disability) (In queue, listening).

S1: I am going to have ice cream.

S3: It's raining.

It appears that the last comment has nothing to do with the conversation in progress. There is lack of transition. The example stated above demonstrates knowledge of turn taking and a real desire to speak, but little knowledge of the rules of topic maintenance.

Topic can be maintained through *different strategies*:

1. *Repetition strategy*—This involves the repetition of the previous utterance in whole or part. It maintains the topic but contributes little to the prepositional development of the topic.
2. *Enhancement strategy*—This would elaborate, extend and develop the topic by providing novel information.

Researchers have found that children with language delays are more likely to use repetition strategy or stereotypic responses (okay, uh huh), strategies that do not develop the topic but do maintain it.

Difficulty in other conversational skills

Lucas (1980) suggested some other problems related to conversation/discourse are:

Topic related problems:

(a) *Topic Closure Difficulties*: The problem involves rephrasing, rewording, or reiterating, because the speaker does not know when to quit. Eg: Mohan, 11: when I was out of the store when it was stolen somebody must have put I in a truck because we were only in there for a few minutes and there was nobody in the sight when we went in there and I don't see how somebody can ride that fast cause there was nobody in sight.......

(b) *Off-Target Responding*: This is a response that is not the one that is expected in the context. The student is unaware of being off target and may find the information too complex to respond to, so changes the topic. Eg: Ramu, 8 (after raising his hand in response to teacher's asking if anyone has to go to the bathroom): Mrs. K, if I study I can pass my spelling test...

(c) *Tangentiality*: In this response, the student hears the topic, associates it with something else, and goes on to that topic. It is sometimes difficult to recognize the association. Eg: Shila, 8, when asked why she was late to school: My mom has a new car. (It turns out that she was late because she missed the bus and so her mom, who has a new car, brought her to school.)

(d) *Topic Identification Problems:* These are evidenced by responses that are related to the previous question or statement, but not to the main topic. The child listens and is attempting to respond appropriately, but cannot determine the correct referent. This student will try again and may appear frustrated, unlike the off-target responder. Eg: Nilu, 8th grade, in response to "why is it important to ask questions about something before buying it?" How much will it cost?

(2) Turn-Taking:

Individuals who have difficulty with turn-taking are often perceived as rude, because they do not follow discourse rules related to turn-taking. They may interrupt the speaker or monopolize the conversation. This inability to follow rules of turn -taking may show up in other areas as well. So they don't respond to verbal initiations by others as frequently as typically developing peers do. During turn taking, Sentence internal overlaps can be seen. This occurs when one person starts to speak after the other person has said a few words but has not completed his turn.

Eg. 1: *Adult: We will go to nanny's place....*
Child: I want to eat pizza.

Here the underlined part indicates overlap which is due to interruption. The child begins to speak without taking into account of the turn in progress. Here, the child introduces which is not related to the content of the adult's turn.

Eg. 2: *Adult: We will go to nanny's place....*

Child: I don't want to go.

Here the overlap is related to adult's context, but the interruption occurs before the adult can complete his turn. Craig and Evans (1989) said that these overlaps are mainly seen in language impaired groups. They also said that linguistic ability is required to understand the form and meaning of the adult's utterance. They also reported that language impaired children did not have the encoding and decoding skills necessary to make appropriate points in the conversation and that they seemed to be still processing the previous sentence information when they interrupted.

Eg: *Adult: Do you need some more chocolates?*

I have asked Sam (brother) to get more.

Child: No

(3) Repair and Revisions:

Many students with disabilities will not repair or revise their language when needed [that is misunderstanding has occurred]. This may result from 2 problems:

(i) They do not always recognize that a repair is needed, because they don't pickup cues that the listener does not understood them.

(ii) They rephrase the sentence or reemphasize the point exactly the same way. (If misunderstanding is due to problems with presupposition, a reinstatement of the original statement will not increase the likelihood of understanding).

Conversely, as a listener, they find difficulties to let the speaker know when they do not understand a message. One reason for this is that they do not always realize that they do not understand. Another reason may be because these students have received so much negative feedback for asking questions and letting people know they don't understand that they quit trying.

S: Raises hand and states he doesn't he doesn't understand.

T: what do you mean you don't understand? I just explained it. We did this yesterday.

Pragmatic disability in some of the disorders

Autism

For children with autism, the use of language for communication purpose remains severe in spite of developments in other language areas. Most children with autism do not develop a range of communicative functions and as a result their communicative and social interactions are limited. They have problem in:

- *Initiating and terminating interaction*- they seem to be deficient in the use of appropriate attention- getting devices such as establishing eye contact etc. they fail to appreciate the conversation such as the need to get the listener's attention, etc.
- Maintaining conversational topics
- Turn taking difficulties
- Using appropriate non-verbal behaviour for the purpose of communication such as eye contact.
- Seldom recognize the need for repairs and also seldom ask for clarifications.

ADHD

DSM IV has listed up the pragmatic features for diagnostic criteria which are as follows:

- Often does not seem to listen when spoken to directly.
- Is often distracted by extraneous stimuli.
- Often talks excessively

- Often blurts out answers before question has been completed.
- Often has difficulty waiting for his/her turn.
- Often interrupts or intrudes on others.

Specific Language Impairment

- They do not use interruptions to gain the turn at speaking.
- Responses to requests for clarification are structurally diffuse.
- Responses to other types of speech acts are likely to be unrelated, inappropriate and variable.
- Demonstrate significantly greater rate of communication breakdowns for narration than for dialogue.

Children with Hearing Impairment

- Hearing impaired children have difficulties in introducing a topic of conversation or in shifting from one topic to another during conversation, because they do not sufficiently consider the needs of the listener (Moeller et al. 1983).
- Problem in the development of communication repair strategies.
- According to Hedge, persons who are hearing impaired may not know how to use the learned language in natural social situations. The following pragmatic communication problems are likely:
  (1) Reluctance to speak
  (2) Limited communication
  (3) Inappropriate speech to the situation or topic.

Aphasia

- *Speech acts and intents*- Aphasic patients have a relatively preserved ability to interpret a variety of speech acts and intents, including the ability to respond correctly to indirect requests but they use a restricted range of speech acts and intents.

- *Topic initiation*-For some aphasic patients, inappropriate initiation is observed. However, they are reported to be relatively good at being sensitive to their partner's interests and previous knowledge (Penn, 1988).
- *Turn taking*– Most aphasic patients rely primarily upon the use of non-verbal behaviours such as nodding or eye gaze (Penn, 1988).
- *Repair and revisions*-The linguistic impairments of the aphasic patients may limit their ability to identify communication breakdowns, to repair them, or both.
- *Maintenance of topic*-Mildly affected aphasic patients frequently demonstrate appropriate discourse maintenance skills, but severe aphasics have been found to produce somewhat lengthy or tangential responses (Penn, 1988).

Bibliography

Akmajian Adrian, Demers A. Richard, Farmer A. Ann, Harnish M. Robert. (1995). Linguistics-An Introduction to Language and Communication (Fourth edition). MIT Press, Cambridge, MA, U.S.A.

Anderson, John M.; and Ewen, Colin J. (1987). Principles of Dependency Phonology. Cambridge: Cambridge University Press.

Anderson, Stephen R. (1992). A-Morphous Morphology. Cambridge: CUP.

Aronoff, Mark. (1993). "Morphology by Itself". Cambridge, MA: MIT Press.

Austin, J. L. (1962) How to Do Things with Words. Oxford University Press.

Baker, Mark C. (2001). The Atoms of Language: The Mind's Hidden Rules of Grammar. New York: Basic Books.

Bakhtin, M. M. (1981) The Dialogic Imagination: Four Essays. Ed. Michael Holquist. Trans. Caryl Press.

Ball, Martin J., Michael R. Perkins, Nicole Müller and Sara Howard (eds). (2008). The Handbook of Clinical Linguistics. Blackwell Publishing Blackwell Reference Online.

Barbara Scholz and Geoffrey Pullum (2006). Robert J. Stainton. ed. "Irrational Nativist Exuberance". Contemporary Debates in Cognitive Science (Oxford /Basil Blackwell): 59–80.

Barnes, Douglas (1971), Language and Learning in the Classroom, Journal of Curriculum Studies. 3:1

Barsalou, L. (1999). Perceptual Symbol Systems. Behavioral and Brain Sciences 22(4)

Bates, E. and Elman, J. and Johnson, M. and Karmiloff-Smith, A. and Parisi, D. and Plunkett, K. (1998). Innateness and Emergentism. A Companion to Cognitive Science (Oxford /Basil Blackwell): 590–601.

Bauer, Laurie. (2003). Introducing Linguistic Morphology (2nd ed.). Washington, D.C.: Georgetown University Press.

Bauer, Laurie. (2004). A Glossary of Morphology. Washington, D.C.: Georgetown UP.

Beard, Robert. (1995). Lexeme-Morpheme Base Morphology. Albany, N.Y.: State University of New York Press.

Bloch, Bernard. (1941). Phonemic Overlapping. American Speech, 16, 278-284.

Bloomfield, Leonard. (1933). Language. New York: H. Holt and Company. (Revised Version of Bloomfield's 1914 An Introduction to the Study of Language).

Bourdieu, Pierre. (1977). Outline of a Theory of Practice. Cambridge University Press.

Brentari, Diane (1998). A Prosodic Model of Sign Language Phonology. Cambridge, MA: MIT Press.

Brian MacWhinney, ed (1999). The Emergence of Language. Lawrence Erlbaum Associates.

Brown, Penelope and Levinson, Stephen (1978), Universals in Language Usage: Politeness Phenomena, pp 56–289 in Goody, Esther [ed] Questions and Politeness. Cambridge University Press. Reprinted Separately in 1987 as Politeness: Some Universals in Language Usage.

Brown, Roger and Camile Hanlon. (1970). Derivational Complexity and Order of Acquisition in Child Speech. In Cognition and the Development of Language, ed. J. R. Hayes. New York: Wiley

Bubenik, Vit. (1999). An Introduction to the Study of Morphology. LINCON Coursebooks in Linguistics, 07. Muenchen: LINCOM Europa.

Carston, Robyn (2002) Thoughts and Utterances: The Pragmatics of Explicit Communication. Oxford: Blackwell.

Chomsky Noam (1959). A Review of B. F. Skinner's Verbal Behavior. Language, 35: 26-58.

Chomsky, N. (1975). Reflections on Language. New York: Pantheon Books

Chomsky, N. and Halle, Morris. (1968). The Sound Pattern of English. New York: Harper & Row.

Clark, Herbert H. (1996). Using Language. Cambridge University Press.

Clements, George N. (1985). The Geometry of Phonological Features. Phonology Yearbook, 2, 225-252.

Clements, George N.; and Samuel J. Keyser. (1983). CV Phonology: A Generative Theory of the Syllable. Linguistic Inquiry Monographs (No. 9). Cambridge, MA: MIT Press.

Coates, Jennifer (1987), Epistemic Modality and Spoken Discourse, Transactions of the Philological Society, 110-31.

Cohen, Anthony P. (1985). The Symbolic Construction of Community. Routledge: New York,

Cole, Peter, ed.. (1978) Pragmatics. (Syntax and Semantics, 9). New York: Academic Press.

Crain, Stephen and Diane C. Lillo-Martin (1999). An Introduction to Linguistic Theory and Language Acquisition. Oxford: Blackwell.

Cruise, Alan (2000). Meaning and Language: An Introduction to Semantics and Pragmatics, Palgrave MacMillan.

Cruise, D.A. (1986) Lexical Semantics. Cambridge.

Crystal, D. (2001). Clinical Linguistics. In M. Aronoff & J. Rees-Miller, The Blackwell Handbook of Linguistics (Oxford: Blackwell), 673-82.

Culler, Jonathan. (1976). Saussure. Fontana.

Culler, Jonathan. (2000). Literary Theory: A Very Short Introduction. Oxford: Oxford University Press.

Cummings, L. (2008). Clinical Linguistics, Edinburgh: Edinburgh University Press Ltd.

de Lacy, Paul. (2007). The Cambridge Handbook of Phonology. Cambridge University Press.

Dijk, Teun A. van. (1977) Text and Context. Explorations in the Semantics and Pragmatics of Discourse. London: Longman.

Dixon, R. M. W. and Aikhenvald, Alexandra Y. (Eds). (2007). Word: A cross-linguistic typology. Cambridge: Cambridge University Press

Dorval, Bruce (1990), Conversational Organization and its Development, Ablex, Norwood, NJ.

Dubois, Sylvie and Hovarth, Barbara. (1998) “Let’s tink about dat: Interdental Fricatives in Cajun English,” Language Variation and Change, 10 (3), pp 245–61.

Duranti, Alessandro. (1997). “Linguistic Anthropology”. Cambridge University Press.

Eagleton, Terry. (1999). Literary Theory: An Introduction. Blackwell Publishers.

Firth, J. R. (1948). Sounds and Prosodies. Transactions of the Philological Society 1948, 127-152.

Fodor, J. (1975). The Language of Thought. Harvard University Press.

Foley, William A. (1998). “Symmetrical Voice Systems and Precategoriality in Philippine Languages”. Workshop: Voice and Grammatical Functions in Austronesian. University of Sydney.

Fromkin, Victoria; Bruce Hayes; Susan Curtiss, Anna Szabolcsi, Tim Stowell, Donca Steriade (2000). Linguistics: An Introduction to Linguistic Theory. Oxford: Blackwell. p. 3.

Gilbers, Dicky; and de Hoop, Helen. (1998). Conflicting Constraints: An Introduction to Optimality Theory. Lingua, 104, 1-12.

Glisan, E.W., & Schrum, J.L. (2010). Teacher's Handbook Contextualized Language Instruction. Boston, MA: Heinle.

Goldsmith, John A (1995). "Phonological Theory". in John A. Goldsmith. The Handbook of Phonological Theory. Blackwell Handbooks in Linguistics. Blackwell Publishers.

Goldsmith, John A. (1979). The Aims of Autosegmental Phonology. In D. A. Dinnsen (Ed.), Current Approaches to Phonological Theory (pp. 202-222). Bloomington: Indiana University Press.

Goldsmith, John A. (1989). Autosegmental and Metrical Phonology: A New Synthesis. Oxford: Basil Blackwell.

Goodall, J. (1986). The Chimpanzees of Gombe: Patterns of Behavior. Cambridge, MA: Belknap Press of Harvard University Press.

Grice, H. Paul. (1989) Studies in the Way of Words. Cambridge (MA): Harvard University Press.

Grice, Paul. "Logic and Conversation". Perspectives in the Philosophy of Language. (2000) ed. Robert Stainton.

Gussenhoven, Carlos & Jacobs, Haike. "Understanding Phonology", Hodder & Arnold, 1998. 2nd edition 2005.

Hall, T. Allen. 2001. Phonological Representations and Phonetic Implementation of Distinctive Features, Mouton de Gruyter.

Halle, Morris. 1983. On Distinctive Features and their Articulatory Implementation, Natural Language and Linguistic Theory, p. 91 - 105

Harris, Roy. (1987). Reading Saussure: A Critical Commentary on the Cours de Linguistique générale. La Salle, Illinois: Open Court.

Harris, Zellig. (1951). Methods in Structural Linguistics. Chicago: Chicago University Press.

Haspelmath, Martin. (2002). Understanding Morphology. London: Arnold (co-published by Oxford University Press).

Hockett, Charles F. (1955). A Manual of Phonology. Indiana University Publications in Anthropology and Linguistics, Memoirs II. Baltimore: Waverley Press.

Hooper, Joan B. (1976). An Introduction to Natural Generative Phonology. New York: Academic Press.

Hoult, T. F., ed. (1969). Dictionary of Modern Sociology. Totowa, New Jersey, United States: Littlefield, Adams & Co.

International Phonetic Association (1999) Handbook of the International Phonetic Association. Cambridge University Press.

Jakobson, Roman, Gunnar Fant, and Morris Halle. 1976. Preliminaries to Speech Analysis: The Distinctive Features and their Correlates, MIT Press.

Jakobson, Roman. (1949). On the Identification of Phonemic Entities. Travaux du Cercle Linguistique de Copenhague, 5, 205-213.

Jakobson, Roman; Fant, Gunnar; and Halle, Morris. (1952). Preliminaries to Speech Analysis: The Distinctive Features and their Correlates. Cambridge, MA: MIT Press.

Jaroslav Peregrin. (2003). Meaning: The Dynamic Turn. Current Research in the Semantics/Pragmatics Interface. London: Elsevier.

Kaisse, Ellen M.; and Shaw, Patricia A. (1985). On the Theory of Lexical Phonology. In E. Colin and J. Anderson (Eds.), Phonology Yearbook 2 (pp. 1-30).

Karanth, P. (2003). Introduction. In P. Karanth & J. Rozario, (Eds), Learning Disabilities in India: Willing the Mind to Learn (pp.17-29). New Delhi: Sage Publications India Pvt Ltd.

Katamba, Francis. (1993). Morphology. Modern Linguistics Series. New York: St. Martin's Press

Kepa Korta and John Perry. (2006) Pragmatics. The Stanford Encyclopedia of Philosophy.

Kim, Uichol (2001). "Culture, Science and Indigenous Psychologies: An Integrated Analysis." In D. Matsumoto (Ed.), Handbook of Culture and Psychology. Oxford: Oxford University Press

Kingston, John. (2007). The Phonetics-Phonology Interface, in The Cambridge Handbook of Phonology (ed. Paul DeLacy), Cambridge University Press.

Labov, William (1966), The Social Stratification of English in New York City, Diss. Washington.

Ladefoged, Peter & Ian Maddieson (1996) The Sounds of the World's Languages. Oxford: Blackwell.

Ladefoged, Peter (1975) A Course in Phonetics. Orlando: Harcourt Brace. 5th ed. Boston: Thomson/Wadsworth 2006.

Ladefoged, Peter. (1982). A Course in Phonetics (2nd ed.). London: Harcourt Brace Jovanovich.

Lakoff, R. (1975). Language and Women's Place. New York: Harper & Row.

Lakoff, Robin T. (2000). The Language War. Berkely, CA: University of California Press.

Laurence R. Horn and Gregory Ward. (2005) The Handbook of Pragmatics. Blackwell.

Leech, Geoffrey N. (1983) Principles of Pragmatics. London: Longman.

Leet-Pellegrini, Helena M. (1980) Conversational Dominance as a Function of Gender and Expertise, pp. 97–104 in Giles, Howard, Robinson, W. Peters, and Smith, Philip M [eds] Language: Social Psychological Perspectives. Oxford: Pergamon Press.

Lenneberg, Eric. (1967). Biological Foundations of Language. New York: Wiley.

Levinson, Stephen C. (1983) Pragmatics. Cambridge University Press.

Levinson, Stephen C. (2000). Presumptive Meanings: The Theory of Generalized Conversational Implicature. MIT Press.

Lyons, John. (1977). (Reprinted in 1996). Semantics, Volume I and II. CUP, Cambridge.

Martinet, André. (1949). Phonology as Functional Phonetics. Oxford: Blackwell.

Matthews, Peter. (1991). Morphology (2nd ed.). CUP.

McLaughlin, Scott. (1998). Introduction to Language Development. Singular Publishing Group, USA.

Mel'èuk, Igor A. (2006). Aspects of the Theory of Morphology. Berlin: Mouton.

Mey, Jacob L. (1993) Pragmatics: An Introduction. Oxford: Blackwell (2nd ed. 2001).

Miller GA. (1977). Spontaneous Apprentices: Children and Language. New York, Seabury Press.

Nakra, O. (1996). Children and Learning Difficulties, New Delhi: Allied Publishers Ltd.

Napoli, Donna Jo (1996). Linguistics: An Introduction. New York: Oxford University Press.

Narang, Vaishna. (2006). Contemporary Themes and Issues in Language Pedagogy, Books Plus, New Delhi.

———— (2009). Acquisition Studies on Indian Bilingual Children. Vol. I. Report of the Project on Mapping, Language, Mind & Brain: Studies in Biolinguistics. Project sponsored by JNU under University with Potential for Excellence Scheme of the UGC, 2002-2007. Yash Publications, New Delhi.

———————— (2009). Communication Disorders: Studies on Aphasia, Acalculia and Dysarthria. Vol. II. Report of the Project on Mapping, Language, Mind & Brain: Studies in Biolinguistics. Project sponsored by JNU under University with Potential for Excellence Scheme of the UGC, 2002-2007. Yash Publications, New Delhi.

Nida, E.A. (1946). Morphology (2nd Ed), The University of Michigan Press, Canada, US.

Nielson, Hanne Riis; Nielson, Flemming (1995), Semantics with Applications, A Formal Introduction (1st ed.), Chicester, England: John Wiley & Sons.

O'Grady, William et al (2005). Contemporary Linguistics: An Introduction (5th ed.). Bedford/St. Martin's.

Otto Neurath (Editor), Rudolf Carnap (Editor), Charles F. W. Morris (Editor) (1955). International Encyclopedia of Unified Science. Chicago, IL: University of Chicago Press.

P. Gardenfors. (2000). Conceptual Spaces. Cambridge, MA: MIT Press/ Bradford Books.

Pamela Grunwell (1987) Clinical Phonology (2nd edition). London: Croom Helm, Pp. 311.

Pike, Kenneth. (1947). Phonemics: A Technique for Reducing Languages to Writing. Ann Arbor: University of Michigan Press.

Pinker, Steven (1994). The Language Instinct: How the Mind Creates Language. New York: Harper Collins.

Potts, Christopher. (2005) The Logic of Conventional Implicatures. Oxford Studies in Theoretical Linguistics. Oxford: Oxford University Press.

Radford Andrew, Atkinson Martin, Britain David, Clahsen Harlad, Spencer Andrew. (1999). Linguistics: An Introduction. CUP, Cambridge.

Ronald W. Langacker. (1999). Grammar and Conceptualization. Berlin/ New York: Mouton de Gruyer.

Sacks et al. (1974) A Simple Systematics for the Organization of Turn-taking for Conversation, Language 50:696-735.

Saussure, Ferdinand de. (2001). Course in General Linguistics. Eds. Charles Bally and Albert Sechehaye. Trans. Roy Harris. La Salle, Illinois: Open Court.

Scalise, Sergio. (1983). Generative Morphology, Dordrecht, Foris.

Shyamala K.C. (2010). Language Disorders in Children. Clinical Linguistics Series-I, CIIL Publications, Mysore.

.... (2010). Bilingual Aphasia. AIISH, Mysore.

..................(2009). *Acquisition/Development of Language and Speech (Chapter).* Self-Learning Material for DHLS Program in Speech-Language Pathology (3rd Edition), AIISH, Mysore.

.........................(2009). *Disorders of Speech and Language (Chapter).* Self-Learning Material for DHLS Program in Speech-Language Pathology (3rd Edition), AIISH, Mysore.

.........................(2009). *Prevention and Early Identification of Communication (Chapter).* Self-Learning Material for DHLS Program in Speech-Language Pathology (3rd Edition), AIISH, Mysore.

Singh, Rajendra and Stanley Starosta (eds). (2003). Explorations in Seamless Morphology. SAGE Publications.

Skoyles JR. (1998). Speech Phones are a Replication Code. Med Hypotheses. 50(2):167-73.

Spencer, Andrew and Zwicky, Arnold M. (Eds.) (1998). The Handbook of Morphology. Blackwell Handbooks in Linguistics. Oxford: Blackwell.

Spencer, Andrew. (1991). Morphological Theory: An Introduction to Word Structure in Generative Grammar. No. 2 in Blackwell Textbooks in Linguistics. Oxford: Blackwell.

Sperber, Dan and Wilson, Deirdre. (2005) Pragmatics. In F. Jackson and M. Smith (eds.) Oxford Handbook of Contemporary Philosophy. OUP, Oxford, 468-501.

Stampe, David. (1979). A Dissertation on Natural Phonology. New York: Garland.

Steven C. Hayes, Dermot Barnes-Holmes, Brian Roche, ed (2001). Relational Frame Theory: A Post-Skinnerian Account of Human Language and Cognition (Hardcover). Plenum Press.

Stump, Gregory T. (2001). Inflectional Morphology: A Theory of Paradigm Structure. No. 93 in Cambridge Studies in Linguistics. CUP.

Swadesh, Morris. (1934). The Phonemic Principle. Language, 10, 117-129.

Thomas, Jenny (1995) Meaning in Interaction: An Introduction to Pragmatics. Longman.

The Social Organization of Doctor-Patient Communication, Center for Applied Linguistics, Washington D.C.

Trager, George L.; and Bloch, Bernard. (1941). The Syllabic Phonemes of English. Language, 17, 223-246.

Twaddell, William F. (1935). On Defining the Phoneme. Language monograph no. 16. Language.

Van Valin, Robert D., and La Polla, Randy. (1997). Syntax: Structure, Meaning and Function. CUP.

Verschueren, Jef, Jan-Ola Östman, Jan Blommaert, eds. (1995) Handbook of Pragmatics. Amsterdam: Benjamins.

Verschueren, Jef. (1999) Understanding Pragmatics. London, New York: Arnold Publishers.

Watzlawick, Paul, Janet Helmick Beavin and Don D. Jackson (1967) Pragmatics of Human Communication: A Study of Interactional Patterns, Pathologies, and Paradoxes. New York: Norton.

Wierzbicka, Anna (1991) Cross-cultural Pragmatics. The Semantics of Human Interaction. Berlin, New York: Mouton de Gruyter.

William O'Grady (April 2008). "Innateness, Universal Grammar, and Emergentism". Lingua 118 (4): 620–631.

www.wikipedia.org (Retrieved, 2011).

Yule, George (1996) Pragmatics (Oxford Introductions to Language Study). Oxford University Press.

Index